A Theologian's Guide to Heidegger

A Theologian's Guide to Heidegger

Hue Woodson

WIPF & STOCK · Eugene, Oregon

A THEOLOGIAN'S GUIDE TO HEIDEGGER

Copyright © 2019 Hue Woodson. All rights reserved. Except for brief quotations in critical publications or reviews, no part of this book may be reproduced in any manner without prior written permission from the publisher. Write: Permissions, Wipf and Stock Publishers, 199 W. 8th Ave., Suite 3, Eugene, OR 97401.

Wipf & Stock
An Imprint of Wipf and Stock Publishers
199 W. 8th Ave., Suite 3
Eugene, OR 97401

www.wipfandstock.com

PAPERBACK ISBN: 978-1-5326-6248-5
HARDCOVER ISBN: 978-1-5326-6249-2
EBOOK ISBN: 978-1-5326-6250-8

Manufactured in the U.S.A.

CONTENTS

PREFACE | ix
ACKNOWLEDGMENTS | xiii

INTRODUCTION: HEIDEGGER AND THEOLOGY | 1
    Heidegger and Theology   1
    How to Read Heidegger Theologically   10
    Heidegger's Role in Postmodern Theology   20

CHAPTER 1: HEIDEGGER'S THEOLOGICAL ROOTS | 30
    Heidegger's Theological Roots   30
    Heidegger and Catholic Freiburg (1919-1923)   33
        "The Philosophical Foundations of Medieval Mysticism" (August 10, 1919)   33
        "Introduction to the Phenomenology of Religion" (Winter 1920/1921)   36
        "Augustine and Neoplatonism" (Summer 1921)   39
        "Colloquium on the Theological Foundations of Kant's *Religion within the Limits of Reason Alone*" (Summer 1923)   45
    Heidegger and Protestant Marburg (1923-1928)   47
        "The Problem of Sin in Luther" (1924)   49
        "Advanced: The High Scholastics and Aristotle: Thomas, *On Being and Essence*; Cajetan, *On the Analogy of Names*" (Summer 1924)   54
        "The Concept of Time" (July 25, 1924)   55
        "Practicum on the Ontology of the Middle Ages: Thomas, *On Being and Essence, Summa contra gentiles*" (Winter 1924/1925)   59
        "History of Philosophy from Aquinas to Kant" (Winter 1926/1927)   60

"Phenomenology and Theology" (March 9, 1927
or July 8, 1927)   64

Heidegger's Return to Freiburg (1928-1944)   67

"Theology and Philosophy" (February 14, 1928)   68

"Augustine: What is Time?: Confessions, Book 11"
(October 26, 1930)   68

"Augustine, Confessions 11: On Time" (Winter 1930/1931)   69

"Philosophizing and Believing: The Essence of Truth"
(December 5, 1930)   70

"The Fundamental Question of Philosophy"
(Summer 1933)   71

Heidegger's Post-Freiburg Years (1944-1976)   76

"The Theological Discussion of 'The Problem of a Non-
Objective Thinking and Speaking in Today's Theology'
—Some Pointers to Its Major Aspects" (March 11, 1964)   76

CHAPTER 2: A HISTORY OF HERMENEUTICS BEFORE AND
AFTER HEIDEGGER | 78

Hermeneutics "Before" Heidegger   79

Defining Hermeneutics Proper   79

Re-contextualizing Ancient Hermeneutics: Augustine's Plato
to Aquinas' Aristotle   80

The Making of Biblical Interpretation and
Biblical Hermeneutics   81

Reformed Hermeneutics: Luther, Calvin, Zwingli   85

Heyne through Eichhorn   92

Schleiermacher's Hermeneutics   93

Strauss and Scientific Hermeneutics   96

Heidegger's Hermeneutics   98

Heidegger's Hermeneutics of "Being"   98

Heidegger's Hermeneutics of "Unconcealment"   101

Theological Hermeneutics "After" Heidegger   104

Existential Hermeneutics: Macquarrie, Bultmann,
Tillich, Rahner   104

Philosophical Hermeneutics "After" Heidegger   112

      Gadamer's Dialectical Hermeneutics   112
      Foucault and the Hermeneutics of the Subject   116
      Derrida and the Hermeneutics of "Deconstruction"   118
      Ricoeur, Hermeneutics of Faith, Hermeneutics of Suspicion   124
      Deleuze and Guattari's Hermeneutics of Rhizomes and Plateaus   125
  Rhetoric, Language and Heidegger: Dialogues in Hermeneutics   128
      Bertrand Russell's "Logical Atomism" and Heidegger's "Being"   128
      Donald Davidson's "Epistemology Externalized" and Heidegger's Unconcealment   130

CHAPTER 3: THEOLOGIZING ON HEIDEGGER'S TERMS | 134
    Plato's Sophist (Winter 1924/1925)   134
    Being and Time (1927)   137
    The Fundamental Concepts of Metaphysics (Winter 1929/1930)   147
    "Letter on Humanism" (December 1946)   154

CONCLUSION: THEOLOGIZING PRIMORDIALITY THROUGH HEIDEGGER | 161

APPENDIX A: THE HEIDEGGER PROBLEM | 169
    The Question Itself: Does Heidegger's Nazism Matter?   171
    Four Assumptions of *Being and Time*   173
    Three Positions on Heidegger   175

APPENDIX B: KARL BARTH | 181
    Contextualizing Barth   182
    Barth and Heidegger   187

BIBLIOGRAPHY | 193

INDEX | 201

PREFACE

A Theologian's Guide to Heidegger provides a uniquely theological introduction to the philosophy of Martin Heidegger, by focusing on not just the relationship between theology and Heidegger, or even the nature of the discourse that must occur between theological concerns and Heidegger's philosophical errands, but by precisely exploring how theology can use Heidegger's philosophy as a means of outlining the scope and task of postmodern theology. In doing so, *A Theologian's Guide to Heidegger* expands upon the current understanding of the relevance of the relationship between Heidegger and theology.

Essentially, *A Theologian's Guide to Heidegger* is directly focused on how postmodern theology can constructively and effectively make use of Heidegger's philosophy within a theological context in a manner that does not just simply synthesis theology and philosophy. Indeed, though there are several "introductions" to Heidegger's thought, all of these examples predominantly exclusively work within a philosophical context. More importantly, though there is an increasing number of texts that explore various relationships between Heidegger and theology, this scholarship does not merely search for theological undertones in Heidegger's philosophy, but, instead, adequately situates Heidegger in postmodern theology with Heidegger's lesser-known theologically-minded texts.

To do this, especially with the postmodern theologian in mind, this book first provides a fairly comprehensive landscape of the relationship between Heidegger and theology, from its earliest roots, Heidegger's participation in it, and the trajectory of the relationship since. From here, a consideration of how Heidegger can be read theologically, offers the theologizing of John Macquarrie, Rudolf Bultmann, Paul Tillich, and Karl Rahner, all of which were influenced by Heidegger in varying degrees and intensity. The historical and philosophical contextualization of these four theologians and how they each theologize puts forth a larger justification of why Heidegger must be read theologically, particularly as a necessary means of transitioning modern theology to postmodern theological thought. What follows this is an explication of Heidegger's role in postmodern theology, which discusses the proliferation of scholarship that makes use of Heidegger's ongoing dialogue with theology within the concerns and issues facing postmodernity.

In Chapter 1 devoted to Heidegger's theological roots, I give an intellectual-biographical account of Heidegger's earliest interactions with theology as a student, which is significantly grounded in his early days at The University of Freiburg as he began his teaching career. These theological roots, as they transition to The University of Marburg, and return to Freiburg, is noted in terms of all Heidegger's seminars, lectures, and talks that are decidedly and purposefully concerned with theology—many of which are lesser-known excursions from philosophy. Among these texts include discussions of texts that are currently lost and a first-time partial translation of a text that has recently been published in German.

Because these seminars, lectures, and talks all shape Heidegger's approach to hermeneutics generally, I proceed, more narrowly, into how Heidegger affects the field of theological hermeneutics. I consider what the history of hermeneutics looked like before Heidegger, how Heidegger contributes to hermeneutics, and what hermeneutics becomes after Heidegger through discussions of the theological, the philosophical, and the rhetorical. Here, in Chapter 2, I will illustrate Heidegger's influences on various thinkers, with influences that are, at times, explicit or implicit in each of their respective thought.

Chapter 3 presents four widely-discussed texts that have garnered a lengthy history of scholarship in Heideggerian studies. These texts constitute an introduction into Heidegger's philosophical thought, but also display terms and terminology that can be comported to Heidegger's theological concerns. Each of these texts can be viewed in reference and in comparison to Heidegger's more explicitly theological texts from Chapter 1—by explicating Heidegger's philosophical terms as they appear in each of the texts in Chapter 3, it becomes all the more possible to theologize on Heidegger's terms, when references these texts with those that appear in Chapter 1. Such a comparative study is essential to establishing the relationship between Heidegger and theology and the relevance therein.

The final section makes note of the four theologians that have had their respective theologies shaped by Heidegger and have become, essentially, proponents of theologizing through Heidegger with philosophical theologies. These four theologians were discussed more exclusively in *Heideggerian*

Theologies, but will be re-litigated and re-evaluated, here, in terms of a specific theological task to which each ascribes and aligns with "the temporal-existential" as an overarching "Heideggerian task." In this manner, our "existential theologians" of John Macquarrie, Rudolf Bultmann, Paul Tillich, and Karl Rahner are considered as theologizing primordiality through Heidegger—what ties each of their respective theologizes, as each focuses on what lies primordially to scripture, tradition, reason, and experience respectively, is individual confrontations with temporality.

ACKNOWLEDGMENTS

First of all, I give thanks for the work of Charles Bambach, John D. Caputo, Richard Capobianco, Susanne D. Claxton, Benjamin D. Crowe, Alfred Denker, Theodore Kisiel, Gregory Fried, Richard Polt, Thomas Sheehan, Anthony C. Thiselton, Iain D. Thomson, Edward (John) Van Buren, Judith Wolfe, and Mark Wrathall.

My thanks to the past and present mentorship of Stacy Alaimo, David R. Brochman, Warren Carter, James O. Duke, Valerie Forstman, David J. Gouwens, Namsoon Kang, Peter Jones, Joretta Marshall, Kevin J. Porter, Masood Raja, Stephen G. Ray, Jr., Timothy Richardson, Kenneth Roemer, Allan Saxe, Jacqueline Vanhoutte, Jim Warren, Kathryn Warren, Jeffrey Williams, Newell Williams, and Kenneth W. Williford.

Thanks to my family at Northway Christian Church of Dallas: Jennifer G. Austin, Judd Austin, Rev. John G. Burton, Chrissy B. Cashion, Tim Gilger, Kim Hetzel, Derry Henry, Ruby H. Henry, Emily Hohnstein, Karen S. Hohnstein, Roger Hohnstein, Rev. Virzola Law, Andrew Reinhart, Kelsey Reinhart, William Schick, Rev. Cheryl Scramuzza, and Rev. Megan Turner.

I also want to give special posthumous thanks to Robert W. (Bob) Bernard (1946-2015), Hubert Dreyfus (1929-2017), William J. Richardson (1920-2016), and James M. Robinson (1924-2016).

Lastly, I am extremely thankful for Samantha Woodson (my wife), Shirley J. Woodson (my mother), and Jeanne McKinnis (my mother-in-law).

INTRODUCTION: HEIDEGGER AND THEOLOGY

Heidegger and Theology

IN A CERTAIN SENSE, scholarship investigating Heidegger's association with theology ultimately dates to Karl Rahner (1904-1984) and his 1936 dissertation at the University of Freiburg entitled *Geist in Welt* (translated later as *Spirit in the World*). The dissertation sought to interpret Thomas Aquinas's epistemology through a comparative study of Joseph Maréchal (1878-1944) and Heidegger—Rahner wanted to consider a reading of Maréchal's transcendental Thomism in relation to an understanding of Heidegger's "existentialism."[1]

At the time, upon the conclusion of Rahner's doctoral studies at Freiburg, Heidegger was in his sixth-year as a member of the philosophy faculty and had completed a short-lived (and inarguably disastrous) tenure as Freiburg's Rector—as a budding Jesuit theologian interested in teaching philosophy, Rahner came unmistakably under the influence of Heidegger's thought and had attended several of Heidegger's courses.[2] However, Rahner's dissertation was under the direction of the theologian, Martin Honecker (1888-1941), who has been noted as an opponent and critic of Heidegger's.[3] Whether it was due to Honecker's professional or philosophical aversion to Heidegger, or due to Honecker's belief that *Geist in Welt* was not sufficiently Catholic nor neo-Scholastic, Honecker rejected Rahner's dissertation. Even though it has been debated as to why Rahner's dissertation "failed"—to the best of my knowledge, there is no documentation citing the exact reasons, and Rahner himself never provided a cause—Rahner would leave Freiburg for the University of Innsbruck. There, not only did Rahner continue decidedly theological studies

---

1. See "Rahner and Heidegger" in *Heideggerian Theologies* (2018).
2. Ibid.
3. Ibid.

and complete a *habilitationsschrift*, but, by July 1937, he would also be appointed *Privatdozent* (or "lecturer"). In 1939, Rahner's "failed" dissertation would be published as *Geist in welt: Zur Metaphysik der endlichen Erkenntnis bei Thomas von Aquin* (*On the Metaphysics of Finite Knowledge in Thomas Aquinas*, translated in 1957). As Rahner's first major work as a theologian, marking the beginning of a scholarly conversation about what kind of relationship exists between theology and Heidegger.

Just three years prior to the emergence of Rahner's translated version of *Geist in Welt*, John Macquarrie (1919-2007) arrived at the end of his doctoral studies in theology at the University of Glasgow under the tutelage of Ian Henderson (1910-1969), after having previously successfully completed philosophical studies with Charles A. Campbell (1897-1974). While at Glasgow, Campbell and Henderson introduced Macquarie to the theological thought of Rudolf Bultmann (1884-1976) and, by extension, Heidegger's thought—essentially, both Campbell and Henderson became important "conduit[s] through which Macquarrie could read Bultmann's Heideggerian approach to New Testament exegesis."[4] On one hand, with Campbell having "exposed Macquarrie to the work of Bultmann and Heidegger, as examples of the intersectionality of philosophy and theology," Henderson, on the other hand, had previously published *Myth in the New Testament* (1952), which served as "the first introduction to the English-speaking word to the controversy over Bultmann's program of demythologizing."[5] Given Henderson's work on Bultmann and his role as Macquarrie's doctoral advisor, Macquarrie would complete his dissertation in 1954 as a study on Bultmann and Heidegger, published the following year as *An Existentialist Theology: A Comparison of Heidegger and Bultmann* (1955).

Like Honecker's likely criticism of Rahner's handling of Heidegger over Maréchal in *Geist in Welt*, Macquarrie's *An Existentialist Theology* is also undoubtedly more about Heidegger than Bultmann. It is also Macquarrie's first work as a theologian. In one of the few assessments of *An Existentialist Theology*, Eugene Long notes that Macquarrie's primary goal in the work is "to contribute to the understanding of the influence of existentialist philosophy on contemporary theological thought."[6] This certainly similarly describes Rahner's approach to *Geist in Welt*, if we see that Rahner's own

---

4. Woodson, *Heideggerian Theologies*, 30.
5. Ibid.
6. Long, *Existence, Being and God: An Introduction to the Philosophical Theology of John Macquarrie*, 4.

concern is with the same influence on the Rahner's reading of Maréchal 's "contemporary theological thought." For Macquarrie especially, he explains *An Existentialist Theology* as something that "sought to show how Bultmann's interpretation of the New Testament as a way of life had drawn upon the analysis of human existence given by Heidegger."[7] It would seem to me that the manner in which Rahner explicates Maréchal's transcendental Thomism "as a way of life" attempts to use Heidegger in the same manner as Macquarrie. The difference, however, is that Macquarrie's critique of Bultmann is dissimilar to Rahner's approach to Maréchal—while Maréchal and Heidegger are very different thinkers that Rahner brings together by way of Aquinas, Macquarrie brings Bultmann and Heidegger together as a means of recognizing Heidegger's influence upon Bultmann by way of what Macquarrie coins an "existentialist theology."

As much as Macquarrie contends that his assessment of Bultmann's use of Heidegger is "uncritical," it remains a significant critique of Bultmann nonetheless.[8] In fact, when comparing Macquarrie's "uncritical" assessment of Bultmann to Rahner's relatively "uncritical" look at Maréchal, the term "uncritical" does not seem to describe what Macquarrie does with Bultmann as it does denote what Rahner does with Maréchal. In this way, we see that Macquarrie is not exactly "uncritical" of Bultmann, since Bultmann's theologizing is more contemporaneously controversial than anything we can say about Maréchal for Rahner. While Rahner simply sees Maréchal as a representative figure in Catholic theology capable of shedding light on Heidegger, Macquarrie does not view Bultmann as a representative figure in contemporary theological thought—rather, the only thing Macquarrie seemingly finds in Bultmann is a means to discover Heidegger by using Bultmann as an intermediary to Heidegger, "just as Macquarrie used Campbell and Henderson as intermediaries to Heidegger."[9] For Macquarrie, Bultmann is merely a means to Heidegger, such that we must be careful when considering *An Existentialist Theology* as a Bultmann-Heidegger "comparison." Rahner's *Geist in Welt* is no more a Maréchal-Heidegger "comparison." Despite what the subtitle of Macquarrie's work proclaims, if it "is not necessarily a comparison, in the

---

7. Macquarrie, "Pilgrimage in Theology," in *Being and Truth: Essays in Honor of John Macquarrie*, xiii.

8. Ibid.

9. Woodson, *Heideggerian Theologies*, 32.

strictest sense of the word,"[10] it certainly seems to handle Heidegger in much the same way as Rahner. As with Rahner's take on Maréchal, it cannot be stressed enough that "Macquarrie seems more interested in staking a Heideggerian position that differs from Bultmann, rather than offering an even-handed, objective study of Bultmann and Heidegger."[11] Because of this, Macquarrie and Rahner, as theologians, share an indebtedness to Heidegger that becomes all the more illuminated in their respective first theological works, particularly when these first studies define the respective trajectories of all their theological works to follow.

In light of the contributions that the first theological works of Macquarrie and Rahner make to the emergence of Heidegger's association with theology in the mid- to late-1950s—if we keep in mind that Rahner's work appeared much earlier, but emerged in translation in the late-1950s—Macquarrie amd Rahner entered into a field of scholarship in theology that included two very important theologians, both of which served as notable colleagues of Heidegger while all were at Marburg in the mid-1920s: Rudolf Bultmann and Paul Tillich (1886-1965).

As it has been noted through Macquarrie's dissertation, by the 1950s, the association between Bultmann and Heidegger was well-known in scholarship into Bultmann's work. Indeed, this association dated to the personal relationship Bultmann and Heidegger had while at Marburg, when the two men sought to collaborate professionally.[12] It is certainly known that Heidegger participated in talks led by Marburg's theology department, having been invited by Bultmann.[13] In fact, "there exists overwhelming evidence that there was an active and open dialogue between Bultmann and Heidegger."[14] In William Dennison's *The Young Bultmann: Context for His Understanding of God, 1884-1925* (2008), we find the recognition that—though rare in Bultmann scholarship focusing exclusively on Bultmann's early professional career—Bultmann and Heidegger "met once a week to discuss theological and philosophical issues."[15] This weekly meetings became "a means for Bultmann to determine how philosophy could speak to

10. Ibid.
11. Ibid.
12. See "Bultmann and Heidegger" in *Heideggerian Theologies* (2018).
13. Ibid.
14. Ibid., 61.
15. Dennison, *The Young Bultmann: Context for His Understanding of God, 1884-1925*, 132.

theological concerns, as well as for Heidegger to ascertain the same [about] theology for philosophical concerns."¹⁶

Heidegger's influence on Bultmann—as it is largely inaugurated by Macquarrie's dissertation—can be found most notably in *Neues Testament und Mythologie* (1941), *Das Evangelium des Johannes* (1941), and *Theologie des Neuen Testaments* (1948). The first of these appeared, in part, in translation as *Kerygma and Myth: a Theological Debate* (1953)—this text included an analysis of Bultmann's seminal essay (delivered as a lecture) "New Testament and Mythology" and his own response to his critics. The second of these, though not translated until 1971, was highly controversial in its treatment of the Gospel of John. The third, though translated in two volumes in 1961 and 1970, made a significant mark on the landscape of New Testament interpretation, offering a full-throated approach to hermeneutics with Bultmann's demythologization program. These three works especially exhibited influences that were wholly outside the theological mainstream and even beyond the boundaries of extremely-conservative and extremely-progressive readings of the New Testament. What Bultmann's demythologizing of the New Testament espoused was a philosophical approach that attracted many critics throughout the 1940s, so that, by the time Macquarrie's assessment appeared in dissertation form, there remained a significant debate over the reasonability of Bultmann's program in one sense and, in another sense, clear overtures made to Heidegger's thought in Bultmann's works leading up to *Theologie des Neuen Testaments*.

There remains an open debate as to the extent to which Heidegger influenced Bultmann's demythologizing. Though, as early as Macquarrie's dissertation, there were clear similarities that allowed Macquarrie's "comparison" to lean heavily towards what Heidegger exerts on Bultmann, David Congdon questions whether Bultmann can be considered as a "Heideggerian theologian," in an article aptly titled "Is Bultmann a Heideggerian theologian?" Having previously published an authoritative study *The Mission of Demythologizing: Rudolf Bultmann's Dialectical Theology* (2015), the 2017 article, as something of a follow-up, "reassesses the Bultmann-Heidegger relationship from three angles," according to Congdon.¹⁷ The most interesting of Congdon's angles is the first: "the essential elements of Bultmann's theology were already in place before he met or learn[ed] from

---

16. Woodson, *Heideggerian Theologies*, 61.
17. See the abstract to Congdon's article, "Is Bultmann a Heideggerian Theologian?"

Heidegger."[18] Even so, Konrad Hammann's biography on Bultmann (2009), translated in 2013, suggests that, particularly given Congdon's overarching argument, Heidegger still shaped Bultmann's overall theological direction.[19] Not only is this shaping apparent in *Theologie Des Neuen Testaments*, but is also especially obvious in the English translation of it as *Theology of the New Testament* (1961). The English translation, as it appeared most notably in London, reignited a debate on Bultmann's demythologization project just as Heidegger's work gained more exposure and influence in France intellectual circles in the 1950s through to the 1960s.

When considering the respective stances that Congdon and Hammann take towards the extent to which Heidegger influenced Bultmann, the same debate can be surely had about Heidegger's influence on Tillich. Though Tillich met Heidegger while the two taught at Marburg, Tillich would only teach there for the 1924-1925 academic year (three terms) before moving on to the Dresden University of Technology. It was while at Marburg that Tillich first began developing a systematic theology which found its way pedagogically into a systematic theology course Tillich would teach in his last term at Marburg—it has been generally argued that Tillich's early work on systematic theology in his Marburg course shows Heidegger's influence. This seems certainly so given that, in Tillich's final term at Marburg, Heidegger had begun early drafts of what would eventually become *Being and Time* and much of this material would find its way into Heidegger's course, *Prolegomena zur Geschichte des Zeitbegriffs* in Summer 1925—to some extent, Heidegger's course, *Platon: Sophistes* in Winter 1924/1925 also has the earmarks of some arguments Heidegger would incorporate in *Being and Time*. With these two courses considered themselves as "early drafts" of *Being and Time*—an argument that has been made most notably by Thomas Sheehan[20] and Theodore Kisiel[21]—it would seem that this "early drafts" certainly had a noteworthy impact on Tillich's approach to the systematic theology he was developing at the time.

Like Bultmann, Tillich shared a comradery with Heidegger that directly affected Tillich's professional career—while Bultmann developed a kinship with Heidegger by way of their common exegetical interests in Martin

18. Ibid.

19. See Hammann, *Rudolf Bultmann: A Biography* (2013).

20. See Sheehan's edited and translated edition of Heidegger's *History of the Concept of Time*.

21. See Kisiel's *The Genesis of Heidegger's Being and Time* (1993).

Luther and the Pauline letters, Tillich developed a similar kinship with Heidegger over shared interests in the thought of Friedrich W. J. Schelling. Tillich's association with Heidegger began, at least in part, by Heidegger's respect for Tillich's two dissertations on Schelling: the first translated as *The Conception of the History of Religion in Schelling's Positive Philosophy* (1911) and the second translated as *Mysticism and Guilt-Consciousness in Schelling's Philosophical Development* (1912). As much as Tillich's reading of Schelling's "positive philosophy" directly influenced Tillich's theological understandings of myth and revelation, Heidegger had a much broader hold on Tillich's eventual synthesizing of philosophy and theology than Schelling. To be sure, Tillich first five major works all—to varying degrees—demonstrate Schelling's early influence on Tillich's thought: *The Religious Situation* (published as *Die religiose Lage der Gegenwart* in 1925), *The Socialist Decision* (1933), *The Interpretation of History* (1936), *The Protestant Era* (1948), and *The Shaking of the Foundations* (1948). Heidegger's influence on Tillich is not fully illustrated until the publication of the first of the three volumes of Tillich's *Systematic Theology* (1951)—it was with the first volume that Tillich began to articulate a theological perspective that can be traced to Tillich's time at Marburg with the systematic theology he taught in his last term there. Not only is Heidegger's fingerprints on the first volume's establishment of Tillich's method of correlation that turns towards an adaptation of Heidegger's question of the meaning of being into "being and the question of God," but Heidegger's influences on Tillich can also be found in Tillich's next five works: *The Courage to Be* (1952), *Love, Power, and Justice: Ontological Analysis and Ethical Implications* (1954), *Biblical Religion and the Search for Ultimate Reality* (1955), *The New Being* (1955), and the *Dynamics of Faith* (1957). What followed were two more volumes of *Systematic Theology* in 1957 (subtitled: *Existence and the Christ*) and 1963 (subtitled: *Life and the Spirit and the Kingdom of God*)—the second, in particular, frequently displays an employment of Heideggerian terminology and language.

The manner in which Tillich expressed his Heideggerian influences by the conclusion of the publication of the three-volume *Systematic Theology* in 1963 would find its way more explicitly by Tillich himself in his "intellectual autobiography," *My Search for Absolutes* (1967). At the time, scholarship into Tillich's use of Heidegger had begun to increase, though not quite as critical as the scholarship into Bultmann's use of Heidegger. To put a finer point on this, Tillich's use of Heidegger followed a new wave of Heideggerian scholarship as Heidegger's reputation broadened beyond French existentialism led by Jean-Paul Sartre and wholly beyond Europe itself, as Heidegger's thought became swept up and assimilated into existentialism as a school of thought. Heidegger resisted this not just in his "Letter on Humanism" (1947), but also in public and private remarks about Sartre's misreading of *Being and Time* through the 1950s and 1960s as existentialism grew in popularity in European intellectual circles—just to be clear, Heidegger did not resist Tillich's nor Bultmann's use of Heidegger's thought in their theological works (and Heidegger is equally silent on Rahner's use of Heidegger in *Geist in Welt*).

Additionally, what made Tillich's work through Heidegger in his *Systematic Theology* volumes all the more noticeable was with the English translation of Heidegger's *Sein und Zeit* as *Being and Time* in 1962 (from the original German publication in 1927) by co-translators Edward Robinson and John Macquarrie. Macquarrie's involvement in the very first translation of *Sein und Zeit* came by way of his previous work on Heidegger in *An Existentialist Theology*. Because of Macquarrie's translation work on *Sein und Zeit*, Macquarrie was afforded the opportunity to publish a series of books throughout the 1960s frequently considering Heidegger's philosophical thought in relation to theology. The first of these is *Twentieth-Century Religious Thought: The Frontiers of Philosophy and Theology, 1900-1970* (1963), which, as Macquarrie notes in the book's preface, was originally conceived as early as 1957, when it was suggested by "some members of the editorial staff at Messrs Harper and Brothers [. . .] that [he] should write the story of religious thought in the present century, with special reference to the relations of philosophy and theology."[22] In the penultimate section of *Twentieth-Century Religious Thought*, Macquarrie briefly discusses Heidegger along with Karl Jaspers (1883-1969) under a very small section entitled "Existentialism in Germany." Macquarrie would discuss Heidegger more thoroughly with respect to theology in *Studies in Christian Existentialism* (1965), a collection of lectures and essays often noting Heidegger in terms of different theological concepts—the collection, as noted by Macquarrie in its preface, includes the lecture "Some Heideggerian Themes and Their Theological Significance" originally delivered in October 1963.[23] Macquarrie's next major work, *Principles of Christian Theology* (1966), becomes a more full-throated expression of Macquarrie's systematic theology, particularly

---

22. Macquarrie, *Twentieth-Century Religious Thought*, 13.
23. See the "Preface" to Macquarrie, *Studies in Christian Existentialism* (1965).

as a means of harmonizing existentialism and orthodox Christian thought. Like Tillich's *Systematic Theology* completed three years earlier, Macquarrie's *Principles of Christian Theology* explicitly makes use of Heidegger in order to conceptualize Macquarrie's understandings of philosophy and theology, such that it can stand alongside not just Tillich's *Systematic Theology*, but also Bultmann's *Theology of the New Testament* as examples of what theologizing with Heidegger looks like. Macquarrie's next three books—*God-Talk: An Examination of the Language and Logic of Theology* (1967), the selected and edited. *Contemporary Religious Thinkers from Idealist Metaphysicians to Existential Theologians* (1968), and *Martin Heidegger* (1968)—all show Heidegger's influence on Macquarrie. While *God-Talk* acts as an expansion of specific arguments raised about theological language in *Principles of Christian Theology* and the very short *Martin Heidegger* acts an intellectual biography of Heidegger's contributions to theology as a "maker of contemporary theology," *Contemporary Religious Thinkers* contains selected readings, including, most notably, Macquarrie's selections from Bultmann and Tillich. In *Existentialism: An Introduction, Guide, and Assessment* (1972), Macquarrie frequently references Heidegger throughout the book and, within an isolated section near the close of the book, he groups together Bultmann, Tillich and Rahner (among others), as "some of the theologians of recent and contemporary times who have been significantly and, in some cases, deeply influenced by existentialist philosophy."[24]

Macquarrie's inclusion of Rahner in the reading of the "existentialist philosophy" in Bultmann and Tillich—setting aside the others Macquarrie places in this group—is likely due to Macquarrie's awareness of Rahner's contemporaneously published theological work, rather than any knowledge Macquarrie may have had about Rahner's connection to Heidegger at Freiburg. The latter can only be ascertained speculatively, since, to the best of my knowledge, Macquarrie never references Rahner having been one of Heidegger's Freiburg students. However, given that Macquarrie is concerned with "recent and contemporary times," he is most certainly referencing Rahner's *Geist in Welt* that had been translated into English as *Spirit in the World* (1968), the English translation of *Hörer des Wortes* as *Hearer of the Word* (1969), *The Trinity* (1970), and some nine volumes in German of *Schriften zur Theologie* by 1970, translated into eight volumes in English as *Theological Investigations* by 1971. Though all of these works come to bear on Macquarrie's understanding of how Rahner's theologizing contributed

---

24. Macquarrie, *Existentialism*, 270-271.

to the "recent and contemporary times" as a kind of theologizing that has been "significantly and, in some cases, deeply influenced by existentialist philosophy," Rahner's most important theological work remained wholly out of Macquarrie's purview at the time of his writing *Existentialism*—that work would be *Grundkurs des Glaubens: Einführung in den Begriff des Christentums* (1976), which would be translated as *Foundations of Christian Faith: An Introduction to the Idea of Christianity* in 1978. In it, Rahner attempts to systematize his theologizing into an overview of his ideas within a framework that is predominantly influenced by Heidegger (even though, to certain extents, Rahner makes use of Kant and Hegel).

Taken together, Bultmann's *Theology of the New Testament*, Tillich's 3-volume *Systematic Theology*, Macquarrie's *Principles of Christian Theology*, and Rahner's *Foundations of Christian Faith* are expressions of the relationship between Heidegger and theology. More importantly, each theologize through Heidegger in a way that allows Heidegger to philosophize through theology—because of this, Bultmann, Tillich, Macquarrie, and Rahner all plays essential roles, through how Heidegger influences them respectively, particularly in the establishment of what Heidegger means to theology across each subsequent decade from the 1940s to the 1950s, from the 1950s to the 1960s, and from the 1960s to the 1970s.

How to Read Heidegger Theologically

Though, while at Marburg, Heidegger developed a working relationship with Marburg's theology department through his friendship with Bultmann, Heidegger's association with theology remained largely complicated, particularly leading up to the publication of *Sein und Zeit*. Even though, as it has been documented in the Bultmann biographies of Hammann and Dennison, Heidegger participated in talks with Bultmann on the Pauline letters[25] and the two men seriously planned to collaborate on an academic project that would synthesize the concerns of philosophy with those of theology,[26] Bultmann is generally believed to be the only member of the Marburg theology department that openly worked with Heidegger, with only Bultmann being known to have personally attended Heidegger's lectures.[27] Though Tillich also had a personal relationship with Heidegger, it is

---

25. See "Bultmann and Heidegger" in *Heideggerian Theologies* (2018).
26. Ibid.
27. Ibid.

mostly unknown to what extent this developed into a professional relationship, such as what Bultmann had with Heidegger—in other words, to the best of my knowledge, there is no direct evidence as to whether Tillich privately worked on any projects with Heidegger, or if Tillich actually attended any of Heidegger's Marburg lectures, even if there is some circumstantial evidence pointing to Tillich's awareness of Heidegger's lectures that many Heidegger scholars believe to serve as "early drafts" for *Sein und Zeit*. With all said, Bultmann—more so than Tillich—became an early ambassador for Heidegger's relationship with theology while at Marburg to the consternation of Bultmann's colleagues in the theology department.

Upon the publication of *Sein und Zeit* and subsequently moving to Freiburg to take the chair of the philosophy department left by Heidegger's mentor, the retiring Edmund Husserl (1859-1938) beginning in the Winter 1928/1929 semester, Heidegger would eventually professionally (and academically) align himself with National Socialism and the Nazi Party in 1933. At that time, Heidegger had been elected Freiburg Rector on April 21 and by November 11, he signed the "Loyalty Oath of German Professors to Adolf Hitler and the National Socialist State," which ultimately aligned Freiburg, by way of Heidegger's leadership, to the same "loyalty oath." Not only did Heidegger's relationship with theology (and Bultmann and Tillich, for that matter) become significantly strained, but Heidegger sought to situate himself as the key philosopher of the Nazi Party, which involved philosophizing the meaning of National Socialism through the thought of key German thinkers such as Hegel, Hölderlin, Schelling, and Nietzsche. While Heidegger's allegiance to National Socialism severely complicated his relationships with his German-Jewish students, Hannah Arendt, Karl Löwith, Hans Jonas, and Günther Anders (all of which had attended courses under Heidegger at Marburg and followed Heidegger to Freiburg), it also strained relationships with other students such as Emmanuel Levinas and even Rahner (who took courses under Heidegger at Freiburg in 1934-1936) to an extent. Even though Heidegger subsequently resigned as Rector in April 1934, he remained a card-carrying member of the Nazi Party at least until 1945—and, during this time, from 1931-1941, the 2014 publication of Heidegger's *Black Notebooks* reveal several instances of Heidegger's anti-semitic beliefs in his private papers. This, in itself, has allowed scholars to more generally re-evaluate Heidegger's relationship with Nazism and, consequently, has brought any relationship between Heidegger and theology all the more questionable and problematic.

Throughout the 1940s, while Bultmann began to more seriously apply Heidegger's "existentialist" thinking to Bultmann's demythologization project towards the New Testament, Heidegger began to increasingly distance himself publicly from National Socialism. By the Winter of 1944, as Heidegger was forced to cancel a course in-progress near the beginning of the Winter 1944/1945 semester in order to be drafted into the *Volksstrum* (or civilian's militia) to fortify the Rhine for the Nazi Forces, Bultmann was in the midst of defending his use of Heidegger in his program of demythologizing while resisting the notions of critics that believed Bultmann's views could be simply reduced to a kind of theological thinking based on Heideggerian categories. By 1949, when Heidegger was officially deemed a "*Mitläufer*" ("follower") by the post-war denazification hearings and had already been banned from teaching for four years, Bultmann published his *Theology of the New Testament* (as *Theologie des Neuen Testaments*) the previous year, which represented, as cited by Robert Morgan in an introduction to the new edition of the work (2007), "the most extensive use of his friend and colleague Martin Heidegger's analysis of human existence" from *Sein und Zeit*.[28] As much as Bultmann was careful to say that his borrowing of Heidegger in his demythologizing was "limited" as a means of countering a broader controversy erupting over the usefulness of demythologizing by New Testament scholars in the years immediately following the publication of *Theology of the New Testament*, Heidegger was readmitted to teaching at Freiburg for the Winter 1950/1951 semester and granted emeritus state the following year. Just as Bultmann continued to confront criticisms over his use of Heidegger theologically, perhaps increasingly so as a result of a general stigma applied to Heidegger's relationship with Nazism by German theologians still reckoning with Nazi atrocities, Heidegger's reputation began to grow rapidly in France throughout the 1950s, along with the growth of French existentialism predominantly spearheaded by Sartre.

Heidegger's popularity in France spread most notably to the U.K., just as Sartre's existentialism gained more philosophical acclaim, all while Bultmann's demythologization began to change the direction of New Testament studies throughout Europe and even in the U.K. It is in this context that Macquarrie's *An Existentialist Theology* emerged at the University of Glasgow—though Macquarrie's work contributed to a growing discussion on the importance of Bultmann's theologizing through Heidegger, to the best of my knowledge, Macquarrie was the first to provide a comparative

---

28. Heidegger, *Being and Time*, xiv.

study of Bultmann with Heidegger. Not only had Macquarrie's "comparison" of the two presented an essential philosophical context to Bultmann's theologizing, but it also further rehabilitated Heidegger within Anglican theological circles by Anglican thinkers that sought to better understand Bultmann's influences (i.e. Charles A. Campbell and Ian Henderson).

While Macquarrie continued to contextualize Bultmann's demythologizing in a follow-up work, *The Scope of Demythologizing: Bultmann and His Critics* (1960), he continued to expand Heidegger's importance: first, with his co-translation efforts of *Sein und Zeit* into *Being and Time* (1962), and, more importantly, with his seminal lecture, "Some Heideggerian Themes and Their Theological Significance," delivered in October 1963, as the Birks Lectures at McGill University in Montreal.

As it is included in Macquarrie's collection, *Studies in Christian Existentialism* (1965), the "Heideggerian themes" with which Macquarrie's assigned "theological significance" are enumerated as: "death and its existential significance," "selfhood and temporality," and "the language of being." To the first "theme," Macquarrie finds that "death occupies such a central place in [Heidegger's] exposition of human existence that he can describe this existence as a being-towards-death."[29] Be that as it may, Macquarrie goes on to suggest that "when [Heidegger] moves from the consideration of human existence to the wider philosophical question of Being, it is still the phenomenon of death that marks out the way into this inquiry."[30] This "wider philosophical question of Being," as Macquarrie sees it, is not grounded on Heidegger viewing the concept of death itself as holding a negative significance on human existence, but, instead, Macquarrie reads Heidegger's articulation of death as something that "becomes integrative rather than destructive for existence."[31] In this regard, Macquarrie writes, "an authentic existence which resolutely anticipates death and understand all living to be also dying transcends the triviality of everyday existence and achieves meaning and unity."[32] Accordingly, Macquarrie believes that, for Heidegger, death "becomes, we must say, creative of selfhood."[33] From this, Macquarrie arrives at another aspect of death that has a positive significance for human existence, such that this

---

29. Macquarrie, *Studies in Christian Existentialism*, 46.
30. Ibid.
31. Ibid., 56.
32. Ibid.
33. Ibid.

significance is two-fold, which Macquarrie describes in the following way: "anxiety in the face of death, has the positive role of recalling man from the forgetting of Being, and awakening him to the wonder of Being."[34] This "wonder," as Macquarrie calls it, is precisely theological in nature, since "from this stems the whole mystical side of Heidegger's thought."[35] It is this "mystical side" that Macquarrie aligns with Christian theology, insomuch as "the positive religious dimensions of Heidegger's thought becomes clear, and these can be traced back to their origin in [Heidegger's] concept of what is generally taken to be the negative phenomenon of death."[36] This leads Macquarrie to a second theme, based on the fact that: "Heidegger's view that death is the master possibility is not, as it sometimes supposed, an expression of nihilism."[37] To the contrary, Macquarrie argues that "it is the recognition in the fullest degree that any resoluteness that can unify the self in more than an illusory way."[38] Given that, as Macquarrie suggests at the very beginning of his discussion of "Selfhood and Temporality," as a second Heideggerian theme, "one of the most serious problems confronting philosophical theology today is that of finding an adequate conception of selfhood."[39] With this in mind, Macquarrie puts forth the idea that Heidegger "has been no less severe than most of his contemporaries in criticizing the traditional (and especially the Cartesian) idea of a substantial self."[40] From here, Macquarrie goes on to say "perhaps to a greater extent than most of his contemporaries [Heidegger] has given us something like a positive account of selfhood which might replace the traditional one; and this new account is, I believe, one that should be of great interest to the Christian theologian."[41] More importantly, according to Macquarrie, "it is such a different model that Heidegger offers us in his explication of selfhood, and the new model is in temporal terms."[42] In Macquarrie's reading of Heidegger's explication of selfhood, "the structure of selfhood is to be conceived in terms of the three dimensions or ecstasies

34. Ibid., 57.
35. Ibid.
36. Ibid.
37. Ibid., 71.
38. Ibid.
39. Ibid., 59.
40. Ibid., 61-62.
41. Ibid., 62.
42. Ibid., 65.

INTRODUCTION: HEIDEGGER AND THEOLOGY

of temporality—the future or what is to come, what has been, and the present."[43] When considering the role that temporality, in light of "the three dimensions or ecstasies of temporality," plays with the meaning of selfhood for Heidegger, Macquarrie concedes that "this kind of language is justified because the self does not have a fixed essence like a thing, but is always ahead of itself, already in its potentiality for being."[44] Macquarrie locates this kind of language in Heidegger's "language of being" as a representation of the varied of meanings of human experience—as a third theme, Macquarrie follows "Heidegger's account of the patterns of such experiences as bring us to the limit of existence and so to the alleged confrontation with Being."[45] Because of this, Macquarrie recognizes that, through his reading of Heidegger, "Being cannot be equated with God, for traditional Christian theology has always conceived of God not as Being but as a being or entity, albeit the supreme entity which has most being, the *ens realissimum*."[46] When reading Heidegger theologically, as Macquarrie certainly does, "theology has suffered from the same defect as Western metaphysics—it has concerned itself exclusively with entities, and has sought to ground entities in another entity (God) without asking about the Being of entities."[47]

With all this said, it is clear that the three "Heideggerian themes" Macquarrie highlights from his reading of Heidegger hold a theological significance to how we read Heidegger theologically. These themes, for Macquarrie, provide a window into how Heidegger speaks necessarily to the concerns of theology and, by extension, how theology speaks necessarily to Heidegger's philosophical concerns. However, the manner in which Macquarrie envisions the kind of dialogue that Heidegger has with theology essentially carries forward the framework began with *An Existentialist Theology*—this certainly seems likely, even though Macquarrie resists limiting how he reads Heidegger theologically to Bultmann's theologizing.

Though Macquarrie is, indeed, the first to point out the manner in which Heidegger holds a general discourse with theology and vice versa, by the time he delivers his lecture "Some Heideggerian Themes and Their Theological Significance," a book had already emerged some four years

43. Ibid.
44. Ibid., 73.
45. Ibid., 81.
46. Ibid., 94.
47. Ibid.

earlier in 1959, which directly challenged Macquarrie's view of the nature of Heidegger's relationship with theology via Bultmann.

The book, *Denken und Sein: Der Weg Martin Heidegggers und der Weg der Theologie* (roughly translated as *Martin Heidegger's Way of Thinking and the Way of Theology*) by Heinrich Ott (1929-2013) presented a take on Heidegger's relationship with theology as based not so much on Butlmann, but more relationally to Barth. Ott's book sparked immense interest between German and American theologians, both of which had already recognized Barth's importance as a consequential modern theologian—this interest also sparked a new series of books, *New Frontiers in Theology*, which sought to explore new studies in modern theology, with only the first in the series focused on what kind of dialogue could be located between Heidegger and theology more broadly. The first volume, in particular, *The Later Heidegger and Theology* (1963), intended to spearhead "encounters between theologians of the Old World and the New."[48] As the editors James M. Robinson and John B. Cobb explain, "this volume explores the special value and relevance of the later Heidegger for Christian theology."[49] In Robinson's introductory essay to the first volume, "The German Discussion of the Later Heidegger," the sense of a "later Heidegger" is defined in terms of the trajectory of Heidegger's thought following Heidegger's "Letter on Humanism" (1946).

Robinson places Heidegger's "letter" in its proper context, as a means of countering Sartre's use of Heidegger towards the development of existentialism.[50] From here, Robinson cites a letter Heidegger writes to Heinrich Ott, in which Heidegger readily concedes that his thought has a relevance for theology, such that, as Heidegger himself says, "as long as anthropological-sociological conceptualizing and the conceptualizing of existentialism are not overcome and pushed to the side, theology will never enter into the freedom of saying what is entrusted to it."[51] Robinson suggests that the relevance Heidegger found in his thinking for the concerns of theology arises from a "turn or change of position" following "The Letter on Humanism."[52] This idea of "a turn," or *Die Kehre*, in Heidegger's thought, between the concerns of *Sein und Zeit* and those that emerge in the philosophical fallout

---

48. See the book jacket of *The Later Heidegger and Theology* (1963).
49. Ibid.
50. Robinson, "The German Discussion of the Later Heidegger," 3.
51. Ibid., 4-5.
52. Ibid., 4.

from "The Letter on Humanism," is an ongoing debate, which need not be rehashed here. Robinson himself does not explicitly contribute to this debate and, instead, simply defaults to Heidegger's own words about "whether he had changed his position."⁵³ Indeed, while keeping the notion of "the turn" in his purview, even Robinson recognizes that "Heidegger's thought began to be debated in philosophical publications as early as 1953"—precisely in France as a result of the popularity of existentialism—he does on to write, "the relevance of this turn for theology was not immediately seen."⁵⁴ With that said, Robinson acknowledges that, through the 1950s, "Heidegger's thought continued to be treated by theologians generally as a single position that had already been classified."⁵⁵ Here, I read Robinson's remarks along two lines. Though it seems to say, on one hand, that theologians of the time did not view Heidegger's thought in terms of having a "change of position" but as a single position extending from *Sein und Zeit*, it is possible to read an implicit reference by Robinson to Macquarrie's work on Heidegger and theology in *An Existentialist Theology*. That "single position," then, most certainly could refer to either Macquarrie's "single position" or Bultmann's "single position" as originally cited by Macquarrie. Whichever the case, Robinson notes that, with the emergence of Heinrich Ott's "monograph" in 1959, "the explosive potentialities of "the later Heidegger" for theology [became] evident [. . .] arguing that the later Heidegger shows us that the philosophy of Heidegger as a whole is more compatible with Barthian theology than with Bultmannian theology."⁵⁶

To make Ott's work all the more important and uniquely significant to the meaning of the relationship between Heidegger and theology in general, Robinson adds that it "was enhanced by Heidegger's positive appraisal of it."⁵⁷ This seems certainly so, given Heidegger's letter to Ott "on the appearance of [Ott's] *Denken und Sein*."⁵⁸ Nevertheless, such an aside—if we can call it that—is curious, since it begs us to compare Ott's work with Macquarrie's by way of Heidegger's possible "appraisal" of Macquarrie's. It is unclear if such an "appraisal"—either positive or even negative, for that matter—actually exists. It is also unclear if Robinson's reference to this is ever

53. Ibid.
54. Ibid., 5.
55. Ibid.
56. Ibid.
57. Ibid.
58. Ibid. See the first footnote on page 5.

so implicitly suggesting that Macquarrie's work does not provide as authentic an assessment of the Heidegger-theology relationship as Ott's work. It is unclear, too, if Robinson's desire, as an American theologian, is to develop a more meaningful relationship with German theologians on Heidegger, to the marginalization of what could be seen as a rival viewpoint made by British theologians, namely Macquarrie—we can note this as possibly being much more than just a coincidence with the publication of *The Later Heidegger and Theology* in such close proximity to Macquarrie delivering his "Some Heideggerian Themes and Their Theological Significance" lecture. It is additionally unclear if Robinson's pitting of Ott against Macquarrie is subtly pointing to a more authoritative command Ott has over Macquarrie on the Heidegger-theology relationship through Bultmann and Barth, since Ott studied at Marburg directly under both Bultmann and Barth. We know, of course, that Macquarrie's "Heidegger" and "Bultmann" are mediated through Campbell and Henderson while Macquarrie was at Glasgow, even with the elevation of Macquarrie's stature in Heidegger scholarship with his participation in the co-translation of *Sein und Zeit* in 1962.

All things considered and remaining silent on Macquarrie, Robinson's case for Ott's view of the Heidegger-theology relationship via Barth is the grounding point for *The Later Heidegger and Theology* volume. Robinson explains that Ott's "monograph" became the basis for a talk Ott gave to the annual meeting of Bultmann's former students, known as the "old Marburgers," in October 1959. The overarching topic for this annual meeting was "the relation of Heidegger to theology."[59] The next meeting was held the following year in October 1960, beginning with Ott's paper, "What is Systematic Theology?" (translated from "*Was ist systematische Theologie?*") and continuing with a debate made with new assessments from Ernst Fuchs (1903-1983) and Gerhard Ebeling (1912-2001)—as noted by Robinson, while Fuchs "published a highly critical review of Ott's book [. . .] in the semester following the meeting, Ebeling conducted a seminar on 'The Philosophy of M. Heidegger and Theology' in which Heidegger himself participated."[60] Robinson notes that Ebeling's theses, as they were originally expressed in the seminar, "have been published together with most of the papers [delivered in the 1960 meeting], in a special issue of the leading Bultmannian periodical, edited by Ebeling, the *Zeitschrift für Theologie und Kirche*."[61] In light of

---

59. Robinson, "The German Discussion of the Later Heidegger," 5.
60. Ibid., 6.
61. Robinson provides the title to Ebeling's essay as "*Verantworten des Glauben in*

the respective work of Ebeling, other old Marburgers, and Ott, Robinson proclaims that—towards the conclusion of a set of preliminary remarks to his introductory essay to *The Later Heidegger and Theology* volume—"it is this debate about the later Heidegger in the German discussion of the last decade that this present essay proposes to analyze."[62]

As Robinson makes clear in what I can be construed as preliminary remarks, in the intervening years between Macquarrie's dissertation, *An Existentialist Theology* (1955) and Macquarrie's lecture, "Some Heideggerian Themes and Their Theological Significance" (1963), Macquarrie's original work on the relationship between Heidegger and theology helped create an alternative view of that relationship that had gained significant momentum by the time Macquarrie delivered the 1963 lecture. With this alternative view having been compiled in *The Later Heidegger and Theology* volume, Macquarrie was undoubtedly aware of its existence, particularly in the same month and year in which he delivers his lecture—at that time, Macquarrie wrote a short book review of the new volume, having appeared in *Theology Today*. Published on October 1, 1963, Macquarrie offers a relatively positive take on what Robinson's introductory essay accomplishes "on the whole," though Macquarrie is careful to note that Robinson's "account differs markedly from those of some other interpreters."[63] The example Macquarrie immediately provides is Thomas Langan's *The Meaning of Heidegger* (1959), to which Macquarrie believes "many American readers will be familiar."[64] Nevertheless, Macquarrie freely concedes that "Robinson is in the main the more reliable guide."[65] The problem, however, for Macquarrie, is that "[Robinson's] essay would have been better had he faced more frankly some of the ambiguities in Heidegger's thought, and had he taken time to digest more fully the mass of material to which he refers in his footnotes."[66] Macquarrie's point here is certainly reasonable, since the German landscape of Heidegger scholarship, which positions Ott, Ebeling, and other old Marburgers in 1959 and 1960, is informed along various

---

Begegnung mit dem Denken M. Heideggers," published in 1961, which I would like to roughly translate as "Answers for Faith in Encountering with the Thinking of M. Heidegger." See Ibid.

62. Ibid., 7.

63. Macquarrie, "New Frontiers in Theology: Vol I, The Later Heidegger and Theology, Edited by James M. Robinson and John B. Cobb," 420.

64. Ibid.

65. Ibid.

66. Ibid.

scholarly fault-lines of engagement with Heidegger during the 1950s. And yet, it may be possible to consider Macquarrie's critique of Robinson and the other American theologians seeking to establish a mode of theologizing with Heidegger as a means of re-articulating and re-establishing the contributions of British theologians (particularly Macquarrie himself) to any theologizing with Heidegger.

Macquarrie would stake this territory again some thirty years later, though, at this time, it would be situated within a growing discussion of Heidegger's relationship with Nazism. On the heels of a series of publications taking a critical assessment of Heidegger's political proclivities towards National Socialism, beginning most notably with Victor Farias' *Heidegger and Nazism* (translated in 1989 from *Heidegger y el Nazismo* in 1987) and Philippe Lacoue-Labarthe's *La fiction du politique* (1987) and continuing to Tom Rockmore's *On Heidegger's Nazism and Philosophy* (1992), Hugo Ott's *Martin Heidegger: A Political Life* (translated in 1993) and Hans Sluga's *Heidegger's Crisis: Philosophy and Politics in Nazi Germany* (1993), Macquarrie would deliver the Hensley Henson Lectures for 1993-1994, entitled *Heidegger and Christianity*. In the preface to the publication of these lectures, Macquarrie writes, "there is little doubt that at the present time the temporal and the historical have acquired a new importance in human thinking."[67] This seems especially so, when considering the context in which Macquarrie delivers the lecture. As such, it is this context—the growing debate on Heidegger's Nazism and the extent to which this negatively impacts how Heidegger can be read theologically—that brings Macquarrie to conclude that "by attending to [Heidegger's] concepts of time and history and also to his views on religion and theology, we may learn something of the impact on Christianity of the contemporary concern with time."[68] How this impact comes to bear separately on Christianity and also on "the contemporary concern with time" is undoubtedly predicated on what kind of role Heidegger is to meaningfully have in postmodern theology.

Heidegger's Role in Postmodern Theology

William J, Richardson (1920-2016), an American philosopher and a Jesuit priest, further established how Heidegger could be read theologically by further grounding Heidegger's role in postmodern theology in the article,

67. Macquarrie, "Preface" to *Heidegger and Christianity*, vii.
68. Ibid., viii.

"Heidegger and Theology" (March 1965).[69] In it, Richardson contributes more explicitly to the discussion between German and American theologians on Heidegger, which had been ignited by the Robinson and Cobb co-edited, *The New Frontiers in Theology* series, focally directed by *The Later Heidegger and Theology* volume. Instead of simply functioning as a book review—as Macquarrie's had been nearly a year and a half earlier—Richardson injects himself into the ongoing "discussion," not just from the standpoint of being an American theologian himself, but also as a Jesuit. More importantly still, Richardson's participation in the "discussion" two volumes in to *The New Frontiers in Theology* series (1963 and 1964) came from the standpoint of the article serving, at least in part, as a modest follow-up to what is widely considered as the first major comprehensive philosophical study of Martin Heidegger, *Heidegger: Through Phenomenology to Thought* (1963).

Generally speaking, what immediately set Richardson's *Heidegger: Through Phenomenology to Thought* apart as a seminal work was its inclusion of an important preface (or "*Vorwort*") to the work written by Heidegger himself in early April 1962.[70] In the preface, Heidegger sets out to respond to "two principal questions" Richardson poses in an earlier letter to Heidegger dated to March 1, 1962.[71] Richardson's first question is devoted to asking, as Heidegger directly quotes from Richardson's original letter: "how are we properly to understand your first experience of the Being-question in Brentano?"[72] Richardson's second question, as directly quoted by Heidegger, is, in part: "granted that a 'reversal' has come-to-pass in your thinking, how has it come-to-pass?"[73] Heidegger's answers to Richardson's "two principal questions" not only guide the framework of Heidegger's "preface" but it also intends to frame more broadly the task and method of Richardson's study. Essentially, Heidegger's responses act as an invocation to *Heidegger: Through Phenomenology to Thought*. I will not explicate Heidegger's responses to Richardson's two questions in detail here, but, rather, I will say that Heidegger hoped that his responses to Richardson would, in Heidegger's words, "help set in motion the manifold

---

69. Appearing in *Theological Studies*, Volume 26, Number 1.

70. Heidegger, "Preface" to Richardson, *Heidegger: Through Phenomenology to Thought*, xxii.

71. Ibid., ix.

72. Ibid., x-xi.

73. Ibid., xvi.

thinking of the simple business of thought, which, by reason of its very simplicity, abounds in hidden plenitude."[74]

Perhaps, with this in mind—what Heidegger calls "the manifold thinking of the simple business of thought"—Richardson ruminates on the meaning of "later Heidegger" as it is used by Robinson. In doing so, in "Heidegger and Theology," Richardson writes that "if the later Heidegger has any relevance for Christians at all, it will extend beyond the field of exegesis."[75] I take Richardson to mean, here, that the role that Heidegger must have in postmodern theology must be more than just one that is limited to hermeneutics. As important as hermeneutics is to theologizing itself, Heidegger's impact on theologizing ventures beyond hermeneutics, as a stand-in for the field of exegesis—in order to "extend beyond" it, Richardson conceives of Heidegger's thought contributing to "the relation between revelation and faith, between faith and speculative thought, between the magisterial function of theological speculation and the magisterial character of the Church."[76] For Richardson, "all these matters would deserve to be rethought in the light of Heidegger's thought, if, indeed, it offers any light at all."[77]

What must be "rethought," as Richardson sees it, is "the ecumenical importance of Heidegger's influence," given that this influence, "especially for us in America, is unquestionable."[78] This, of course, is exemplified in the inquiries included in *The New Frontiers in Theology* series. From these, Richardson seeks a new line of inquiry that is uniquely oriented to the concerns of Catholicism, from which he is able to ask: "does the later Heidegger have any relevance for the Catholic exegete or theologian?"[79] Because such a question leads Richardson to recount what Heidegger once suggested to be the relevance of "his effort" as "be[ing] considered in terms of an analogy: as philosophical thinking is to Being, so theological thinking (the thinking of faith) is to the self-revealing God."[80] With respect to this, and the extent to which Heidegger's words "covers a multitude of sins," Richardson intends to "simply try to understand the relationship between Being and thinking for the later Heidegger, and then restrict our

---

74. Ibid., xxii.
75. Richardson, "Heidegger and Theology," 87.
76. Ibid.
77. Ibid.
78. Ibid.
79. Ibid.
80. Ibid.

attention to only one way in which its application, by analogy, might be suggestive to the Catholic thinker."[81]

As much as Richardson's "Heidegger and Theology" is chiefly concerned with what relevance Heidegger has for the Catholic exegete or theologian, it is more than just a way for Richardson to have a voice carrying forward the discussions across two volumes of the Robisnon-Cobb co-edited *The New Frontiers in Theology* series. Indeed, as much as the article duly serves as a kind of pedagogical follow-up to the methodological nature of *Heidegger: Through Phenomenology to Thought*—if we see "Heidegger and Theology" recapitulating Heidegger's progress from phenomenology to thought as predicated on Heidegger's desire to "simply try to understand the relationship between Being and thinking"—the article lends itself to another contextualization, which Richardson makes explicit, though in passing.

At the time of Richardson's writing of "Heidegger and Theology," what was undeniably in his purview was the Second Consultation on Hermeneutics, which had been convened by the Graduate School of Drew University on April 9-11, 1964. We know, of course, from "Heidegger and Theology," that Richardson was aware of the conference at Drew, as well as the conference's theme, "The Problem of Non-objectifying Thinking and Speaking in Theology." Though the only comment Richardson makes about the conference itself is that such a theme contains "Heideggerian terminology of the purest water," there seems to be a subtle judgment concealed in it.[82] That judgment is reared again rather passively, though directed poignantly at the paper that opened the conference at Drew and its author to which Richardson describes as "one of Bultmann's disciples (no friend of Heidegger)."[83]

It need not seem strange that Richardson is not more forthcoming in "Heidegger and Theology" about his opinions of the conference at Drew nor more full-throated in what he means by suggesting that the author of the paper that opened the conference was nothing more than "one of Bultmann's disciples" and, as Richardson viewed it, "no friend of Heidegger." We know only from Richardson's footnote that these indictments are directed at Hans Jonas (1903-1993), who had been both a student of Bultmann and Heidegger.

The year before Richardson's "Heidegger and Theology" appeared, Jonas' opening address at Drew—which is coincidently titled "Heidegger and

---

81. Ibid.
82. Ibid.
83. Ibid., 94.

Theology"—intended to engage with, as Jonas himself explains, "a number of 'theses' which Martin Heidegger had sent to serve as a basis for the [conference]."[84] These "theses," or "themes," preceding Jonas' address arose from a paper Heidegger sent, *in absentia*,[85] as a "theological discussion," written on March 11, 1964, about a month before the conference officially convened.[86] Heidegger's "theological discussion" begins by asking: "what is it that is worth questioning in [the problem of a nonobjectifying thinking and speaking in today's theology]?"[87] From here, Heidegger suggests that "as far as I see, there are *three themes* that must be thought through."[88] These three themes, for Heidegger, arise, if I may be very brief here, from "determin[ing] what theology, as a mode of thinking and speaking, is to place in discussion," "stat[ing] what is intended by objectifying thinking and speaking," and "decid[ing] to what extent the problem of a nonobjectifying thinking and speaking is a genuine problem at all."[89] As Heidegger construes the individual meanings of these themes, he asserts that "the third theme comprises the theological consequences of the first and second, when they are treated sufficiently."[90]

Subsequently, Jonas begins his opening address by orienting it immediately towards Heidegger's "third theme," by stating that "the problem of objectification, and with it that of reversing or partially unmaking it, was bequeathed to Western theology from its origin in the mating of the Biblical word with the Greek *logos*."[91] What eventually follows this is Jonas' questioning "objectification" itself, which brings him to ask "if the adoption of the 'seeing' approach from Greek philosophy was a misfortune for theology, does the repudiation or overcoming of that approach in a contemporary philosophy provide a conceptual means for theology to reform itself, to become more adequate to its task?"[92] Jonas wonders, then, if it can "lead to a new alliance between theology and philosophy"[93]—he not only

---

84. Jonas, "Heidegger and Theology," 235.
85. Heidegger was too sick, at the time, to attend in-person.
86. See the appendix to Heidegger, "Phenomenology and Theology," 54.
87. Ibid.
88. Ibid.
89. Ibid., 54-55.
90. Ibid., 55.
91. Jonas, "Heidegger and Theology," 236.
92. Ibid., 239.
93. Ibid.

INTRODUCTION: HEIDEGGER AND THEOLOGY

wonders what kind of "new alliance" is afforded after, for example, "the medieval one with Aristotlianism has broken down."⁹⁴ For Jonas, the question becomes what philosophizing is most adequate to theologizing, when "what theology needs in this relationship is the otherness of philosophy, not its similarity."⁹⁵ It is on this point that Jonas outlines the otherness of Heidegger to "what theology needs" in a relationship with Heidegger. Essentially, Jonas finds an incompatibility between theology and Heidegger, such that Jonas proclaims that there is a profound pagan character in Heidegger's thought.⁹⁶ Robert W. Funk would later summarize Jonas' assertions, in "Colloquium on Hermeneutics" (October 1964), by writing that "Jonas believes that Heidegger's primal thinking thinks away from and beyond God."⁹⁷ Duly summarized in this manner, Funk suggests that "the upshot of Jonas' analysis comes to expression in three further points," with the last of these—and perhaps the most important of the three—the notion that "Jonas believes that Heidegger's attempt to shift the initiative to being, so seductive to Christian theology, is in fact the most enormous hybris in the whole history of thought."⁹⁸ It is particularly with respect to this third point, as characterized by Funk, which brings Jonas to believe that Heidegger cannot claim to an authority that "through him speaks the essence of things itself [. . .] which no thinker should ever claim."⁹⁹

Because Jonas' academic and professional career was so indebted to Heidegger, such a dismissal of Heidegger and especially so in the context of the conference at Drew received a great deal of attention at the time. Funk, too, certainly sees the significance in it in the account of it presented in "Colloquium on Hermeneutics." *The New York Times* ran a cover article on Jonas "breaking" with Heidegger, dated April 11, 1964, under the scathing subtitle "Conference at Drew Is Told Philosopher's Work Lacks Meaning for Christians."¹⁰⁰

In light of this noteworthy "break," particularly at an event as noteworthy as the conference at Drew, and in a way noteworthy enough to be on the front page of *The New York Times*, Richardson responded to Jonas' critiques

---

94. Ibid.
95. Ibid., 240.
96. Ibid., 248.
97. Robert W. Funk, "Colloquium on Hermeneutics," 295.
98. Ibid.
99. Ibid.
100. See *The New York Times*, April 11, 1964 article.

and criticisms of Heidegger just sixteen days following the conclusion of the conference at Drew—on April 27, 1964, having already been scheduled to deliver the annual Suarez Lecture at Fordham University, as detailed briefly in Martin Woessner's *Heidegger in America* (2010), Richardson "intended to discuss the topic of Heidegger's thinking as it related to the question of God, but at the last minute he abandoned his planned remarks and addressed instead Jonas' charges themselves."[101] Richardson's paper, as it was published in Spring of 1965, is entitled "Heidegger and God—and Professor Jonas." Not only does Richardson view Jonas' opening address at the conference at Drew as "offer[ing] the most damning evaluation possible of Heidegger's attitude toward God," but Richardson also proposes that "we renounce the luxury of a purely philosophical meditation, and pick up the gage where Dr. Jonas has thrown it down." Richardson locates his purpose in challenging Jonas' prosecution of Heidegger on the belief that "philosophy does have an obligation to be relevant."[102] More than that, Richardson finds himself guided by the sense that "a statement for the prosecution warrants a statement for the defense, in order that justice, which is to say truth, may have its way."[103] In order to do Heidegger "justice," with the intention of allowing truth to "have its way," Richardson situates the problem with Jonas' characterization of Heidegger's relationship with theology by questioning "the meaning of the [conference] at Drew," challenging "the substance of the Jonas attack," and contextualizing "its value."[104]

Though Richardson's "Heidegger and God—and Professor Jonas" was not published until Spring of 1965—in the same month as Richardson's "Heidegger and Theology" was published—it should certainly not be construed as strictly a coincidence that Jonas published his opening address to the conference at Drew as an essay included in Jonas' *The Phenomenon of Life: Toward a Philosophical Biology* (1966). In fact, it seems likely that Jonas did this to explicitly counter Richardson's characterization of Jonas' handling of Heidegger's relationship with theology, particularly since, given Funk's account of Jonas' position, Jonas seemingly wished to further contextualize, in his own terms, his "break" with Heidegger and the meaning of Heidegger's role in postmodern theology.

101. Martin Woessner, *Heidegger in America*, 116.
102. Richardson, "Heidegger and God—and Professor Jonas," 14.
103. Ibid.
104. Ibid.

INTRODUCTION: HEIDEGGER AND THEOLOGY

Clearly, the difference between Richardson and Jonas on the viability of Heidegger towards theology is irreconcilable. The Richardson-Jonas debate, as it arose in the mid-1960s, has understandably developed into what extent it is even possible to theologize through Heidegger, with Heidegger's association with Nazism either becoming a non-factor in Heidegger's contribution to theology (for Richardson) or disqualifying Heidegger alltogether from theological discourse (for Jonas).

Several articles inserted themselves into this debate through the rest of the 1960s, which, to the best of my knowledge, include only: Charles E. Scott's "Heidegger Reconsidered: A Response to Professor Jonas" (April 1966) and "Heidegger, the Absence of God, and Faith" (July 1966), John N. Deely's "The Situation of Heidegger in the Tradition of Christian Philosophy" (April 1967), Frederick Sontag's "Heidegger, Time, and God" (October 1967), Thomas F. O'Meara's "Tillich and Heidegger: A Structural Relationship" (April 1968), and Peter C. Hodgson's "Heidegger, Revelation, and the Word of God" (July 1969)

With the exception of Macquarrie's *Martin Heidegger* (1973), the following appeared through the 1970s: John R. Williams' "Heidegger and the Theologians" (1971) and "Heidegger, Death, and God" (March 1972), Sueo Oshima's "Barth's 'Analogia Relationis' and Heidegger's Ontological Difference" (April 1973), Joseph Kockelmans' "Heidegger on Theology" (October 1973), Robert Masson's "Rahner and Heidegger: Being, Hearing, and God" (1973), Annemarie Gethmann-Siefert's *Das Verhaltnis von Philosophie und Theologie im Denken Martin Heideggers*. (1974), Eugene T. Long's "John Macquarrie on Language, Being, and God" (December 1976), John D. Caputo's "The Problem of Being in Heidegger and Aquinas" (January 1977), John R. Williams' *Martin Heidegger's Philosophy of Religion* (1977), Charles Habib's "A Christian Reflection on Martin Heidegger" (1977), Jeffrey Goldstein's "Buber's Misunderstanding of Heidegger: Being and the Living God" (1978), Carl A. Raschke's "The End of Theology" (June 1978), and Joan Stambaugh's "The Question of God in Heidegger's Thought" (July 1979).

Work in the 1980s include: John Caputo's "Heidegger's God and the Lord of History" (Autumn 1983), Robert L. Hurd's "Heidegger and Aquinas: A Rahnerian Bridge" (1984), William Portier's "Ancilla invita: Heidegger, the Theologians, and God" (June 1985), Thomas O'Meara's "Heidegger and His Origins" Theological Perspectives" (May 1986), Robert S. Gall's *Beyond Theism and Atheism: Heidegger's Significance for Religious Thinking* (1987), David E. Klemm's "Toward a Rhetoric of Postmodern Theology: Through

Barth and Heidegger" (October 1987), Michel Haar's "Heidegger and the God of Hölderlin" (January 1989), Vincent Guagliardo's "Aquinas and Heidegger: The Question of Philosophical Theology" (1989).

Excluding Macquarrie's *Heidegger and Christianity* (1994), the 1990s include the following studies: George Kovacs' *The Question of God in Heidegger's Phenomenology* (1990), Jeff O. Prudhomme's "The Passing-by of the Ultimate God" (October 1993), Allen Scult's "Hermeneutics and the Rhetoric of Biblical Theology" (January 1994), Pero Brkic's *Martin Heidegger und die Theologie: Ein Thema in dreifacher Fragestellung* (1994), Claude Ozankom's *Gott und Gegenstand: Martin Heideggers Objektivierungsverdikt und seine theologische Rezeption bei Rudolf Bultmann und Heinrich Ott* (1994), David R. Crownfield's "The Question of God: Thinking after Heidegger" (April 1996), Yong Huang's "God as Absolute Spirit: A Heideggerian Interpretation of Hegel's God-Talk" (December 1996), Jeff O. Prudhomme's *God and Being: Heidegger's Relation to Theology* (1997), Sonia Sikka's *Forms of Transcendence: Heidegger and Medieval Mystical Theology* (1997), Sonia Sikka's "Questioning the Scared: Heidegger and Levinas on the Locus of Divinity" (July 1998), Laurence P. Hemming's "Heidegger's God" (1998), Catriona Hanley's "Heidegger on Aristotle's 'Metaphysical' God" (January 1999), Anthony Godzieba's "Prolegomena to a Catholic Theology of God Between Heidegger and Postmodernity" (July 1999), and James K. A. Smith's "Liberating Religion from Theology: Marion and Heidegger on the Possibility of a Phenomenology of Religion" (August 1999).

From 2000 to the present, notwithstanding my own *Heideggerian Theologies: The Pathmarks of John Macquarrie, Rudolf Bultmann, Paul Tillich, and Karl Rahner* (2018), a broad landscape of scholarship exploring the relationship between Heidegger and theology can be found in the following studies: Catriona Hanley's *Being and God in Aristotle and Heidegger: The Role of Method in Thinking the Infinite* (2000), Laurence Hemming's *Heidegger's Atheism: The Refusal of Theological Voice* (2002), Benjamin Crowe's *Heidegger's Religious Origins: Destruction and Authenticity* (2006), Timothy Stanley's "Heidegger on Luther on Paul" (2007), Benjamin Crowe's *Heidegger's Phenomenology of Religion: Realism and Cultural Criticism* (2008), Istvan Feher's "Religion, Theology, and Philosophy on the Way to Being and Time: Heidegger, the Hermeneutical, the Factical, and the Historical With Respect to Dilthey and Early Christianity" (2009), Timothy Stanley's *Protestant Metaphysics after Karl Barth and Martin Heidegger* (2010), Russell Matheson's "Phenomenology and Theology: Situating Heidegger's

Philosophy of Religion" (2011), Judith Wolfe's *Heidegger and Theology* (2014), Duane Armitage's "Heidegger's God" (2014), Judith Wolfe's *Heidegger's Eschatology* (2015), Peter J. Fritz's "Catholic Theology and Heidegger" in *The Oxford Handbook of Catholic Theology* (2015), Duane Armitage's *Heidegger's Pauline and Lutheran Roots* (2016), Martin Nitsche's "A Place of Encounter with a Divine: Heidegger on the Spatiality of Religious Experience" (January 2017), Peter Costello's "Heidegger and Scripture: The Calling of Thinking in our Abandonment" (January 2017), Tarek Dika's "Finitude, Phenomenology, and Theology in Heidegger's *Sein und Zeit*" (2017), the Marten Bjork and Jayne Svenuungsson co-authored, *Heidegger's Black Notebooks and the Future of Theology* (2018), Peter S. Dillard's *Non-metaphysical Theology after Heidegger* (2018), John R. Betz's "After Heidegger and Marion: The Task of Christian Metaphysics Today" (October 2018), and Norman Swazo's "Heidegger's Destruktion of Theology: 'Primordial Faith' and 'Recognition' of the Messiah" (January 2019).

CHAPTER 1: HEIDEGGER'S THEOLOGICAL ROOTS

Heidegger's Theological Roots

WHILE, FROM 1903 TO 1906, when attending the State Gymnasium in Constance, and subsequently, from 1906 to 1909, when attending the State Berthold Gymnasium in Freiburg, Heidegger remained "with residence at the archdiocesan Gymnasium Seminary in preparation for archdiocesan priesthood."[1] By July 13, 1909, when he was awarded his high school baccalaureate "with the highest possible overall grade," having studied a variety of academic subjects including religion, Latin, Hebrew, Greek, and philosophy, Heidegger selected theology on a "statement of intent regarding university studies."[2] As a student entering the University of Freiburg, Heidegger's academic "theological roots," as I refer to them, can be situated in his acceptance into Freiburg's Department of Theology for the Winter 1909/1910 semester. At that time, Heidegger was still preparing for archdiocesan priesthood, "with residence at the archdiocesan Theological Seminary."[3]

With the exception of a course on logic, during Heidegger's first semester at Freiburg, as detailed in noteworthy accounts by Thomas Sheehan (1988) and John Van Buren (2002), Heidegger was enrolled in the following theology/religion courses with the following lecturers: "Encyclopedia of Theological Disciplines" (Rev. Julius Mayer[4]), "Introduction to the Sacred Scripture of the Old Testament" (Rev. Gottfried Hoberg), "Exegesis of Paul's Letter to the Romans" (Rev. Simon Weber), "General History of

---

1. Van Buren, *Supplements*, 18.
2. Ibid.
3. Ibid.
4. Please note that there is a discrepancy between Van Buren's spelling of this last name (Meyer) and what appears in Sheehan's version (Mayer). I have erred on Sheehan's spelling, due to his earlier publication.

the Church, Part One" (Rev. Georg Pfeilschifter), and "Theory of Religion" (Rev. Heinrich Straubinger).[5]

With the exception of a course on metaphysics, in Heidegger's second semester at Freiburg in Summer 1910, he was enrolled in the following theology/religion courses with the following lecturers: "Messianic Prophesies" (with Hoberg), Hermeneutics, with the History of Exegesis (with Hoberg), "Introduction to the Sacred Scripture of the New Testament" (with Weber), "General History of the Church, Part Two" (with Pfeilschifter), and "Theory of Revelation and of the Church" (with Straubinger).[6]

With the exception of a survey course on the history of the German constitution, in his third semester at Freiburg in Winter 1910/1911, Heidegger was enrolled in the following theology/religion courses with the following lecturers: "Introduction to Catholic Dogmatics: The Doctrine of God" (Rev. Carl Braig), "Exegesis of the Holy Gospel According to John" (with Weber), "General Moral Theology, Part One through Three" (with Mayer), "The Doctrine of Property" (with Mayer), "Catholic Canon Law, Part One: Introduction, Sources, and Constitution" (Rev. Emil Göller), "General History of the Church, Part Three, The Age of the Enlightenment" (with Pfeilschifter), and "The History of Medieval Mysticism" (Rev. Joseph Sauer).[7]

With the exception of a course on the Renaissance, in his fourth semester at Freiburg in Summer 1911, Heidegger was enrolled in the following theology/religion courses with the following lecturers: "Theological Cosmology: The Creation, Preservation, and Governance of the World" (with Braig), "Special Moral Theology, Parts One and Two (with Mayer), and "The Christian Art of the Nineteenth Century and the Present" (with Sauer).[8]

As noted by Sheehan, throughout the Summer of 1911, Heidegger suffered from ill-health that posed "negative consequences for his ecclesiastical plans."[9] By Fall of 1911, Sheehan observes that "when [Heidegger] returned to Freiburg [for the upcoming Winter 1911 semester], Heidegger had moved out of the theological seminary [. . .] he had also transferred out of theology."[10] Essentially, at this point, Heidegger "abandon[ed] career

---

5. Van Buren, *Supplements*, 18.
6. Ibid.
7. Ibid.
8. Ibid.
9. Sheehan, "Heidegger's Lehrjarhe," 95.
10. Ibid.

plans for the priesthood."[11] It seems that this was mostly due to Heidegger's "preference at this point [being] to study with Husserl," who, at the time, was teaching at the University of Göttingen.[12] Instead of doing so, Heidegger was accepted into Freiburg's Department of Natural Sciences and Mathematics in Winter 1911/1912. Though Heidegger was enrolled mostly math and sciences courses for the semester, with the exception of two science courses and two philosophy courses, it has been detailed by both Sheehan and Van Buren that, during this semester, Heidegger audited a three theology/religion courses with the following lecturers: "Dogmatic Theology" (with Braig), "Gospel of John" (with Prof. Edward Schwartz), and "Hellenic Mystery Religions" (with Prof. Richard Reitzenstein). For the following Summer 1912, Winter 1912/1913, and Summer 1913, Heidegger was enrolled in mostly math courses, with a single science course and a handful of philosophy courses sprinkled throughout. On July 26, 1913, Heidegger had left the Department of Natural Sciences and Mathematics, was accepted to the Department of Philosophy, and was recommended by the Department of Philosophy "for the doctoral degree in philosophy summa cum laude," based on his dissertation, submitted a month prior, "Theory of Judgment in Psychologism: Critical and Positive Contributions to Logic."[13] On August 20, 1913, Heidegger applied for a Von Schaezler Grant, in order, as cited by Van Buren, "to dedicate himself to the study of Christian philosophy and to pursue an academic career"—by September 29, 1913, he was awarded the grant for the 1913-1914 academic year with the expectation, as purported by Van Buren, that Heidegger "would remain true to the spirit of Thomistic philosophy."[14] Heidegger renewed the grant twice (on September 20, 1914 and on December 13, 1915), under the premise that, as Van Buren quotes, "his academic life's work [would be] oriented to making the wealth of ideas inherited from Scholasticism applicable to the future intellectual struggle for the Christian ideal of life in Catholicism."[15]

---

11. Van Buren, *Supplements*, 19.
12. Sheehan, "Heidegger's Lehrjarhe," 95.
13. Van Buren, *Supplements*, 20.
14. Ibid.
15. Ibid., 21.

CHAPTER 1: HEIDEGGER'S THEOLOGICAL ROOTS

Heidegger and Catholic Freiburg (1919-1923)

From 1915-1917, Heidegger taught five lecture courses and seminars in the role of a *"Privatdozent"* or lecturer (or what Sheehan refers to as "instructor"): two in Winter 1915/1916, two in Summer 1916, and one in Winter 1916/1917. At present, none of these early philosophy courses have been published into Heidegger's *Gesamtausgabe*. For that matter, the extent to which these lectures and seminars can be listed at all suggests that they are housed in the Deutsche Literaturarchiv in Marbach—Sheehan, in particular, can be thanked for the listing of these four early lectures. Though Heidegger did not teach from Summer 1917 to Winter 1918/1919—this amounted to a total of four semesters—due Heidegger's "conscription into war service," Heidegger delivered an informal talk on August 2, 1917 entitled "On the Essence of Religion" (translated from "Über das Wesen der Religion"). This talk was selected from an ongoing compilation of notes for a planned treatise on what Heidegger titled as the "Phenomenology of Religious Consciousness/Life" that he began in 1916 and continued through to August 1919, which would later become conscribed into a text for a planned lecture "The Philosophical Foundations of Medieval Mysticism."

"The Philosophical Foundations of Medieval Mysticism"
(August 10, 1919)

Included as the third of three texts in *The Phenomenology of Religious Life* (as GA 60, translated from *Phänomenologie des religiösen Lebens*), "The Philosophical Foundations of Medieval Mysticism" (translated from "*Die philosophischen Grundlagen der mittelalterlichen Mystik*") is the title ascribed to a lecture course that Heidegger intended to deliver in the Winter 1919/1920.

Having finished his habilitation thesis in 1916 on Duns Scotus (originally submitted the previous year) and becoming Edmund Husserl's assistant in January 1919, the Winter 1919/1920 semester was Heidegger's third semester in the role of a *"Privatdozent"* or lecturer. At the time, it has been suggested that Heidegger's interests were in phenomenology and Neo-Kantian ontology, particularly as a means of further investigating Scotus's doctrines of categories—in light of this, it is believed that Heidegger's concerns, when entering the Winter 1919/1920 semester, was primarily with, as explained by John Van Buren in a rare account of this early period in Heidegger's career, "moving from religion to ontology in order to rethink the latter historically with aid of the former."[16] Nevertheless, according to Van Buren, Heidegger's plans for the "The Philosophical Foundations of Medieval Mysticism" lecture "will go in the opposite direction of applying his new ontology to a phenomenology of mysticism."[17] Van Buren notes that the lecture course was to have been taught alongside two other courses for Winter 1919/1920—one devoted to "Selected Problems of Recent Phenomenology" and the other a "Seminar in Connection with Natorp's *General Psychology*." Instead of carrying this forward as planned, Van Buren points out that "Heidegger replaced the course on mysticism with an expansion of the course on phenomenology from a one- to a two-hour course, which was then retitled 'Basic Problems of Phenomenology.'"[18] It is remains unclear why Heidegger made this choice, even though the official reason given was "lack of time."[19] Van Buren chooses to make use of Kisiel's suggestion—from *The Genesis of Heidegger's Being and Time*—that "[Heidegger] felt that he had still not adequately worked out the philosophical conceptuality and methodology needed for executing the concrete analyses of his phenomenology of religion."[20] Even though Kisiel may indeed be correct about this, it remains impossible to know if this was precisely the reason why Heidegger abandoned the planned "The Philosophical Foundations of Medieval Mysticism."

The editors of the text explain in the "afterword" to GA 60 that "the manuscript that was left behind makes it known that [Heidegger] began working it out on August 10, 1919, and on August 14 attempted a continuation and then broke it off."[21] Apparently, by August 30, Heidegger made a formal request to Freiburg's Department of Liberal Arts "for a change in the lecture course." The editors provide Heidegger's reasons for this change from Freiburg archival documents, which, just as Van Buren has noted, seems to be based on Heidegger's believing he did not have enough time, since, in Heidegger's words, he had "counted on a longer autumn break."[22] From this, it seems that Heidegger experienced some trouble working

16. Van Buren, "Heidegger's Early Freiburg Courses, 1915-1923," 143.
17. Ibid.
18. Ibid., 144.
19. Ibid.
20. Ibid.
21. Heidegger, *The Phenomenology of Religious Life*, 261.
22. Ibid.

through what he planned for "The Philosophical Foundations of Medieval Mysticism," such that, as Heidegger claims in his request for change of lecture course, "a working-through of the material—one that meets stringent demands—for the announced lecture course [. . .] is impossible."

What currently remains of the undelivered "The Philosophical Foundations of Medieval Mysticism" is a text made up of nothing more than a series of outlines and sketches. Essentially, it is an incomplete text, which begins with Heidegger stating that, though the "formulation is ambiguous," he intends to be guided by the assertion that "phenomenological research into religious consciousness is the driving problem and method."[23] The "driving problem, for Heidegger, is what he calls the "renunciation of constructive philosophy of religion," what he describes as "non-absorption in the purely historical as such," and the need to "[trace] back to the genuinely clarified and genuinely originally seen phenomena to pure consciousness and its constitution."[24] In order to do this, Heidegger wishes to develop a phenomenological "primordial" understanding of religious consciousness in a way that can be ascertained "out of the historical."[25]

Thematically, Heidegger argues that the lecture would proceed "purely according to the history of philosophy," such that the term "philosophical foundations" would point to "the metaphysical presuppositions, the phenomenological views, ethical doctrines, and above all the scientific aspect of the sphere of experience, the psychological positions of medieval mysticism."[26] Though Heidegger begins a section on "Mysticism in the Middle Ages" and carries subsequent sections exploring the phenomenological attitude towards religious experience through to a section on "Irrationality in Meister Eckhart"—Eckhart (1260-1328) being a pivotal figure at the intersection of medieval philosophy and Christian mysticism—he proceeds into a section on Friedrich Schleiermacher's second address, "On the Essence of Religion" (1799, included in *On Religion: Speeches to its Cultured Despisers*). From here, he eventually (and very briefly) considers Hegel's "original, earliest position on religion" along with its consequences rooted in the "decisive influence of Kant."[27] After this, Heidegger returns to Schleiermacher, but, this time, he provides a brief consideration

23. Ibid., 231.
24. Ibid.
25. Ibid.
26. Ibid.
27. Ibid., 248.

of Schleiermacher's *The Christian Faith* (1821-1822), with respect to the "phenomenology of religion in general."[28] What follows, then, before the manuscript breaks off, is a section entitled "The Holy," in which Heidegger offers "preparations for the review" of Rudolf Otto's *The Idea of the Holy* (1917)—Otto (1869-1937), a Lutheran theologian, influenced most notably by Kant and Schleiermacher, would help develop the study of the science of religion, which would later develop into the branches of philosophy of religion, the history of religion, and the psychology of religion.

"Introduction to the Phenomenology of Religion" (Winter 1920/1921)

As the first of three texts included in *The Phenomenology of Religious Life* (GA 60), the editors of "Introduction to the Phenomenology of Religion" (translated from *Einleitung in die Phänomenologie der Religion*) note, in the afterword to the volume, that "the manuscript of the lecture course is lost."[29] Interestingly, because of this, the editors rely on "five sets of notations" made by students that attended the course—each annotation made by each student, according to the editors, "allow for the approximate reconstruction of the train of thought and articulation of the lecture course."[30] It must be noted that not all of these annotations are found with Heidegger's other papers in the Deutsche Literaturarchiv in Marbach, known as the "DLA" (it is from this archive, in particular that Heidegger's *Gesamtausgabe* has been catalogued)—only three are found in the DLA, while the other two "are kept in the Husserl Archive of Leuven."[31] This presented a problem for the editors when attempting to reconstruct the lecture course. Essentially, this reconstruction was not just simply a combination of all the annotations made into a main text of the lecture course—an adjudication of phrases and terms across the annotations into a coherent text—but it also includes, "reproduced" in a series of appendices, Heidegger's own "handwritten notes from the context of the lecture course."[32] Heidegger's notes, which consist of what the editors describe as "single pages in a folder" in the DLA, act as supplementary material to what the editors have reconstructed

28. Ibid., 249.
29. Ibid., 255.
30. Ibid.
31. Ibid.
32. Ibid.

from student annotations, "because the pages are immediately related to the work of the lecture course and, in the absence of the originally handwritten lecture, are the only remaining original documents pertaining to the lecture course."[33]

Structurally, the main text of "Introduction to the Phenomenology of Religion" is less than 100 pages, and is comprised of two parts: a "methodological introduction" and a "phenomenological explication"—the first is associated with "philosophy, factical life experience, and the phenomenology of religion," and the second is focused on "concrete religious phenomena in connection with the letters of Paul." Given this structure, the lecture course seems to be constructed around, first, presenting a methodology guided by Heidegger's examination of "the formation of philosophical concepts and factical life experience," "current tendencies of the philosophy of religion" by way of philosophy of religion of Protestant theologian and an authority in the field, Ernst Troeltsch (1865-1923), "the phenomenon of the historical," and "formalization and forma indication," before proceeding into a phenomenological interpretation of three Pauline letters: the letter to the Galatians, the first letter to the Thessalonians, and the second letter to the Thessalonians, in order to conceptualize the "characteristics of early Christian life."

In light of what Heidegger left undelivered in "The Philosophical Foundations of Medieval Mysticism," it is clear that "Introduction to the Phenomenology of Religion" is concerned with, as Van Buren found missing in the undelivered lecture from the previous semester, "work[ing] out the philosophical conceptuality and methodology needed for executing the concrete analysis of [Heidegger's] phenomenology of religion." In this regard, then, what we find in "Introduction to the Phenomenology of Religion" is, as Van Buren points out, "Heidegger ventur[ing] in the opposite direction of concretizing the formal indications of his ontology in a phenomenology of religion."[34] At the time, Heidegger was rethinking his ontology while concurrently composing a review of Karl Jaspers's *Psychology of Worldviews* (1919)—Van Buren points out that Heidegger was at work on this review "between 1919 and 1921."[35] With "Jaspers' appropriation of Kierkegaard"[36] as a means of psychologically articulating the meaning of

33. Ibid.
34. Van Buren, "Heidegger's Early Freiburg Courses, 1915-1923," 144.
35. Ibid.
36. Ibid.

"worldview" and Heidegger having delivered a lecture course on the subject during the Winter 1919 (in what is known as a War Emergency Semester), entitled, "The Idea of Philosophy and the Problem of Worldviews" (in GA 56/57, translated from *Die Idee der Philosophie und das Weltanschauungsproblem*), Heidegger's rethinking of ontology is most certainly tied to his rethinking of "worldview." By the time Heidegger delivers "Introduction to the Phenomenology of Religion," he is, still, ultimately concerned with developing a thoroughgoing conceptualization of "worldview"—exactly a year after his first investigation of it—and situates an understanding of "worldview" in his "phenomenological explication" of three of Paul's eschatological letters, with respect to, according to Van Buren, an "analysis of kairological time and the nonobjectifiability of God."[37]

This second part of "Introduction to the Phenomenology of Religion"—more so than the first—frequently receives scholarly attention, particularly in an effort to understand the relationship between Heidegger and theology. Aside from what Van Buren briefly discusses, the two earliest and most important accounts on the significance of Heidegger's phenomenological confrontation with Paul's eschatology in the second part of the lecture can be found in Thomas Sheehan's "Heidegger's 'Introduction to the Phenomenology of Religion,' 1920-1921" (1979-1980) and a large portion of "The Religion Courses" section of Kisiel's *The Genesis of Heidegger's Being and Time* (1993). For Kisiel, though making note to an account additionally given by Otto Pöggeler, "the more complete gloss by Sheehan makes the 'phenomenon of factic life-experience' central to Part One, but never mentions its climax in the formal indication."[38] Kisiel's own account, however, is more thorough than Sheehan's, with Kisiel devoting some forty pages to discussing "Introduction to the Phenomenology of Religion." Kisiel includes the curious fact that the lecture broke off at a point after the end of its first part—what Kisiel calls "*curses interruptus*"—which occurs on November 30, 1920, seemingly, as cited by one of notations made by Oskar Becker, "owning to the objections of nonmajors"[39]—the objections were to the progress, or lack thereof, made in the first part of the lecture. These "objections," as Kisiel describes, were "the direct result of student complaints made to the Dean of the Philosophical Faculty over the lack of religious content in a course

---

37. Ibid.
38. Kisiel's footnotes to *The Genesis of Heidegger's Being and Time*, 527.
39. Ibid., 171.

on the philosophy of religion."⁴⁰ Because these objections directly forced Heidegger to end the first part in favor of commencing the second party earlier than Heidegger had planned, Heidegger does not provide a more complete use of formalization and formal indication—to which, given the interruption—is unfortunately short and incomplete—which Kisiel believes to be "at the very heart and soul of the early Heidegger."⁴¹ Since Heidegger is never able to express more fully how he intended to explain his use of formalization and formal indication as part of a turn away from methodological introduction to the phenomenological explication, Kisiel finds that "the single most important casualty of the premature interruption of the methodological considerations of this course, which was centered upon the 'self-understanding of philosophy.'"⁴²

"Augustine and Neoplatonism" (Summer 1921)

Included as the second of three texts in *The Phenomenology of Religious Life* (GA 60), the main text for the lecture, "Augustine and Neoplatonism" (translated from "*Augustinus und der Neuplatonismus*"), as noted by the editors, originally "consists of nineteen handwritten pages in folio format."⁴³ The editors thusly describe these handwritten pages in the following way: "along the left side Heidegger wrote the progressive text, [while] on the right side he left room for notes, insertions, citations, supplements, as well as explanations of the translations."⁴⁴ Structurally, the main text of the lecture contains some fifteen to twenty marginal notes per manuscript page, with one of these manuscript pages containing as many as thirty—because, the editors explain, "many of them [are] not only underneath one another, but [are] also in outlined bundles next to each other, often again with further insertions and supplements, and, accordingly, most of the time with a loss of grammatical sequence."⁴⁵ Consequently, since "marginal notes are without clear reference to the continuous text," the editors rendering of a complete coherent text was made all the more difficult when considering

---

40. Ibid., 172.
41. Ibid.
42. Ibid.
43. Heidegger, *The Phenomenology of Religious Life*, 259.
44. Ibid.
45. Ibid.

the state of the lecture as it is.[46] As with "The Introduction to the Phenomenology of Religion," in an effort to adjudicate the problem of the manuscript, the editors also relied on, in this case, "handwritten annotations" from students attending the "Augustine and Neoplatonism" lecture—these students included Oskar Becker, Fritz Schalk, and Karl Löwith, whereby all of their "writings were repeatedly collated."[47]

In its edited form, the "Augustine and Neoplatonism" lecture contains, essentially, two parts: an introductory part and the main part—the introductory part, in just ten pages, provides "interpretations of Augustine," while the main part, which extends some 57 pages in length, focuses on a "phenomenological interpretation of *Confessions*; Book X." In the very brief "introductory part," Heidegger examines three interpretations of Augustine of Hippo (354-430) in three very brief sections of no more than a page in length for: Ernst Troeltsch (which also appears in part one of "The Phenomenology of Religion" lecture), Adolf von Harnack (1851-1930), and Wilhelm Dilthey (1833-1911).

Before entering into a discussion of these three interpretations proper, Heidegger first gives some preliminary remarks on the lecture itself, by announcing that "the task set before us is a limited one; to what extent it is limited will become clear, at least negatively, in its demarcation from other interpretations and evaluations of Augustine."[48] That task, as Heidegger outlines it, is predicated on the "latter" interpretations and evaluations that "concur in their high esteem of Augustine's cultural-historical impact."[49] For Heidegger, these "latter ones"—those that he eventually presents as belonging to Troeltsch, Harnack, and Dilthey (to which we can include Heidegger here)—situate their respective interpretations and evaluations of Augustine in term of two contexts that Heidegger points out. Heidegger's first point is this: Augustine's role in the development of medieval theology, whereby "the medieval reception of Aristotle was able to assert itself—if at all—only in a sharp confrontation with Augustinian directions of thought."[50] This especially comes to bear on medieval mysticism—which, as we know, Heidegger attempted to explore but failed to deliver in an earlier lecture planned for Winter 1919/1920—as what Heidegger describes as "a vivification of theological

46. Ibid.
47. Ibid.
48. Ibid., 115.
49. Ibid.
50. Ibid.

thought and practical-ecclesiastical religious ritual which, in essence, goes back to Augustinian motifs."⁵¹ From here, Heidegger offers a second point of context is this: "Augustine was subject to a renewal in the Catholic Church, in particular in seventeenth-century France (Descartes, Malebranche, Pascal, Jansenism, Bossuet, Fénelon)." It is in light of this that Heidegger further contextualizes this point by surmising that "what is at work in this is not really Augustine, but an Augustinianism which is more appropriate to the doctrine of the Church, and which slightly violates the dogmatic boundaries only in ontologism."⁵² Here, with this in mind, we find Heidegger directly criticizing the contemporary work of Max Scheler (1874-1928) in a parenthetical aside that makes the following charge: "what Scheler is doing today is merely a secondary reception of these circles of thought dressed up in phenomenology."⁵³ This sort of charge against Scheler's use and abuse of phenomenology is most certainly Heidegger's attempt to distinguish his own phenomenology, as much as it is about understanding Augustinianism more narrowly. In this essence, Heidegger argues that "Augustinianism has a twofold meaning: philosophically, it means a Christian Platonism turned against Aristotle; theologically, a certain conception of the doctrine of sins and of grace (freedom of the will and predestination)."⁵⁴ Based on this twofold conceptualization of Augustinianism, Heidegger concludes his preliminary remarks to the "introductory part" with surmising that "Augustine was a subject to a reconsideration through the awakening of the critical science of history in the nineteenth century."⁵⁵ Given this historical context along with the contingency "of the research of the last decades," Heidegger contextualizes what will become his own phenomenological interpretation of Augustine (not provided until "the main part") by "characteriz[ing] briefly the three most prominent interpretations and evaluations from which the following attempt distinguishes itself, and with regard to which it essentially limits itself."⁵⁶ According to Heidegger, these "three most prominent interpretations," as it has been aforementioned, belong to how Augustine is hermeneutically-handled respectively by Troeltsch, Harnack, and Dilthey.

51. Ibid.
52. Ibid.
53. Ibid.
54. Ibid.
55. Ibid.
56. Ibid.

While Heidegger reads Troeltsch's interpretation of Augustine, as it is expressed in Troeltsch's *Augustin, die christliche Antike und das Mittelalter. Im Anschluß an die Schrift* (1915), which can be roughly translated as *Augustine, the Christian Antiquity, and the Middle Age: Following Scripture*), "from the perspective of a general, universally-historically oriented philosophy of culture," Heidegger ultimately locates a problem in this.[57] It is to this problem that Heidegger asks: "how one is to establish oneself in the world, make oneself at home in it with decency and adjusted to progress, after one has already fallen for paganism?"[58] To answer this, Heidegger problematizes Troeltsch's use of Augustine, as one that "establishes the problem of culture as the essence of a universal-historical study of history [such that] the study becomes, to a considerable extent, 'encompassing,' but equally blurred and merely the material of an educational orientation."[59]

As much as "Harnack understands Augustine and his significance differently," Heidegger reads Harnack's interpretation of Augustine as a "presentation [that] is based on a much greater familiarity with Augustine's writing than is found in the case of Troeltsch and his—in this respect—*too* universal presentation."[60] As Heidegger reads "Harnack's presentation," Heidegger defines it "on the basis of the task of a history of dogma, as [Harnack] formulated it."[61] In doing so, Heidegger construes, from Harnack, "the problematic of the history of dogma [is] thus conceived [so that] what is peculiar to Augustine does not, according to Harnack, appear as the formation of a new dogmatic system, but as the re-vivification of the old one on the basis of personal experience and piety, and, in the closest connection with this piety, the integration of the new fundamental thoughts of the doctrine of sin and grace."[62] This "general evaluation" can be found primarily in Harnack's *Dogmengeschichte* (1914, roughly translated as *History of Economic Thought*).

Dilthey's interpretation of Augustine, for Heidegger, is "in the context of a historical pursuit of the formation of historical consciousness and an epistemological basis for the human sciences."[63] Heidegger locates this

57. Ibid., 116.
58. Ibid.
59. Ibid.
60. Ibid., 117.
61. Ibid.
62. Ibid.
63. Ibid.

interpretation in Dilthey's *Introduction to the Human Sciences* (1883, translated from *Einleitung in die Geisteswissenschaften*). Interestingly enough, this section on Heidegger's understanding of Dilthey's interpretation of Augustine is reconstructed from Oskar Becker's notes on Heidegger, which begins with Becker writing: "[Dilthey] traces knowledge back to descriptive psychology, to 'experience' (in the sense of self-observation, internal perception)."[64] Becker follows this with an initial question—a question that is seemingly a question posed by Heidegger himself—that asks: "now, what is the significance of Christianity, and of Augustine in particular, for the foundation of the human sciences?"[65] To this, Becker writes, assumedly based on Heidegger's answer, "a change in the life of the soul goes along with Christianity [insomuch as] the life of the soul turns back to itself."[66] Becker goes on to write: "a new vivacity comes to humanity through the experience of the great model of the personality of Jesus."[67] With respect to this, Becker asks a second question—undoubtedly Heidegger's—that asks: "what is the significance of this altercation for the purposive complex of science?"[68] Through Heidegger, Becker argues that "with Christianity, the limit of ancient science, which merely concerned itself with the representation of the outer world, has been overcome: the life of the soul becomes a scientific problem."[69] This brings Becker, by way of Heidegger, to suggest that "[Dilthey] shows how Christianity becomes a doctrine and a philosophy under the influence of ancient science."[70] The next question Becker presents is this: "what is Augustine's significance in this process?"[71] The significance, as Heidegger reads it, is "in the face of ancient scepticism, Augustine ascertained the absolute reality of internal experience [. . .] in the absolute consciousness of God [. . .] the human soul is changeable; it requires an unchangeable basis [such that] this is the internal experience of God's existence."[72] Becker cites Augustine's *De trinitate* (published around 417) here. The conclusion that Heidegger reaches, as relayed by

64. Ibid., 118.
65. Ibid.
66. Ibid.
67. Ibid.
68. Ibid.
69. Ibid.
70. Ibid.
71. Ibid.
72. Ibid.

Becker, is that "Dilthey says that what Augustine wished to accomplish was accomplished first by Kant and Schleiermacher [and] thus, Dilthey entirely misunderstands the inner problem of Augustine."[73]

What follows this "introductory part" is Heidegger's "main part" of the lecture, which involves, as aforementioned, a "phenomenological interpretation" of Augustine's *Confessions* (written between 397-400), with Heidegger's chief focus on Book X. Before discussing Confessions, Heidegger begins by noting Augustine's "*Retractationes*" written "towards the end of his life, around 426 or 427," which went about "correct[ing], and improv[ing] what, to him, now seem[ed] problematic" with the earlier *Confessions*.[74] Heidegger provides an "account of the motives which provoked this reassessment," with a section quoted from *Retractationes*.[75] Afterwards, Heidegger proceeds to *Confessions*, with a parenthetical note about "the preface is to be explicated from an existential perspective." [76] This comes to bear on Heidegger's focus on Book X, which he suggests "can be easily demarcated from the others books [of *Confessions*], as Augustine here no longer relates his past, but rather tells what he is now,"—that situatedness, as Heidegger finds it in Augustine's understanding of "the now," is, as Heidegger quotes from Augustine, "in the very time of the making of my confessions."[77] It is respect to this meaning of "the now" that Heidegger enters Book X, by grouping its first seven chapters in terms of "the motif of *confiteri* [to confess] before God and the people," "knowledge of oneself," "the objecthood of God," and "the essence of the soul."[78] Next, Heidegger groups Chapters 8-19 together under "*The* memoria"—note the emphasis on "the"—and Chapter 20-23 under "of *the beata vita*"—note the emphasis here. Heidegger, then, considers Chapters 24-27 under "the how of questioning and hearing," with Chapters 24-27 under "the *curare* (being concerned) and Chapters 30-34 under "the first form of *tentatio: concupiscentia carnis*." Heidegger isolates Chapter 35 as "the second form of *tentatio: concupiscentia oculorum*," following with Chapters 36-38 under "the third form of *tentatio: ambition saeculi*." Finally, Heidegger isolates Chapter 39 as "self-importance," before concluding the lecture with a section entitled "*Molestia* [Trouble]—The Facticity of Life,"

73. Ibid.
74. Ibid., 127.
75. Ibid.
76. Ibid., 127-128.
77. Ibid., 128.
78. Ibid., 129-132.

predicated on "the how of the being of life" and "*molestia*—the endangerment of having-of-oneself."

The manner with which presents the "Augustine and Neoplatonism" is undoubtedly related to the earlier, "Introduction to the Phenomenology of Religion"—there is a connection between the two as what Kisiel calls Heidegger's "religion courses." Kisiel notes the collection as "not just a matter of bringing the discussion down to the student level, that this methodological treatment of the formal indication is followed by two guiding conceptual schematisms, extracted from the texts of Paul and Augustine, of the dynamics of becoming Christian."[79] Not only do we find Heidegger revisiting "the factical life experience" from the earlier, "Introduction to the Phenomenology of Religion lecture in a more nuanced way in the use of "the facticity of life" in the present lecture "Augustine and Neoplatonism," but we also see that Heidegger is still concerned ultimately with "the early characteristics of Christian life"—though this, in the earlier lecture, is devoted to how these characteristics are conceptualized in the "eschatological" Pauline letters, with his turn toward Augustine, Heidegger is reconsidering these characteristics in terms of "*molestia*," or what he poignantly describes as "a burden of life, something which pulls life down."[80] This, in itself, is reconsidered in light of a two-fold significance in the meaning of "*molestia*" as "a How of experiencing, a burden to, and an endangering of, having-of-oneself—in full facticity."[81]

"Colloquium on the Theological Foundations of Kant's *Religion within the Limits of Reason Alone*" (Summer 1923)

In what was to be his last semester teaching at Freiburg, Heidegger taught a total of four courses in Summer 1923: one lecture course, *Ontology—The Hermeneutics of Facticity* (GA 63, translated from "*Ontologie. Hermeneutik der Faktizität*") and three seminars (which currently remained unpublished). Of the three seminars, two are phenomenological interpretations of Aristotle—one is a beginner's seminar on Aristotle's *Nicomachean Ethics* and the other is a continuation of upper-level practicum of a comparative study of Book 6 of Aristotle's *Nicomachean Ethics*, *De anima*, Book 7 of *Metaphysics* from the previous Winter 1922/1923. The third seminar of

---

79. Kisiel, *The Genesis of Heidegger's Being and Time*, 218.
80. Heidegger, *The Phenomenology of Religious Life*, 181.
81. Ibid., 183.

this period is the "Colloquium on the Theological Foundations of Kant's *Religion within the Limits of Reason Alone*," which, Sheehan highlights, was based on selected texts, dedicated to advanced students, and was co-taught with Julius Ebbinghaus (1885-1981).

Not only is the "Colloquium on the Theological Foundations of Kant's *Religion within the Limits of Reason Alone*" seminar currently unpublished, but it also remains uncertain as to the exact structure of this course. Given that it holds an importance for being delivered in Heidegger's final semester at Freiburg, it is especially important as the first theology course Heidegger delivers since "Augustine and Neoplatonism" in Summer 1921. Nevertheless, it seems that little is actually known about the course or its content—though Van Buren claims, in *The Young Heidegger* (1994) that the course "explored the influence of Luther on Kant and German Idealism,"[82] this claim remains spurious. Only Sheehan provides some anecdotal information, proposing, in a footnote to the course listed in *Becoming Heidegger*, co-edited with Kisiel, that "we might perhaps get an idea of the upshot of this seminar from Julius Ebbinghaus, 'Luther und Kant,' *Luther-Jahrbuch* IX (1927), 119-55."[83] Sheehan goes on to say that "this joint colloquium developed from the habit that the two had since 1921 of spending one evening a week together to read the works of the young Luther and Melanchthon," which Ebbinghaus himself recounts in a text not published until 1975. From Sheehan's anecdote, we can surmise that Heidegger co-teaching with Ebbinghaus on Kant was likely a close reading of *Religion within the Limits of Reason Alone* (1793). Aside from that, it is impossible to know, at this point in time, how Heidegger and Ebbinghaus divided their teaching efforts, as much as it is difficult to say which "selected" portions of text held theological significance for the unknown pedagogical objectives of the seminar itself.

With Kant's text itself generally having an immense influence on the history of theology and the philosophy of religion, it remains debatable about how *Religion within the Limits of Reason Alone* is to be interpreted, particularly with respect to the distinction, in it, that Kant makes between rational religion and historical religions—for Kant, rational religion was "bare" to extent that it presents religious truths, while historical religions, though clothed, are incapable of expressing religious truths. With this in mind, we can certainly see how such a text would come into Heidegger's

---

82. Van Buren, *The Young Heidegger*, 149.
83. Kisiel and Sheehan, *Becoming Heidegger*, lvii.

purview—keeping in mind his previous interests in Troeltsch—especially as a precursor to additional work on explicitly devoted to Kant in Winter 1923/1924 (an unpublished talk to the Kant Society), Winter 1926/1927 (GA 23), Winter 1927/1928 (GA 24), and *Kant and the Problem of Metaphysics* in 1929 (GA 3).

Heidegger and Protestant Marburg (1923-1928)

Upon becoming an associate professor in the Philosophy Department at the University of Marburg in October 1923—"with the rights and privileges of a full professor"[84]—Heidegger began teaching there in the Winter 1923/1924 semester. In that first Marburg semester, Heidegger taught three courses: one lecture course on phenomenological research (GA 17) and two seminars (one for beginners and another for advanced students) that are given the title "Phenomenological Practicum"—the beginners were taught Husserl's *Logical Investigations* and the advanced were taught Aristotle's *Physics*. It must be noted that neither of the two seminars from Winter 1923/1924 have been published.

Even without knowing the exact content and format of the two unpublished seminars are currently unknown—even if we can assume that they do exist, at least in the Deutsche Literaturarchiv in Marbach—we can be sure that, across three courses in this semester, Heidegger was interested in further developing the approach to phenomenological interpretation as it had previously and frequently been delivered in Freiburg seminars. Yet, at the close of his first Marburg semester, Heidegger remains equally interested in theological investigations, such that these interests increased in frequency over the course of Heidegger's time at Marburg, beginning most notably with Heidegger's talk on "The Problem of Sin in Luther." What this talk illustrates, as observed by Brian H. Bowles in an introduction to the text as it appears in *Becoming Heidegger*, that "the move to 'Protestant Marburg' [. . .] gave Heidegger immediate and uninhibited opportunity to demonstrate his long familiarity with the Lutheran opus."[85] That familiarity has been dated to as early as 1918, when Heidegger "began to read Luther closely"[86] and did so "sometimes with like-minded colleagues like Julius

---

84. Ibid., xxxvii.
85. Ibid., 183.
86. Ibid.

Ebbinghaus,"[87] with whom Heidegger would co-teach the colloquium on Kant in Summer 1923. Bowles also notes that, sometime in 1921, "a small grant through Husserl allowed Heidegger [. . .] to obtain the complete Erlangen edition of Luther," which Heidegger made use of in his Freiburg lectures and seminars.[88]

Indeed, there is a "record of evidence"[89] that shows not only Heidegger's familiarity with Luther's work, but also Luther's influence on Heidegger—this seems especially so, given Van Buren's belief that Heidegger's "colloquium" on Kant co-taught with Ebbinghaus sought to explore "the influence of Luther on Kant," even if it is impossible to know for sure to what extent Heidegger's knowledge of Luther figured into the specific (and currently unknown) content of the "colloquium." However, what is undoubtedly clear is that Heidegger's prior work on Luther had an influence on Heidegger's contribution to Bultmann's seminar on Paul for Winter 1923/1924—Bowles points out that "the record of the seminar shows that Heidegger made his first significant contribution in a discussion of the Lutheran thesis of the justification of faith through God's act of judgment, and therefore the relationship between faith and ethical action."[90] This contribution is dated to January 10, 1924, with respect to an exegesis of Romans 6 on the topic of "living in faith—Bowles explains that "Heidegger's exegesis [. . .] spilled over, in the following weeks, into questions of the fulfilment of ethical commands and the special demands imposed on Christians."[91] These "special demands imposed on Christians," as such, were certainly carried forward from Heidegger's understandings of the "characteristics of early Christian life" seen in the "Introduction to the Phenomenology of Religion" lecture (Winter 1920/1921) and the "*molestia* (trouble)" as "the facticity of life" seen in the "Augustine and Neoplatonism" lecture (Summer 1921). Because of this, it is especially possible to see Heidegger's exegesis of Romans 6, as part of Bultmann's larger seminar, as connected to Heidegger's exegesis of Paul's letter to the Galatians and Paul's first and second letters to the Thessalonians in the "Introduction to the Phenomenology of Religion." It is this exegetical focus that contextualizes, as Bowles asserts, "a discussion of the demands of conscience, guilt, decision [. . .], and freedom

87. Ibid.
88. Ibid.
89. Ibid.
90. Ibid.
91. Ibid.

sets the state for Heidegger's two-part commentary that concludes the semester" for Bultmann's seminar on Paul.

"The Problem of Sin in Luther" (1924)

Towards the end of the Winter 1923/1924 semester, Heidegger participated in the "last two hours" or the last two sessions of a seminar Bultmann already had in-progress called "Paul's Ethics,"[92] as a course belonging to the Department of Theology. Heidegger's participation has been dated to February 14 and 21, 1924, with Heidegger's talk, "The Problem of Sin in Luther," being described by Bowles as "attempt[ing] to lead the theological question of sin, faith, and man's relation to God back to more properly philosophical territory."[93] Heidegger's dialogue with Luther is grounded on Heidegger translating Luther's theology philosophically. In light of this, in particular, "despite these apparent correspondences," Bowles writes, "there exists between [Heidegger and Luther] a radical incommensurability."[94] According to Bowles, "for in Heidegger, in opposition to Luther, there is no room to talk about the 'original righteousness' of the human being."[95] Bowles continues to write, "in fact it is precisely from this perspective that one would have to reconsider the aforementioned parallels between the two on the issues surrounding the determination of the being of the human," to the extent that, as Bowles later summarizes, "Heidegger's relation to Luther will always be a strained relation."[96]

What further strains how Heidegger relates to Luther is through the text itself—it is in the fact that Heidegger's actual manuscript of "The Problem of Sin in Luther" is currently unpublished and, according to Van Buren, is "presumably lost."[97] In other words, a manuscript of Heidegger's talk on Luther has not been published in the *Gesamtausgabe* and, given Van Buren's claim about it being "presumably lost" means that it is unclear if it exists in the Deutsche Literaturarchiv in Marbach among an unknown and unseen amount of Heidegger papers that have not seen the light of day within the *Gesamtausgabe* volumes that have appeared or planned for future publication.

92. Ibid., lx.
93. Ibid., 184.
94. Ibid.
95. Ibid.
96. Ibid.,185.
97. Van Buren, *Supplements*, 31.

Thusly, in pondering whether or not the actual manuscript exists at all, I can only speculate, since it is largely impossible to know for sure. Be that as it may, all that has been published is a student transcript of Heidegger's "The Problem of Sin in Luther," which first appeared in the Bernd Jaspert edited volume, *Sachgemäße Exegese: Die Protokolle aus Rudolf Bultmanns Neutestamentlichen Seminaren 1921-1951* (1996, rendered by Kisiel/Sheehan as *Exegesis Going to the Things Themselves: The Protocols from Rudolf Bultmann's New Testament Seminars*)—from this, what has been translated in Van Buren's *Supplements* (2002) and the Kisiel-Sheehan co-edited *Becoming Heidegger* (2007) is a protocol paper composed by a unnamed student that attended Bultmann's "Paul's Ethics" seminar.

As transcribed by the unnamed student (and using the translation in *Becoming Heidegger*), Heidegger begins his talk on "The Problem of Sin in Luther" with the following remarks: "the problem of sin will here be treated not as an object of religious contemplation but as a theological problem [and] Luther's theology will be elucidated from the perspective of this question."[98] Heidegger concedes that "the object of theology is God" and, with that in mind, theology's "theme is the human being in regard to how he is placed before God."[99] In beginning here, the relationship between God and human being is a theological problem grounded in not just the meaning that can be made out of God as "the object of theology," but also the meaning that can be made out of human being as "the theme of theology." The underlying relationship between object and theme is construed through the extent to which human being is articulated in terms of "how [it] is placed before God." In this way, what Heidegger is most concerned with, as a prerequisite for a theological problem, is in the fact that, as Heidegger defines, "to be human is at the same time also to be *in* the world, and so that human beings also have before them the entire problematic of the world."[100] There exists a fundamental and inevitable tension between what it means "to be human" and what it means to be "*in* the world"—the emphasis Heidegger places on "*in*," then, is at the intersection of humanity's world and the world's human, such the problem that Heidegger wishes to explore is in what kind way humanity interprets itself against the world and in what manner does the world interpret itself against the human.

---

98. Kisiel and Sheehan, *Becoming Heidegger*, 185.
99. Ibid.
100. Ibid.

With the "problematic" of humanity and the world, Heidegger finds that "Luther's theological questioning assumed a particular basic direction in starting from the problem of sin."[101] From here, Heidegger questions what the meaning of "sin" is, "when humanity's relation to God is discussed as a theological problem?"[102] Sin, as a theological problem, "is closely tied to the question of the original state [*Urstand*] of humanity in *iustitia originalis* [original righteousness]."[103] In other words, for Heidegger, the meaning of being human and the meaning of world are meanings that must be separated—or hermeneutically adjudicated—until the meaning of being human is not corrupted by what that meaning becomes in light of the meaning of the world. What Heidegger is orienting his own question of the meaning of being human towards is a worldlessness, which is predicated on "asking about human *being* at the moment of its emergence from the hand of God."[104] Taking note to the emphasis Heidegger places on "being" in human being," what we see is a pre-*Being and Time* articulation of the question of the meaning of being as that which is primordial to the degree to which worldhood conceals what being is "at the moment of its emergence from the hand of God."

It seems to me, then, that the theological problem is how the meaning of being can be truly assessed without the concealedness of the world, so that being, without world, can be engaged "at the moment of its emergence from the hand of God." There is most certainly some foreshadowing here, if we see Heidegger's wrestling with this theological problem as becoming, eventually, a philosophical problem that finds itself way into the heart of *Being and Time*—in fact, it is possible to view this theological problem as a precursor to what is generally believed (i.e. Kisiel) to be the "primitive form"[105] of *Being and Time* in "The Concept of Time" that Heidegger was presumably composing concurrently as a "so-called review article"[106] and subsequently completed on July 25, 1924 as a talk, just five months after delivering "The Problem of Sin un Luther." For that matter, when taking a closer look what Heidegger means by saying "at the moment of [humanity's] emergence from the hand of God," what we find, in turn, is a theological reference to the

---

101. Ibid.
102. Ibid.
103. Ibid.
104. Ibid.
105. Kisiel, *The Genesis of Heidegger's Being and Time*, 477.
106. Heidegger, *The Concept of Time*, vi.

meaning of being in a "prelapsarian" sense versus what the meaning of being has become in a "postlapsarian" way—it is decidedly focusing on the former over the latter, in order to locate the meaning of being without the hermeneutical domination of the latter over the former.

The theological problem, here, is that "being" and "world" cannot be separated from one another, since both are inextricably linked to "postlapsiarianism," or what has occurred to the meaning of being human after the Fall. To look towards *what it means to be human* "at the moment of its emergence from the hand of God" means looking towards a conceptualization of "prelapsarianism" or the situatedness of the meaning of being human before the Fall.

Seen this way, Heidegger recognizes another tension between "prelapsarianism" and "postlapsarianism," insomuch as, according to Heidegger, "the human being must, on the one hand, be regarded as the *summum bonum* [highest good] of creation and, on the other hand, be so created that the Fall and the being of sin become possible but are not blamed on God."[107] This gives Heidegger reason to surmise that "the idea of redemption also depends upon the way in which original sin and the Fall are considered."[108] The idea of redemption seeks to confront humanity's *corruptio* as a means to unconceal humanity's *iustitia originalis*—if viewed in this manner, as Heidegger certainly seems to posit, the following stands all the more true: "for the more the radicality of sin is underrated, then the more redemption is disparaged and the more God becoming human in the Incarnation loses its necessity."[109] Having understood it this way, this brings Heidegger to ascertain that, "we thus find in Luther's thought the fundamental tendency that the *corruptio* of man's being can never be grasped radically enough," particularly to counter, challenge, or oppose scholasticism. [110]

Heidegger follows this assessment of Luther's handling of humanity's *corruptio* by pointing to Luther's "tendency towards this problematic" as an occurrence that takes place in Luther's "early period" as much as it does in his later thought.[111] The examples Heidegger provides from Luther's early period are: "The Question of Man's Capacity and Will without Grace" (1516), "Disputation against Scholastic Theology" (1517), and *The*

107. Kisiel and Sheehan, *Becoming Heidegger*, 185.
108. Ibid.
109. Ibid., 186.
110. Ibid.
111. Ibid.

CHAPTER 1: HEIDEGGER'S THEOLOGICAL ROOTS

Heidelberg Disputation (1518)—with respect to each of these, Heidegger offers brief exegetical work of Luther's words.

It must be noted that, thus far, all of the aforementioned presentation of Heidegger's argument about how the problem of sin is handled by Luther constitutes only the first session of the "The Problem of Sin in Luther" talk, as it was held on February 14, 1921, from what has been transcribed from an unnamed student in attendance of the talk. In the next session held on February 21, 1914, Heidegger presents examples from Luther's later thought. Before going so, Heidegger outlines "the problem of sin and *iustitia originalis*" in Scholasticism, suggesting that "Luther rebels against this and instead appeals to *experientia* [experience], insomuch as "the *natura hominis* is *corruptia*."[112] In other words, humanity by nature of being humanity "is itself sin [. . .] sin is thus not something tacked onto the moral condition of humans but is rather their essential core."[113] According to Heidegger, "with Luther, sin becomes a concept encompassing existence, which his emphasis on *affectus* already indicates."[114]

In locating where in Luther's later thought such sentiments are exemplified, Heidegger cites Luther's lecture course on Genesis in 1544, considering the following points: 1.) "the difference of opinions" between Scholastics and Luther, 2.) "the Fall through sin," 3.) "the movement of sin," 4.) "the situation of the human being who alienates himself from God is still a relation to God," 5.) a summarization of how points 1-4, "show how Luther's orientation in regard to sin is completely different from that of Scholasticism and how [Luther] understands sin as a fundamental antithesis to faith."[115] Following on this, Heidegger finds that the field of his contemporary protestant theology "does not demonstrate the understanding of sin" as Heidegger has assessed it and, therefore, "the understanding of the relation of God and man."[116] With this in mind, Heidegger concludes the talk by citing a "remark" from Kierkegaard on Luther's role in the broader relationship between Catholicism and Protestantism "on the spiritual ground" of the former to the extent that the latter is "only a corrective to" the former.[117]

---

112. Ibid., 188.
113. Ibid.
114. Ibid.
115. Ibid., 189-191.
116. Ibid., 191.
117. Ibid.

"Advanced: The High Scholastics and Aristotle: Thomas, *On Being and Essence*; Cajetan, *On the Analogy of Names*" (Summer 1924)

Three months after delivering the talk, "The Problem of Sin in Luther," the Summer 1924 semester began, in which Heidegger delivered two courses: a lecture course on Aristotle (in GA 18) and a seminar on Aristotle. While the lecture course, entitled *Basic Concepts of Aristotelian Philosophy* was undoubtedly directed at a larger, beginning group of students, the seminar was for smaller group of upper-level, advanced students—though both courses were essentially on the subject of Aristotle, only the content of the latter, the seminar, is comported theologically.

Based on its title, "Advanced: The High Scholastics and Aristotle," translated from *Fortgeschrittene: Die Hochscholastik und Aristoteles*, is a comparative study between Aristotle and Scholasticism. In order to more fully understand what is being compared, I wish to parse, for a moment, how I have rendered "*Hochscholastik*." To be clear, I have followed the translation of "high scholastics" from Kisiel-Sheehan, rather than Van Buren's translation of "late scholasticism." It is not to say that one translation is more correct than the other, since "*Hochscholastik*," as a term, can be generally rendered either way—yet, if we think of the term more literally, "high scholastic" would be more appropriate than Van Buren's rendering. Nevertheless, translating "*Hochscholastik*" into either referencing "high" or "late" is immensely tricky, when considering that there is a fundamental difference between the period known as "high scholasticism" and what is known historically as "late scholasticism" (or even second scholasticism)—the former, occurring in the 13th and early 14th centuries, is focused largely on a recovery of Greek philosophy, the latter, occurring in the 16th and 17th centuries, includes the emergence of Scotist (followers of John Duns Scotus), Thomist (followers of Thomas Aquinas), and Jesuit (led by the Society of Jesus with Ignatius Loyola) variations of scholasticism.

Given the subtitle, within the context of scholasticism and Aristotle, Heidegger is focused on the thought of the Italian philosopher/theologian Thomas Aquinas (1225-1274) and the thought of Italian philosopher/theologian Thomas Cajetan (1469-1534). When considering where Aquinas and Cajetan are placed within scholasticism (or what we might call Italian scholasticism more specifically), Aquinas belongs to what I have defined as "high scholasticism," while Cajetan belongs to what has been called "late scholasticism." Essentially, Aquinas is known for his use of Aristotle, which involved synthesizing Aristotelian philosophy with Christian thought and his influential work *Summa Theologica* (written 1265-1274, but unfinished), while Cajetan is known for his study of the philosophy of Aquinas, especially in Cajetan's extensive commentaries on Aquinas' *Summa Theologica* (written 1507-1522).

We see, then, that Aquinas and Cajetan are in a theological-philosophical lineage that begins with Aristotle, as much as we know that Heidegger frequently taught both lectures and seminars devoted to Aristotle, including the lecture delivered concurrently with the "Advanced: The High Scholastics and Aristotle" seminar. We know, too, that this seminar, from its subtitle, focuses on Aquinas' *On Being and Essence* (written 1252-1256, translated from *De ente et essentia, ad fratres socios*) and Cajetan's *On the Analogy of Names* (1498, translated from *De nominum analogia*). We can certainly assume that Heidegger sought to draw a comparison between Aquinas and Cajetan through an exegesis of their respective texts, though we might question, nonetheless, why Heidegger did not explicitly compare Aquinas' *On Being and Essence* with Cajetan's commentary on Aquinas' *On Being and Essence* (1495). And yet, it is uncertain if Cajetan's commentary on *On Being and Essence* figures, at all, into Heidegger's reading of Aquinas against Cajetan. Indeed, the content of "Advanced: The High Scholastics and Aristotle" is largely unknown, since neither a manuscript of the seminar nor a student transcript/protocol has been published in the *Gesamtausgabe*—for that matter, it is impossible to know if a text from this seminar actually exists or if some form of the text is housed in the Deutsche Literaturarchiv in Marbach.

"The Concept of Time" (July 25, 1924)

After the end of the Summer 1924 semester, Heidegger's "The Concept of Time" ("*Der Begriff der Zeit*") lecture was delivered to the Marburg Theological Society on July 25, 1924, which has been compiled along with another text, a treatise, entitled "The Concept of Time" also dated to 1924 in GA 64. The two texts are largely concerned with the same themes—these themes, as they are respectively presented in both the lecture and the treatise, were eventually broadly incorporated in *Being and Time*. More directly, what we find in both the lecture and the treatise find their way, in varying degrees, into the following lecture courses: *Plato's Sophist* (Winter 1924/1925), *History of the Concept of Time* (Summer 1925), *Logic: The Question of Truth* (Winter 1925/1926), and *The Basic Problems of Phenomenology* (Summer 1927), all of which contribute to early drafts of *Being and Time*, the first of which is dated from March to November 1926. Nevertheless, the lecture and the treatise sharing the title "The Concept of Time" are widely considered as containing the earliest discussions of what would become revised and recapitulated into *Being and Time*—it is the treatise of "The Concept of Time" that was thought of, according to Hans-Georg Gadamer, as "the original form" or "*Urform*" of *Being and Time*,[118] which is, in turn, made explicit in the 2011 translation of the treatise by Ingo Farin and Alex Skinner.[119]

However, though both texts of both the lecture and the treatise are housed in the Deutsche Literaturarchiv in Marbach, both are transcribed copies of Heidegger's original manuscripts, with both originals currently being lost. While the transcribed copy of the treatise was made by Heidegger's wife, Elfride (1893-1992)—a handwritten copy, in fact, that was used for the 2004 German publication of what numbered about 100 pages printed pages—the much smaller lecture (of about 22 printed pages) was presumably transcribed by a student in attendance. And yet, even though the two texts share the title, "The Concept of Time," and are largely similar thematically, and could have been concurrently written, only the lecture is theologically comported.

The lecture of "The Concept of Time" begins with "reflections [that] are concerned with time," predicated on answering the guiding question: "what is time?"[120] Heidegger begins to answer this question by supposing that "if time finds its meaning in eternity, then it must be understood starting from eternity." In this way, through the meaning of eternity, Heidegger locates this meaning as, perhaps, "something other than the empty state of perpetual being, the ἀεί, if God were eternity."[121] Heidegger goes on to add, "the way of contemplating time initially suggested would necessarily remain in a state of perplexity so long as it knows nothing of God, and fails to understand the inquiry concerning him."[122] From here, Heidegger proceeds to suppose that "if our access to God is faith and if involving

---

118. See Gadamer, "Martin Heidegger und die Marburger Theologie," in *Heidegger: Perspektiven zur Deutung seines Werks*, 169.
119. See Heidegger, *The Concept of Time: The First Draft of Being and Time*.
120. Heidegger, *The Concept of Time*, 1.
121. Ibid.
122. Ibid.

oneself with eternity is nothing other than this faith, then philosophy will never have eternity."[123]

It is on this point that we see that Heidegger's concern with the meaning of time is grounded on what theologizing about time tells us about time, rather than what reveals itself when philosophizing about time. Said this way, we see that philosophizing about time "will never have eternity" in the same manner as theologizing does "have eternity." It seems, too, that Heidegger finds a limitation to philosophizing about time that never conceptualizes "eternity" along the spectrum of the meaning of time—only theologizing can conceive of "eternity" and thusly, it is only when we are theologizing about time that we are able to fully conceptualize the meaning of time. In this regard, the question of the meaning of time is fundamentally tied to the meaning of eternity, such that, as Heidegger believes, "we will never be able to employ eternity methodologically as a possible respect in which to discuss time."[124] Because the meaning of eternity depends as much on the meaning of time as time does eternity, this relationship, as Heidegger sees it, can only be ascertained theologically, since "philosophy can never be relieved of this perplexity."[125] Due to this perplexity, Heidegger goes on to assert that "the theologian, then, is the legitimate expert on time."[126] For Heidegger, the theologian's task of theologizing about time can be outlined in "several respects," two of which Heidegger provides as: (1) "theology is concerned with human existence as Being before God [insomuch as] it is concerned with the temporal Being of such existence in its relation to eternity," and (2) "Christian faith is in itself supposed to stand in relation to something that happened in time."[127] Both of these "respects" considered, Heidegger contends that "the philosopher does not believe."[128] Not only does the philosopher "not believe," if recognizing that this sentiment is an indictment of philosophizing about time, but, according to Heidegger, "if the philosopher asks about time, then he has resolved *to understand time in terms of time* or in terms of the ἀεί, which looks like eternity but proves to be a mere derivative of being temporal."[129] Note the emphasis Heidegger places on "to understand time in

123. Ibid.
124. Ibid.
125. Ibid.
126. Ibid.
127. Ibid.
128. Ibid.
129. Ibid., 1-2.

terms of time"—this emphasis marks the limitations of philosophizing about time, since this kind of philosophizing only thinks "in terms of time," rather than in terms of more than just time.

What immediately follows this careful distinction between theologizing about time and philosophizing about time is a lengthy set of considerations about time that "are not theological."[130] These considerations are, of course, philosophical, working through an understanding of time scientifically through Einstein's relativity theory, then Aristotle, then Augustine's Eleventh Book of *Confessions*, and then an explication of Dasein's relationship to time, or "the Being of temporality."[131] Interestingly enough, Heidegger does not mention theology or what I have called theologizing about time again, and arrives, by the very end of the lecture, at the question: "what is time?" It becomes, now, "Who is time?"[132] In turn, it is considered "more closely" as "are we ourselves time?"[133] Then, "closer still," Heidegger asks: "am I my time?"[134] Though these questions are philosophical in nature, Heidegger is undoubtedly leaning theologically with them, so that he is actually theologizing about time, particularly when he finds that "I come closest to [time], and if I understand the question correctly, it is then taken completely seriously."[135] Philosophizing about time, then, does not take the meaning of time "completely seriously," and only theologizing about time puts forth a "questioning [that] is thus the most appropriate manner of access to and of dealing with time as in each case mine."[136] Essentially, due to the limitations of philosophizing about time and the extent to which theologizing about time is limitless, a consideration of Dasein "would be: questionable."[137]

---

130. Ibid., 2.
131. Ibid., 21.
132. Ibid., 22.
133. Ibid.
134. Ibid.
135. Ibid.
136. Ibid.
137. Ibid.

CHAPTER 1: HEIDEGGER'S THEOLOGICAL ROOTS

"Practicum on the Ontology of the Middle Ages: Thomas, *On Being and Essence, Summa contra gentiles*" (Winter 1924/1925)

In the Winter 1924/1925 semester, Heidegger taught two courses: a lecture course on Plato (in GA 19) and the seminar on Thomas Aquinas. As with the previous semester, it is certainly easy to assume that the lecture course was directed towards a larger group of beginning-level students, while the seminar was for a smaller group upper-level or "advanced" students. Like the seminar from the previous Summer 1924, this seminar associated with Winter 1924/1925 has Aquinas as its focus, even though, unlike the seminar from the previous semester, Heidegger chooses to devote it to Aquinas exclusively, rather than as a comparative study between two thinkers. Here, too, though Heidegger's concern is with Aquinas, it is a comparative study of sorts between two text written by Aquinas—here, Heidegger again grounds the seminar on *On Being and Essence*, but seemingly compares it to another Aquinas text, *Summa contra gentiles* (written 1261-1263).

I use "seemingly" because, as with the seminar from the previous semester, the "Practicum on the Ontology of the Middle Ages: Thomas, *On Being and Essence, Summa contra gentiles*" seminar is currently unpublished in the *Gesamtausgabe* and it seems largely uncertain if an actual text of the seminar or even a student transcript/protocol actually exists in the Deutsche Literaturarchiv in Marbach. Because of this, it is impossible to know anything specific about the content of the seminar. That is to say, it is impossible, now, to precisely know how Heidegger discussed Aquinas' two texts, keeping in mind that *On Being and Essence* is a philosophical treatise and *Summa contra gentiles* can be categorized as a systematic work. Nevertheless, what we can surmise is that the seminar is likely more theological in nature than it is philosophical—this, perhaps, seems to be much the reason why this seminar was delivered in conjunction with the lecture on Plato.

The title of the seminar, translated from *Übungen zur Ontologie des Mittelalters*, can be described as either a "practicum" (by Kisiel-Sheehan) or as "exercises" (by Van Buren), since the German word "*Übungen*" can be rendered either way. Aside from that, what we have in the rest of title gives us a general idea about subject of the seminar—"ontology of the middle ages." However, it is unclear if Heidegger provided that title himself or if it was a title given to the course by Marburg's Department of Philosophy, with Heidegger providing the focus on Aquinas. Though this cannot be adjudicated, the title "ontology of the middle ages" says a lot—it shows us that the seminar sought to explore the question of the meaning of being within the historical context of the Middle Ages. More than that, since Heidegger is focusing on Aquinas, we find that this question of the meaning of being is investigated within the period of the High Middle Ages, or what we can think of as High Scholasticism. Since this period, with Aquinas as a central figure, became interested in merging the concerns of Aristotelian philosophy with those of thirteenth-century Christian thought. It is on this point alone that it becomes all the more curious why Heidegger matched this upper-level seminar on Aquinas with the lower-level lecture on Plato, when upper-level students were customarily concurrently enrolled in an upper-level course and lower-level course delivered by the same professor—in Heidegger's case, this was certainly common, insomuch as Heidegger was known to provide expanded discussion and more in-depth elucidations in upper-level seminars for students that were also enrolled in the lower-level lecture course.

"History of Philosophy from Aquinas to Kant" (Winter 1926/1927)

For the Winter 1926/1927 semester, Heidegger taught two courses: a lecture course entitled "History of Philosophy from Thomas Aquinas to Kant" (GA 23, translated from *Geschichte der Philosophie von Thomas von Aquin bis Kant*), and an upper-level seminar that served as a practicum for the lower-level lecture course. Though the associated "practicum" (or "Übungen") remains unpublished and it is unclear if it is held in the German Library Archive—and, for that matter, if it indeed exists, it is impossible, now, to know if it is actually a manuscript from Heidegger himself or if it is a student transcript—the "History of Philosophy from Thomas Aquinas to Kant" lecture was published in 2006 as part of the *Gesamtausgabe*, though it currently remains untranslated. As noted by the editors of GA 23, the original manuscript of "History of Philosophy from Thomas Aquinas to Kant" is held in the German Library Archive, accompanied by transcriptions of the lecture, presumably by students enrolled in the course.[138]

Heidegger begins "History of Philosophy from Thomas Aquinas to Kant" with an "introduction" outlining "philosophy as phenomenological ontology" ("*Philosophie als phänomenologische Ontologie*").[139] In doing so, Heidegger provides a "display of [the] lecture" ("*Anzeige dieser Vorlesung*"), predicated on "how to display this lecture on 'newer philosophy': from

---

138. Heidegger, *Geschichte der Philosophie von Thomas von Aquin bis Kant*, 245.
139. Ibid., 1.

Descartes to Kant" ("*wie man diese Vorlesung über 'neuere Philosophie' anzuzeigen pflegt: von Descartes bis Kant*").[140] Heidegger begins by highlighting Descartes' "new principle—the ego, subject, consciousness, reason" ("*neues Prinzip—das Ich, Subjekt, Bewußtstein, Vernunft*"),[141] which, for Heidegger, constitutes an "alignment of the approach up to Hegel—*Geist*" ("*Ausrichtung des Ansatzes bis zu Hegel—Geist*").[142] Note that "*Geist*" has been left untranslated, since, when translated as either "spirit" or "mind," these translations fail to capture the very essence of *Geist* at its most fundamental meaning. Still, with respect to Heidegger's understanding and conceptualization of Hegel's *Geist*, Heidegger arrives at the following assertion: "the new philosophy since Descartes is the Protestantism of the thinking *Geistes*" ("*die neuere Philosophie seit Descartes ist der Protestantismus des denkenden Geistes*").[143] Here, specifically on this point, Heidegger makes a turn towards Aquinas, which, as we know, not only predates Descartes, but also served as an influence on the development of Descartes' thinking. Heidegger's "announcement" ("*Ankündigung*")[144] of Aquinas in this context—not just historical but also philosophical—is subsequently grounded on what can be seen as disclaimers. These disclaimers, as I call them, are presented in the following way:

> [. . .] not to annex a few centuries outside; not to pay due attention to the neglected Middle Ages, or even to the Catholicism of the thinking *Geistes* in medieval scholasticism—i.e. not only its attachment to the great tradition of Ancient Philosophy, but its strong roots in it.[145]

The above has been translated from the following:

> [. . .] *nicht, um einige Jahrhunderte äußerlich anzugliedern; nicht, um dem vernachlässigten Mittelalter die schuldige Beachtung zu schenken oder gar dem Katholizismus des denkenden Geistes in der mittelalterlichen Scholastik—d. h. nicht nur ihre Gebundenheit an die große Tradition der antiken Philosophie, sondern ihre kräftige Verwurzelung in dieser.*

140. Ibid.
141. Ibid.
142. Ibid.
143. Ibid.
144. Ibid.
145. Ibid.

Heidegger goes on to say:

> In fact, we will seek to understand in this direction. It is only expressive that one does well not to speak of Protestantism or Catholicism, because this philosophy has nothing to do with both as a manifestation of the Christian religion, but the conviction that the fundamental problems of the ego [. . .] and the problem of newer philosophy can only be understood at all from the Middle Ages and indeed from its general doctrine of being.[146]

This has been translated from the following:

> *In der Tat werden wir in dieser Richtung zu verstehen suchen. Nur ist ausdrücklich zu sagen, dass man gut daran tut, weder von Protestantismus noch Katholizismus zu reden, weil diese Philosophie mit beiden als Ausprägung der christlichen Religion nichts zu tun hat, sondern Überzeugung, dass die fundamentalen Probleme des Ich [. . .] und die Problematik der neueren Philosophie überhaupt nur zu verstehen sind vom Mittelalter her und zwar aus dessen allgemeiner Lehre vom Sein.*

In focusing on this "doctrine of being" ("*Lehre vom Sein*"), Heidegger asks a guiding question: "but if from the Middle Ages, then why Thomas [Aquinas]?" ("*Wenn aber vom Mittelalter her. Warum dann gerade Thomas?*").[147] To answer this guiding question, Heidegger recognizes that the "reception of Aristotle" expressed in Aquinas' commentaries of Aristotle's thought is what makes Aquinas a key figure not just in the Middle Ages but also the development of the doctrine of being itself. It is this that is construed into the "possibility of scientific theology" ("*möglichkeit der wissenschaftlichen Theologie*"), Aquinas' "Summa," and the larger "harmony of Christian-Catholic faith and ancient philosophy in their perfected Aristotelian form" ("*Harmonie von christlich-katholischem Glaubensgehalt und antiker Philosophie ihrer vollendeten form Aristotelisch*").[148]

What follows this, through the "introduction," is Heidegger's conceptualization of the "concept and method of philosophy" ("*begriff und method der philosophie*"), in the purview of Aquinas.[149] It is in the same purview that Heidegger concludes the "introduction" with a recognition of the "positive sciences and philosophy" ("*positive wissenschaften und*

---

146. Ibid.
147. Ibid., 2.
148. Ibid., 3.
149. Ibid., v.

philosophie") oriented most notably towards "philosophy as transcendental philosophy" (*"philosophie als transzendentalphilosophie"*) and, for Heidegger, "philosophy as phenomenological ontology" (*"philosophie als phänomenologische ontologie"*).[150] In the final section devoted to this, just before Heidegger's "summary" (*"zusammenfassung"*) of the whole of the introduction, Heidegger outlines two subsections: "what is phenomenology?" (*"was ist phänomenologie?"*) and "from the concept of phenomenon" (*"zum phänomenbegriff"*).[151]

After the introduction, Heidegger provides five chapters, with each devoted to a thinker, beginning with Aquinas, and continuing with Rene Descartes (1596-1650), Baruch Spinoza (1632-1677), Gottfried Leibniz (1646-1716), and Christian Wolff (1679-1754). We can see, then, particularly when remaindering the title of the lecture course itself, that the presentation of each thinker in a devoted chapter is unfolded as a survey of each in brief summarization—in this way, we can see that the "History of Philosophy from Aquinas to Kant" lecture is, undoubtedly, a survey course and, perhaps, the very structure of the course was dictated by Heidegger as an orientation towards how he wished to ground phenomenology in the roots of Aquinas, Descartes, Spinoza, Leibniz, and Wolff, with a special emphasis placed on Aquinas.

In the first chapter (*"erster abschnitt"*), from the thirteen sections beginning with Heidegger's assessment of Aquinas' "task-position and literature" (*"Aufgabenstellung und Literatur"*), "from life and work" (*"Zu Leben und Werk"*), and "disputed questions of truth" (*"Quaestiones disputatae de veritate"*), the most important portions of Heidegger's Aquinas chapter that hold theological significance are in the sections entitled "The Ontological Sense of *Vertitas (Adaequatio)*" (*"Der ontologische Sinn der veritas [adaequatio]"*), "God and the Cause of Evil" (*"Gott und die Ursache des Übels"*), "Eternity and Time" (*"Ewigkeit und Zeit"*), and "The Proofs of God: The Very Foundations of Medieval Ontology" (*"Die Gottesbeweise. Die eigentlichen Fundamente der mittelalterlichen Ontologie"*). Within "The Ontological Sense of *Vertitas (Adaequatio)*," Heidegger includes a discussion of "first philosophy as theology" (*"Erste Philosophie als Theologie"*), which, in short, reads into Aquinas' use of Aristotle's "first philosophy" as a grounding for the kind of theology developed from the Middle Ages through Aquinas.[152]

150. Ibid., vi.
151. Ibid., vi.
152. Ibid., 60-61.

Within "Eternity and Time," Heidegger provides a discussion of "the godlessness of philosophy" ("*Die Gott-losigkeit der Philosophie*"), which, in short, attempts to confront philosophy's godlessness with the meaning of God to the meaning of theology as a way of construing the meaning of eternity and, ultimately, time as an unfolding "temporality in the phenomenological reflection of existence itself" ("*Zeitlichkeit in phänomenologischer Besinnung des Dasin selbst*").[153]

"Phenomenology and Theology" (March 9, 1927 or July 8, 1927)

Heidegger's lecture, "Phenomenology and Theology" ("*Phänomenologie und Theologie*"), was delivered more than once, with the first time occurring to Evangelical Theologian's Society in Tübingen and a second version occurring in Marburg. The second version of the lecture was entitled "Theology and Philosophy" and it is dated to February 14, 1928—this second version, as it were, is said to have contained only the second part of the larger lecture "Phenomenology and Theology," which Heidegger explains in a letter (see "Theology and Philosophy"). However, there is a disagreement over the date of the first version—it can be dated to either March 9, 1927 or July 8, 1927.

The two dates ascribed to the first version of "Phenomenology and Theology" can be found in the listing included in the Kisiel-Sheehan co-edited *Becoming Heidegger* (2007) and an earlier inclusion co-edited by by James G. Hart and John C. Maraldo that appears in *The Piety of Thinking* (1976) and in the William McNeill edited, *Pathmarks* (1998). While the earlier version of the text (1976 and 1998) is dated to March 9, 1927, the later version of the text (2007) is listed as dating to July 8, 1927. The conflicting dates to this first version of the "Phenomenology and Theology" lecture points either to two different texts of that first version or to an error in the date of the Evangelical Theologian's Society to which the lecture was given. Because Kisiel-Sheehan and McNeill disagree on the date of the lecture, it is difficult to know what the exact date is without attending to the actual manuscript, which is undoubtedly held in the Deutsche Literaturarchiv in Marbach and eventually published in the *Gesamtausgabe*.

What further complicates the dating of the first version of "Phenomenology and Theology" is that it is included in two volumes of the *Gesamtausgabe*: GA 9 and GA 80—the text in GA 9, entitled *Wegmarken*, first

153. Ibid., 80.

published in German in 1967, has been included in both *The Piety of Thinking* and *Pathmarks*, while the text contained in GA 80, entitled *Vorträge*, recently published in German in 2016.

At the beginning of the lecture, Heidegger finds that "the popular understanding of the relationship between theology and philosophy is found of opposing faith and knowledge, revelation and reason."[154] When considering this relationship along the lines of its "popular understanding," Heidegger puts forth what is the "popular understanding" of how theology is defined separately from philosophy. For philosophy, Heidegger sees it as "that interpretation of the world and of life that is removed from revelation and free from faith."[155] Having said that, Heidegger views theology as "the expression of the creedal understanding of the world and of life—in our case a Christian understanding." Given these two definitions, as Heidegger defines them, "philosophy and theology give expression to a tension and a struggle between two worldviews [such that] this relationship is decided not by scientific argument but by the manner, the extent, and the strength of the conviction and the proclamation of the worldview."[156] Even so, Heidegger concedes to the fact that "we, however, see the problem of the relationship *differently* from the very start." Consequently, according to Heidegger, "it is for us rather a question about the *relationship between two sciences*."[157]

When considering more broadly the question of the meaning of being in terms of "ontic sciences [that] in each case thematize a given being that in a certain manner is always already disclosed *prior* to scientific disclosure," Heidegger concludes that "we call the sciences of being as given—of a *positum*—positive sciences."[158] As a way of contrasting with ontology, which Heidegger construes as "keep[ing] beings in view, but for a modified attitude," Heidegger avoids a further explication of ontology, though we can ascertain that Heidegger does not see ontology as a positive science, and arrives at the thesis, with emphasis: "*theology is a positive science, and as such, therefore, is absolutely different from philosophy.*"[159] Based on this thesis, Heidegger points out that "the task of our discussion will be to characterize theology as a positive science and, on the basis of this characterization, to

154. Heidegger, "Phenomenology and Theology," 40.
155. Ibid.
156. Ibid.
157. Ibid.
158. Ibid., 41.
159. Ibid.

clarify its possible relationship to philosophy, which is absolutely different from it."[160] The task of this discussion becomes delineated by "obtain[ing] a threefold division: (a) the positive character of theology; (b) the scientific character of theology; (c) the possible relation of theology, as a positive science, to philosophy."[161]

While Heidegger views "the positive character of theology" as "the founding disclosure of a being that is given and in some way already disclosed," he suggests that "theology itself is something that everywhere in world history gives testimony to its intimate connection with Christianity itself as a whole."[162] What this means, for Heidegger, is that "theology cannot be the science of Christianity as something that has come about in world history, because it is a science that itself belongs to the history of Christianity, is carried along by that history, and in turn influences that history."[163]

In following on this with "the scientific character of theology," Heidegger notes that "theology is the science of faith," by way of four interconnected suppositions[164] As such, "theology is the science of that which is disclosed in faith, of that which is believed."[165] Additionally, theology is "the science of the very comportment of believing, of faithfulness," to the extent that theology "is the science of faith, not only insofar as it makes faith and that which is believed its object, but because it itself arises out of faith."[166] Lastly, for Heidegger, theology "is the science of faith insofar as it not only makes faith its object and is motivated by faith, but because this objectification of faith itself, in accordance with what is objectified here, has no other purpose than to help cultivate faithfulness itself for its part."[167]

In the final section of the lecture focused on "the relation of theology, as a positive science, to philosophy"—which I would argue is likely the section that makes up the "Theology and Philosophy" lecture dated to February 14, 1928—Heidegger begins by asserting that "if faith does not need philosophy, the *science* of faith as a positive science does."[168] Note the

---

160. Ibid.
161. Ibid., 43.
162. Ibid.
163. Ibid.
164. Ibid., 45.
165. Ibid., 46.
166. Ibid.
167. Ibid.
168. Ibid., 50.

emphasis placed in "science" here. On this point, Heidegger continues to say that "the positive science of faith does not need philosophy for the founding and primary disclosure of its *positum*, Christianness, which founds iself in its own manner."[169] To further situate the relationship between theology and philosophy, Heidegger offers what appear to be two directives: the first, "philosophy is the formally indicative ontological corrective of the ontic and, in particular, of the pre-Christian content of basic theological concepts,"[170] and secondly, "philosophy is the possible, formally indicative ontological corrective of the ontic and, in particular, of the pre-Christian content of basic theological concepts [even though] philosophy can be what it is without functioning factically as this corrective."[171]

Heidegger's Return to Freiburg (1928-1944)

Following the publication of *Sein und Zeit* in April 1927 and following Husserl's retirement after Husserl (who taught his last course at Freiburg on July 25, 1928) as Professor of Philosophy, Heidegger officially assumed Husserl's chair in philosophy at Freiburg, officially starting in the Winter 1927/1928 semester.[172] In this semester, Heidegger taught one lecture course on a phenomenological interpretation of Kant (GA 25) and two upper-level phenomenological practicum seminars—with all these courses focused on phenomenology, there was some expectation on Husserl's part that Heidegger would continue Husserl's work on phenomenology and be, to some extent, Husserl's true successor at Freiburg. During a break in this semester, in a period of December 5-9, 1927, Heidegger presented a talk, "Kant's Doctrine of the Schematism and the Question of the Meaning of Being" in Cologne with Scheler and (apparently without Scheler) in Bonn (in GA 26).[173]

---

169. Ibid.
170. Ibid., 52.
171. Ibid., 53.
172. This is based on the teaching records, to which Kisiel and Sheehan agree.
173. Sheehan notes that the actual text to this talk is dated January 26, 1927, which means that it was written almost a year before Heidegger actual delivered it. But also, the dating of the text confirms that it was written while Heidegger was still part of Marburg faculty, rather than at Freiburg.

"Theology and Philosophy" (February 14, 1928)

Delivered on February 14, 1928, "Theology and Philosophy" is a talk Heidegger gave at Marburg, which occurred, when judging by the date, at the very end of the Winter 1927/1928 semester. The content of this talk is currently unknown, even though it is certainly possible to surmise from this title that Heidegger's subject is on the relationship between theology and philosophy. Though it is clear that the talk was given at Marburg, it is currently unknown whether it was delivered within Marburg's Department of Philosophy or to Marburg's Department of Theology. Indeed, it may be possible to suppose that it was delivered to the latter, given the title of the talk itself and Heidegger's proclivity for collaborating with the Department of Theology (by way of Bultmann)—be that as it may, the exact location of the talk remains unknown. In the notes to *The Genesis of Heidegger's Being and Time*, Kisiel references a footnote to the typescript of "Theology and Philosophy" made by Heidegger, in which Heidegger explains that this talk was a "change in title from the ["Phenomenology and Theology"] talk."[174] The fact that Kisiel points to an existing typescript of "Theology and Philosophy" suggests that, though the text of the talk has remained unpublished—and excluded from any of the volumes of the *Gesamtausgabe*—it does exist in the Deutsche Literaturarchiv in Marbach. Interestingly enough, in addition to pointing this out, Kisiel also refers to a letter Heidegger exchanged with Elizabeth Blochmann (1892-1972), collected in *Briefwechsel: 1918-1969* (1989), which Heidegger directly references the "Theology and Philosophy" talk as "essentially the content of the second part" of the "Phenomenology and Theology" talk that was delivered the previous year.

"Augustine: What is Time?: Confessions, Book 11" (October 26, 1930)

Delivered on October 26, 1930 as a talk at the Benedictine monastery of Beuron, "Augustine: What is Time?: Confessions, Book 11" ("*Augustinus: Quid est tempus? Confessiones lib. XI*") is not only given just prior to the "Augustine, Confessions 11: On Time" in Winter 1930/1931, but is undoubtedly an expansion of "The Concept of Time" lecture from July 25, 1924.

More importantly, being that Heidegger's talk "Augustine: What is Time?" is delivered towards the end of the break between Summer 1930

---

174. Kisiel, *The Genesis of Heidegger's Being and Time*, 560.

and Winter 1930/1931, it is certainly possible to contextualize the talk as serving as a supplement to the Winter 1930/1931 seminar. We may be able to see the talk as an early draft of the later seminar, particularly if we take note to the similar titles and subject matter—we need not look any further than Heidegger's focus on Book 11 of *Confessions*. This seems especially so in light of Heidegger's use of the Latin, "*Quid est tempus*" for "what is time," which is also implicated in the later seminar, though, in the later lecture, Heidegger also uses "*de tempore*."

Though Heidegger's seminar on Augustine assists us in understanding Heidegger's talk at Beuron, there is another seminar in Winter 1930/1931, as noted by the editors to GA 83, entitled "Seminar Book: Exercises for Beginners" which serves as a "background" for the talk at Beuron.[175] The editors of GA 83 also note that this "Seminar book" was "not announced" ("*nicht angekündigt*"), which, in itself, denotes that the seminar for beginners was not delivered in Winter 1930/1931—clearly, in pointing this out, the editors are speaking of two different seminar courses, though they do not explain the circumstances around the "Seminar book" becoming "not announced" and, in turn, not delivered. If all of this is so, it may be possible to suppose that the undelivered "Seminar book" Heidegger oriented towards beginners became either the "background" ("*Hintergrund*")[176] for the Beuron talk or, in my view, the whole of the talk itself—the latter is certainly more true than the former, particularly when comparing the text in GA 83 that is supposedly dated to October 25, 1930 with the text included in the recently published *Vorträge* (GA 80).

"Augustine, Confessions 11: On Time" (Winter 1930/1931)

Heidegger's upper-level seminar entitled, "Augustine, Confessions 11: On Time" ("*Augustinus, Confessiones XI [De Tempore]*"), which was taught in the Winter 1930/1931 semester, alongside another upper-level seminar on Plato's *Parmenides* (co-taught with Wolfgang Schadewaldt [1900-1974]) and a lower-level lecture on Hegel (GA 32). Both upper-level seminars are compiled in GA 83, with the "Parmenides" seminar constituting barely thirteen pages in length, and the "Augustine" seminar at just short of 30 pages in length—the "Parmenides" seminar, more so than the "Augustine," seems to be a supplement to the Hegel lecture, given that Heidegger ties

---

175. Heidegger, *Seminare: Platon-Aristoteles-Augustinus*, 668.
176. Ibid.

Hegel into the very end of the "Parmenides" seminar. Nevertheless, both the "Parmenides" and "Augustine" seminars perform close readings of Plato's *Parmenides* and Augustine's *Confessions* respectively—however, it is only the "Augustine" seminar that provides a more careful, thoughtful and focused close reading than the "Parmenides."

Focused on a close reading of Book 11 of *Confessions*, Heidegger begins with an introduction that briefly considers Aristotle's understanding of time, before Heidegger concentrates more exclusively on an interpretation of Book 11's Chapters 14-30. It must be noted that Heidegger's handling of Aristotle's notion of time in reference to Augustine is undoubtedly an extension of Heidegger's prior lecture, "The Concept of Time" from July 25, 1924—not only can the prior lecture be situated in the purview of "Augustine, Confessions 11: On Time," but more generally with respect to *The Basic Problems of Phenomenology* from Summer 1927 also contributes to how Heidegger comports himself in "Augustine, Confessions 11: On Time." If we view "Augustine, Confessions 11: On Time" in light of how Heidegger theologizes about time in "The Concept of Time," Heidegger theologizes in much the same manner here, culminating with defining the meaning of time as "extent—sprawled awareness" ("*Aus-dehnung—Ausgestrecktheit*") and a consideration of time as "existence" (as the Latinized "*existentia*").[177]

"Philosophizing and Believing: The Essence of Truth" (December 5, 1930)

Dated in December 5, 1930, "Philosophizing and Believing: The Essence of Truth," by its title, seems to suggest that it was a talk—or what might be called a conference lecture—Heidegger directed towards theological issues rather than strictly philosophical concerns. We know this because the talk was delivered at the Evangelical-Theological Association at Marburg. Judging from the date of its delivery, Heidegger presented it about a month into the beginning of the Winter 1930/1931 semester, while he concurrently taught three courses: a lecture course on Hegel (GA 32) and two advanced seminars (one on Augustine's *Confessions*, the other on co-taught Plato's *Parmenides*). It may be possible to suggest that the advanced seminar on *Parmenides* could contextualize the unpublished "Philosophizing and Believing: The Essence of Truth" talk. This seems so, if the advanced seminar, included in GA 83, published but untranslated,

177. Ibid., 69.

thematically handles a similar notion of truth as an interplay of "philosophizing" and "believing," as seen later in Heidegger's Winter 1942/1943 lecture, *Parmenides* (GA 54). If viewed this way, not only would the earlier *Parmenides* seminar shed some light on how Heidegger theologizes "the essence of truth" in the "Philosophizing and Believing: The Essence of Truth" talk, but it would also bring forth a means of recognizing Heidegger's philosophical theologizing in both the earlier and later *Parmenides* courses. It is also noted that, barely a week after presenting "Philosophizing and Believing: The Essence of Truth," Heidegger would eventually deliver the talk, "On the Essence of Truth" at Freiburg—Kisiel highlights the significance of the close proximity of the two talks. More importantly, based on the "data taken from a transcript of the [talk]," Kisiel writes that the earlier talk's "variant title suggests that Heidegger from the start adapted his oft-repeated [talk] 'On the Essence of Truth' to his context and audience."[178] This, of course, is true, especially since, in the following Winter 1931/1932, Heidegger delivered another course, "On the Essence of Truth" or "*Vom Wesen der Wahrheit*" (GA 34) and yet another version in Winter 1933/1934 (in GA 36/37). With all of this in mind, the exact content of "Philosophizing and Believing: The Essence of Truth" remains unknown, though we can certainly surmise from Kisiel that it does exist in "transcript" in the Deutsche Literaturarchiv in Marbach.

"The Fundamental Question of Philosophy" (Summer 1933)

In Summer 1933, Heidegger taught three courses: a lecture course entitled "The Fundamental Question of Philosophy" (translated from "*Der Grundfrage der Philosophie*") and two seminars—these two seminars were an advanced seminar entitled "*Oberstufe: Der Satz vom Widerspruch*" (which can be translated as "Advanced; The Sentence of Contradiction") and a lower-level seminar entitled "*Unterstufe: Der Begriff der Wissenschaft*" (which can be translated as "Lower-Level: The Concept of Science"). While the two seminars are currently unpublished—though we can presume that they are likely collected in the Deutsche Literaturarchiv in Marbach, given that they are catalogued in an appendix to William Richardson's *Heidegger: From Phenomenology to Thought*—"The Fundamental Question of Philosophy" is included in GA 36/37 (in *Being and Truth*) with the lecture, "On the Essence of Truth," delivered the following semester in Winter 1933/1934.

178. Kisiel, *The Genesis of Heidegger's Being and Time*, 562.

What must not be overlooked is that, just before the Summer 1933 semester, in the interim following the Winter 1932/1933 semester, Heidegger was elected rector of Freiburg on April 21, 1933. On May 1, 1933, Heidegger joined the Nazi Party and delivered his inaugural address as rector on May 27, just as the Summer 1933 semester began. In the position as rector, Heidegger expressed his support for Hitler, the Nazi Party, and the "German revolution" that had been championed by National Socialism itself—it is in this capacity that Heidegger's delivery of "The Fundamental Question of Philosophy" lecture course is all the more interesting, especially if it is considered as holding theological significance.

Where this significance occurs theologically is in the "main part" of "The Fundamental Question of Philosophy," occurring after an introductory section in which Heidegger explains what "the fundamental question" is in terms of "the fundamental happening of our history."[179] In this introduction—which may be worth discussing very briefly—Heidegger discusses "the spiritual-political mission as a decision for the fundamental question,"[180] and proceeds into a discussion of "the Greek questioning in poetry and thought," precisely as "the inception of philosophy."[181] Following on this, Heidegger includes in his introductory remarks an explication of "what philosophy is not"[182] and ends the introduction section with "the fundamental question of philosophy and the confrontation with the history of the Western spirit in its highest position: Hegel."[183] For Heidegger, Hegel's "highest position" in "the history of the Western spirit," becomes something that must be confronted.

Entering the "main part," now, entitled "The Fundamental Question and Metaphysics: Preparation for a Confrontation with Hegel," Heidegger explores "the development, transformation, and Christianization of traditional metaphysics"—Heidegger, ultimately, arrives at a "fundamental question" presented as "what is man?"[184] This question is predicated on "metaphysics as [a] natural tendency," grounded on "constantly tending toward it" and "at the same time a constant error (transcendental illusion)."[185]

179. Heidegger, *Being and Truth*, 15-22.
180. Ibid.
181. Ibid.
182. Ibid.
183. Ibid.
184. Ibid.
185. Ibid.

From this, Heidegger suggests that "in spite of everything, [Kant's thought] remains in the received Christian world."[186] Heidegger goes on to construe this as "*today's Christianity* and *its theology*—traditional metaphysics and the decisive question?"[187] Afterward, in assessing "Kant's critical question regarding the possibility of metaphysical cognition and the classical division of metaphysics,"[188] Heidegger begins to consider "the Christian transformation of the concept of metaphysics"[189] as "knowledge of the supersensible (*trans physicam*)"[190] and, eventually, as a further explication "on the influence of the Christianization of the concept of metaphysics."[191]

Near the conclusion of the "main part" of "The Fundamental Question of Philosophy," as Heidegger confronts Hegel more directly as "the completion of metaphysics as theo-logic," the use of this term "theo-logic" holds a theological significance for Heidegger. Yet, when Heidegger enters the final section of the lecture entitled "the fundamental character of Hegelian metaphysics. Metaphysics as theo-logic," Heidegger asks "in what way is [metaphysics] 'theo-logic'?"[192] Note the emphasis Heidegger places on hyphenating the term as "theo-logic"—in separating the word from what we expect to be rendered as "theologic," Heidegger is able to separately define "theo" in relation to "logic."

To question *in what way is [metaphysics] 'theo-logic'* Heidegger rephrases this question to "*in general*: what does that mean?"[193] In turn, Heidegger concedes in the "negative: it does *not* mean 'theology.'"[194] It is on this point that Heidegger explains what he means, by first asserting that "theology has as its task the knowledge of God, divine things and their relation to man and world." Since, as Heidegger defines, "-logy" is a "*system of assertions* about [something]," this brings him to conclude that "theology is a particular kind of cognition with a special *domain of knowledge* and its own *standards* for knowledge."[195] In order to be more specific about how he

186. Ibid.
187. Ibid.
188. Ibid.
189. Ibid.
190. Ibid.
191. Ibid.
192. Ibid., 56.
193. Ibid.
194. Ibid.
195. Ibid.

conceives of the meaning of "theology" itself, Heidegger illustrates it "in a double sense: (1) as *natural theology*, based on reason alone and the natural cognitive powers of human beings; (2) as *revealed theology, on the basis of* faith and *for* faith and the community of a church."[196] Heidegger goes on to think of "*theology* [as] delimited in this way from physiology, geology, biology, philology."[197] This brings Heidegger consider all said about "theo-logic" in the "positive [. . .] thus *logic*, in such a way that it is essentially related to and *grounded* in θεός, *the Christian God*."[198] With evoking "the Christian God," Heidegger finds that "our question is divided in two: (a) in what way is Hegel's metaphysics *logic*? and (b) in what way is this theo-logic?"[199] The first of these questions—as it relates to Hegel's metaphysics of logic—is handled in terms of three fronts of inquiry: "the science of logic as authentic metaphysics,"[200] "metaphysics as logic in its higher form" or as "the logic of the logos as logic of the pure essentialities,"[201] and "the higher logic as logic of reason."[202]

All considered brings Heidegger to assert that "logic as the system of the absolute self-consciousness of God"—this, in itself, is what Heidegger wishes to define as "theo-logic."[203] To this, Heidegger asks: in what way is this 'logic' '*theo*-logic'?" Note the emphasis, again, on "theo." From here, Heidegger suggest that the answer to this "has already basically been given, inasmuch as 'logic' is the science 'of' the absolute."[204] For Heidegger, this ultimately points to "the absolute as absolute '*identity*.'"[205] This "absolute identity" becomes, according to Heidegger, "the making-possible of the absolute actuality of the actual [such that] absolute actuality is the essential whole of essentialities, that is, of the concepts of essence as thought absolutely."[206] Through what Heidegger points to in Hegel's *Logic* (1812), "*metaphysics as science of the Being of beings is 'logic'* and this logic is the logic 'of' the

196. Ibid.
197. Ibid.
198. Ibid.
199. Ibid.
200. Ibid., 57.
201. Ibid.
202. Ibid., 59.
203. Ibid.
204. Ibid.
205. Ibid., 60.
206. Ibid.

absolute, that is, God."²⁰⁷ Heidegger considers "God," in this way, "not just a *genitivus objectivus*: exhibition of God, but also *genitivus subjectivus*: the essence of God as *he essentially unfolds as absolute spirit*."²⁰⁸ Subsequently, as Heidegger sees the meaning of *absolute spirit* and how God "essentially unfolds" as it, "logic is the system of the absolute self-consciousness of God; it is essentially related to God and grounded in God [to the extent that] *Hegel's metaphysics is logic in the sense of theo-logic*."²⁰⁹

Though Heidegger follows with a recapitulation section entitled "the completion of Western philosophy in metaphysics as theo-logic and the questionworthiness of this 'completion,'" the conclusion to the lecture entitled "Confrontation and Engagement" must be addressed, particularly if we are to understand the historical context in which Heidegger places his approach to Hegel's metaphysics and, in turn, the historical context in which can place what Heidegger has theologized up to this point. What we have in "Confrontation and Engagement" is no direct mention of God nor "theo-logic," but, instead, a means of confronting and engaging the meaning of metaphysics for the German people and the German state. Whether or not Heidegger is continuing to theologize, in a sense, about what National Socialism means for the German people and the German state is certainly up for debate. Though he abstains from referring to "theo-logic," it may be possible to locate another version of "theo-logic" in how he construes the relationship between National Socialism, the German people, and the German state—this "theo-logic," through Hegel's metaphysics, is most certainly oriented towards the meanings of "absolute identity" and "absolute actuality." We need not further parse what the implications are to this kind of thinking, particularly if we note that this kind of thinking is not just philosophical in nature, but is decidedly and purposefully leaning towards the theological. We see, through the use of the theological, that Heidegger arrives at the notion that "the German people [do] not belong among those peoples who have already lost their metaphysics [. . .] we are a people that must *first gain* its metaphysics and *will* gain it—that is, we are a people that still has a fate."²¹⁰ On this point, there appears to be a theologizing at play—Heidegger is theologizing about what awaits the German people and the German state, once "his" people are able to "*first gain* its metaphysics."

207. Ibid.
208. Ibid.
209. Ibid., 61.
210. Ibid.

Heidegger's Post-Freiburg Years (1944-1976)

Following the Winter 1944/1945, which was interrupted when Heidegger was drafted for service into the *Volksstrum* to assist in fortifying the Rhine for the German army in what would be the last year of World War II, Heidegger would be condemned by post-war denazification hearings as a "follower," the second lowest incrimination level of Nazi war criminals. As the hearing lasted from late 1946 until early 1949, it was determined by French military authorities that Heidegger was to be banned from teaching or being involved with any university activities due to his prior involvement with the Nazi Party. Nevertheless, Heidegger would be readmitted to teaching at Freiburg for the Winter 1950/1951 semester, eventually receiving emeritus status, teaching regularly until 1958, and being invited to give an assortment of talks until 1973—it is during this lattermost period that the first conference in North America devoted to Heidegger's philosophy was established in 1964 and held at Drew University, having been directly influenced by a letter sent to it by Heidegger and subsequently becoming the annual conference known now as The Heidegger Circle.

"The Theological Discussion of 'The Problem of a Non-Objective Thinking and Speaking in Today's Theology'—Some Pointers to Its Major Aspects" (March 11, 1964)

Dated to March 11, 1964 and given as a letter to supplement or even provide direction to the theological discussion that took place on April 9-11, 1964 at Drew University in Madison, NJ, the content of the text entitled, "The Theological Discussion of 'The Problem of a Non-Objective Thinking and Speaking in Today's Theology'—Some Pointers to Its Major Aspects" has been associated rather closely with the "Phenomenology and Theology" lecture. This is certainly so in *The Piety of Thinking* and *Pathmarks*, both of which present the former as an appendix to the latter. In such a presentation, though the two texts are thematically associated with the relationship between theology and philosophy, we must not forget that the two text are separated by more than fifty years. More importantly, when keeping in mind that the "Phenomenology and Theology" lecture was delivered earlier in Heidegger's career, particularly in very close proximity to the publication of Being and Time, the "The Theological Discussion of 'The Problem of a Non-Objective Thinking and Speaking in Today's Theology'—Some

Pointers to Its Major Aspects" letter was composed towards the end of Heidegger's career, particularly during a period of professional rehabilitation. We can read only this letter against Heidegger's disastrous association with National Socialism and, in turn, read into it a confrontation with Sartre's existentialism. But, even more importantly, this purpose of this letter is fundamentally different from the purpose of the earlier lecture, "Phenomenology and Theology"—it is, here, in the letter that Heidegger not only does not mention phenomenology, but he is also predominantly concerned with contextualizing what he sees as today's theology.

CHAPTER 2: HERMENEUTICS BEFORE AND AFTER HEIDEGGER

THE RELATIONSHIP BETWEEN HEIDEGGER and theology is based on the role that hermeneutics plays in the separate development of both—essentially, hermeneutics is what ties the manner in which Heidegger tends to philosophize from a theological standpoint and the degree to which we understand the very meaning of theologizing to what theology is. Not only is hermeneutics itself integral to Heidegger's philosophizing and the mode of theologizing with which he often engages himself, but hermeneutics is also essential to theology, since hermeneutics itself is what allow theologizing to take place. We have seen, in one sense, that hermeneutics is the means by which Heidegger is able to confront theology from a philosophical point of view and theologize about Augustine, Aquinas, and Luther in ways that substantatively contribute to how each figure is conceptualized theologically. In another sense, however, hermeneutics is a significant force, by which theologians such as Augustine and Aquinas, in particular, are able to make use of Plato and Aristotle respectively, in an effort to synthesize Platonism and Aristotelianism with Christian thought. For Heidegger's handling of Luther, we find that hermeneutics becomes the means by which Heidegger conceptualizes the concept of sin through philosophizing it as a problem in Luther's theology, to the extent that this contribution brought a new hermeneutical lens to Bultmann's course on "Paul's Ethics." In this way, as evidenced, for example, especially through Bultmann's collaborations with Heidegger, the interdisciplinary discourse that occurs between Heidegger and theology is grounded on hermeneutics, insomuch as this discourse illustrates that the relationship between Heidegger and theology is an intra-disciplinary one—it is a relationship in which Heidegger speaks to theology as necessarily as theology speaks to Heidegger and, consequently, this ongoing conversation suggests that what remains concealed about Heidegger can be unconcealed through making meaning out of theology and what theology conceals can be unconcealed through making meaning out of Heidegger.

Hermeneutics "Before" Heidegger

Defining Hermeneutics Proper

Hermeneutics is more than just interpretation. In order to truly explain the influence of Platonic thought on Augustinian hermeneutics, the term "interpretation" becomes greatly limiting. Instead, when considering "hermeneutics," I would argue that it is, in fact, a "meaning-making" process—it is about what I would call making the "metaphysical" into the "ontological."

To be clear, when I use the proposition *making the metaphysical into the ontological*, I am describing hermeneutics as a hermeneutical practice utilizing a distinct hermeneutical lens. Instead of considering hermeneutics in the traditional sense of interpreting texts, my use of the term will be directed more towards the theological: interpreting or explaining religious concepts, theories, and principles. As such, *making the metaphysical into the ontological* as hermeneutics is the process of interpreting a transcendental idea by translating its abstraction through concretization—making the abstract (the metaphysical) into the concrete (the ontological).

My sense of the "transcendental idea" is Kantian, where it is derived from what Immanuel Kant argues in his *Critique of Pure Reason*. For Kant, the term is personified as a pure concept of reason.[1] The "pure" aspect to any concept, or object—that is, when it is a "transcendental idea"—is one predicated on being *a priori*. As such, this kind of object of understanding is something that is represented, or objectified, prior to all experience. These *a priori* concepts, through the process of a more rigorous experiential objectification, according to Kant, "indicate the synthetic unity which alone makes possible an empirical knowledge of objects."[2] What this means, then, is that, when there is an encounter with an object of understanding, particularly one that is a transcendental idea, there is an initial knowledge of it as a "mere logical form" before there is a deeper, deliberative knowledge of it as an "empirical form." Knowledge of an *a priori* object of understanding, as Kant argues, "[is] not to be obtained by mere reflection but only by inference."[3] The relationship

---

1. Kant, *Critique of Pure Reason*, 315.
2. Ibid.
3. Ibid., 308.

between a "mere logical form" and an "empirical form," just as Kant contends, is bridged by "mere reflection." So, what arises from such a relationship is the relationship between what Gottlob Frege calls sense and reference,[4] where what can be logically inferred about an a priori object of understanding becomes an empirical point of reference.

So, during the process of *making the metaphysical into the ontological*, Augustine, like Plato, are engaged with interpreting an abstract idea into a concrete idea—the "metaphysical" and the "ontological" are grounded respectively on the "sense" of something of transcendental value and, subsequently, grounded on the "reference" of something of empirical value.

The relationship between "sense" and "reference," as making the metaphysical into the ontological, arises in Book 6 of *The Republic*. In it, Socrates explains that "Forms" are objects of intellection and are, as such, relegated to the highest part of the "intelligible class" towards truth and knowledge. This is furthered in the next book, Book 7, which Socrates illustrates the "Allegory/Simile of the Cave." In this "allegory/simile," Socrates argues that "Forms" are merely projections of things seen as second-hand representations—in this respect, "Forms" are predicated on "sense" and "reference." When "Forms" are projected on the walls of a "cave," the human mind has only a "sense" of them and obtains a "reference" embodied only representations of what truly "is."[5]

Re-contextualizing Ancient Hermeneutics: Augustine's Plato

I would like to draw a comparison between Plato and Augustine in relation to the field of "hermeneutics." As the "Great Synthesizer," Augustine is considered pivotal to the development of early Christianity during the Early Medieval period, synthesizing elements of Platonic philosophy with the fundamentals of Christian tradition. Augustine's chief concern was with biblical interpretation, which brought about a radically new approach to the reading a text, understanding what a text says to the reader, and the extent to which a text grounds a reader's "meaning-making" process. This, of course, had a tremendous influence on the systemization of Christianity

---

4. Gottlob Frege's notions of "sense" and "reference," which, of course, owe their theory and praxis to Kant, but also, for that matter, Ferdinand de Saussure's idea of the "sign." Frege, "On Sense and Reference," 61.

5. Plato, *The Republic*, 509d-516d.

in the wake of critical disputes with dogma and faith, especially during the first three centuries before Augustine.

For Augustine, Platonic philosophy provides an essential ideological framework towards philosophizing about the Christian faith. I would argue that this is not just important with respect to Augustine's work in hermeneutics in the fourth century C. E., but essential to understanding the ideological trajectory of hermeneutics over the course of the last seventeen centuries.

Nevertheless, the starting point in hermeneutics is with Augustine. One way to describe Augustine's "hermeneutics"—specifically, once Augustine embraced and incorporated Platonic thought in a way that none of his theological predecessors had done—is as a "hermeneutics of Love." Augustine's hermeneutical task, in brief, is focused on first approaching the text as a whole, then considering the parts—such as individual words, and the relationships between words. I find that Augustine's notions of the text and words are respectively analogous to Plato's view of the State and the individual. But, more importantly, through Platonic influence on Augustine's hermeneutics, I would like to argue that Augustine's "hermeneutics of Love" is a re-articulation of Plato's theory of justice as it is outlined in *The Republic*—my intent is to discuss Plato's theory of justice as a "hermeneutics of Justice." In this regard, then, Augustine's approach to hermeneutics is one that is ultimately concerned with justice—or, perhaps, about ethics and morality. Essentially, what becomes an important part of Augustine's hermeneutical lenses is the situatedness of the reader when encountering a text—the reader should have a balanced soul beforehand. In my view, since Augustine's hermeneutist should have a "balanced soul," I would argue that Augustine's concept of soul is based on Plato's tripartite concept of the soul as appetitive, rational, and spirited.

The Making of Biblical Interpretation and Biblical Hermeneutics

So, if we begin with discussing hermeneutics as "biblical interpretation," it becomes possible to ascertain what David Jasper means in *A Short Introduction to Hermeneutics* by offering the following: "hermeneutics [. . .] is about 'interpretation' or even 'transmission,' and especially the interpretation of sacred texts."[6] As Jasper argues, this sense of "interpreting" is focused on "transmitting" the words of any given sacred text from the sense of it being

6. Jasper, *A Short Introduction to Hermeneutics*, 7.

"divinely inspired" or "the Word of God" into something quantifiable. In other words, "biblical interpretation" is rooted in "transmitting" the words of a given sacred text to a reader. In effect, what is transmitted between the text and the reader is meaning and understanding. I do not mean "meaning" and "understanding" in an arbitrary sense, but in a more specialized sense: I am thinking particularly about translation. I would argue, then, that, as a way of outlining what hermeneutics means in terms of "biblical interpretation," we are talking specifically about the translation of a sacred text from one language into another.

For example, "biblical interpretation" is occurs in the translation of the Hebrew Bible and the New Testament from their respective original Hebrew and Greek languages into the language of the reader. For a reader—not necessarily an English-language reader, but any reader that wishes to translate a sacred text from a foreign language into their native language—"biblical interpretation" is utilized by simply finding out what a sacred text says. It is a simple consideration of the words as those words they are, where the reader does not add or delete anything from what is there. In this sense, the "meaning" and "understanding" that a reader wishes to establish from their encounter with a sacred text is grounded in literally parsing the words of that text into something more meaningful and understandable—finding a foreign language's equivalents in a native language. At this rather basal level, "biblical interpretation" is involved mainly with "meaning" and "understanding" at its lowest possible denominator. It simply does not go any further than the words on the page, their interrelationships with one another in any given sentence, and the fundamental semantic value in the accumulative proliferation of those words.

Obviously, when we talk about "biblical interpretation," a reader's encounter with a text is never limited to the lowest possible denominator. This is precisely related to what I would call "Platonic hermeneutics"—the idea that what is seen is not all that is seen, but a limitation of what can be seen, since "seeing" has semantic elasticity. Essentially, what a reader discovers is that a text contains much more semantic elasticity to it, which ventures further than what can be called "literal." When we consider the "fundamental semantic value of the words as an accumulation of a collection of signs," the reader must be aware that a text has multiple layers of "meaning" and "understanding." This multiplicity is relegated to and regulated by whatever degree of "meaning" and "understanding" that a reader teases from a text.

What the reader experiences, then, as Jasper suggests, is the "slippage between intention and meaning, or worse, between the slipperiness of written words and human understanding."[7] This "slipperiness" becomes particularly important for the Early Christian Church, specifically during the first three to five centuries of the development of Christianity following Jesus. During this time, "intention" and "meaning" are critical issues that move hermeneutics from simple "biblical interpretation" to complex "biblical hermeneutics"—it becomes a vital concern to do more than simply quantify what a sacred text says verbatim, but to peel back the many semantic layers seething beneath what is literally there. This movement is especially prevalent in the hermeneutical practices that Church Fathers applied to the formulation of Early Church doctrine. One important example can be found in the formulation of creed statements during the Councils of Nicaea in 325 C.E., Constantinople in 381 C.E. and Chalcedon in 451 C.E. Each of these Councils was dedicated to weighing "intention" and "meaning" in the sacred texts that developed within the Christian tradition –the overarching issue debated in these Councils revolved around an immensely important, yet elusive question: what does the text say in relation to what the text probably means and, in turn, in relation to what the text most certainly does not mean? This is an issue of "biblical hermeneutics": a concern with conceptualizing "meaning" and "understanding" from a text that goes beyond and deeper than the simple quantification of the words.

By the time we move into "biblical hermeneutics," it is safe to say that we are dealing with more than just the words on the page—we are doing more than just engaging the text in terms of, as I have mentioned, "what is literally there." I call this, of course, the "quantification of the words." When we embark on "biblical hermeneutics," we, as readers, are injecting our subjectivity into our reading experience. In this regard, we are merging "what is literally there" with our own preconceived notions, prior knowledge, opinions, assumptions, embedded theologies, and so on. Our lived experience before we come in contact with the text engulfs our reading experience. This "subjectivization" of the reading experience is one that, perhaps, makes it possible for a reader to "read into" a sacred text and extract from that "reading" anything conceivable. In effect, that means making the sacred text mean whatever a reader chooses it to "mean" and, likewise, understanding whatever they want to "understand" from it. Jasper makes my point particularly clear when he discusses Augustine's "greatest

7. Ibid., 14.

contribution to the development of hermeneutics" and subsequently argues the following "in brief":

> [. . .]for Augustine, any reading of Scripture must be disciplined by a careful and thorough analysis of its language and grammatical structures in order to prevent wild and groundless exposition. Words are *signs* –that is, they refer to something as signifiers and are not to be confused with the thing to which they refer. As we shall see later, this is a remarkably modern insight into the nature of language.[8]

This "modern insight," as Jasper calls it, is an insight into theoretical and practical components that inevitably go into what it means "to do" hermeneutics. Jasper recognizes that Augustine understands that the "nature of language" is comprised of "signs." These signs are "signifiers" that, if I may extend Jasper just a bit further, correspond to something "signified"—in other words, the chain of letters that make up a word is a "signifier," something quantified concretely, which is represented by an abstract image, or something "signified."

With Platonic influences in tow, I would argue that Augustine's notion of the "sign" merely sets the "hermeneutical" stage for the Protestant Reformation of the Sixteenth Century which, as Jasper rightly argues, "affected the greatest revolution in hermeneutics . . . that the church in the West has known."[9] This becomes particularly significant when we consider that two of the chief leaders of the Reformed movement, Martin Luther (German) and John Calvin (French), both "read into" Scripture something that allowed them to conclude that the Church needed "reform." With Platonic hermeneutics lurking in the background, Lutheran and Calvinistic hermeneutics—if I may refer to them as such—carefully weighed "intention" and "meaning" in the Scripture to the theological extent that they realized that, in short, there were unnecessary excesses and inappropriate dogma in the Church.

What eventually arises out of the Reformed movement is the necessity to find "meaning" and "understanding" for sake of "meaning and understanding," rather than being dependent on what Authority dictates "meaning and understanding" are. Luther's and Calvin's approaches to hermeneutics involved elevating the reader's individualized experience with a given text with the intended purpose of performing what I would

8. Ibid., 40.
9. Ibid., 56.

like to call "subjective meaning-making." The Lutheran-Calvinistic approaches paved the way for the likes of Immanuel Kant and Friedrich Schleiermacher of the Eighteenth Century. First, Jasper delineates Kant's approach to hermeneutics as one that "questioned the objectivity of the world 'out there' [where] he was not suggesting that it does not exist, but rather that it is only possible to perceive and understand it on our own terms, and not absolutely."[10] Now, as for Schleiermacher, Jasper describes him as having "insisted that reading is an art and that the reader of a text must be as much an artist as its author."[11] Based on how Jasper outlines Kant's and Schleiermacher's approach to hermeneutics, I would contend that Kant and Schleiermacher were not just concerned with the "subjectivization" of the reader's experience with a given text, but also the objectification of the text itself. I would argue that this is precisely what Plato was also concerned with: the sense that there is a difference between "subjectivization" and objectification" when encountering objects of understanding. In this way, both Kant and Schleiermacher—though they are on opposing sides of German Idealism—are aware that "meaning and understanding" are more than just a subjective enterprise but is, by association, an objective one. It is not strictly about how a reader is doing their subjectivizing, but how they are allowing the text to do its objectifying—this goes back to the notion of "reading into" a text.

Reformed Hermeneutics: Luther, Calvin, Zwingli

To understand the Lutheran view and interpretation of the Bible is to first become aware that Martin Luther (1483-1546) "sought to make the Word of God the starting point and final authority for his theology [where] the Bible was for him of paramount importance, and it was in it that he found an answer to his anguished quest for salvation."[12] This means, more than anything, that Luther found in the Word of God salvation, something from which he could connect to the message of the Christ, Christ's work of atonement, the forgiveness of sins, and the overall message of the gospel.[13] Quite

10. Ibid, 78.
11. Ibid., 84
12. Gonzalez, *The Story of Christianity: Volume II: The Reformation to the Present Day*, 47.
13. Tillich, *A History of Christian Thought: From Judaic and Hellenistic Origins to Existentialism*, 244.

literally, for Luther, the message of the gospel as it appears in the Bible suggests that "the Word of God is none other than God."[14] This, of course, is a premise that Luther takes directly from the first verse of the Gospel of John,[15] but, more specifically, it is the notion that the "Bible itself declares that, strictly speaking, the Word of God is none other than God the Son, the Second Person of the Trinity, the Word who was made flesh and dwelt among us."[16] To arrive at such a conclusion, Luther believed that "the Bible is the Word of God, because [,] in it [,] Jesus, the Word incarnate, comes to us"[17] and, because of this, therein rests the Word's final authority.[18] This final authority, in the Lutheran perspective, is an authority that is over the church, the Pope, and even tradition. In effect, the Word of God, or the Scriptures, provides "a more trustworthy witness to [the] gospel than the pope's corrupt church, or even the best in Christian tradition."[19] To that end, what Luther arrived to with this logic is his doctrine of the authority of Scripture above the church, which ascertains that the church had not made the Bible any more than the Bible had made the church, but that the gospel made both the Bible and the church.[20] More importantly, it is with the doctrine of the authority of Scripture above the church that Luther argues against the pope, alone, being allowed "to interpret the Scriptures or to confirm the interpretation of them [as though] they have assumed the authority of their own selves."[21] To Luther, the interpretation of the Scriptures was not meant to be limited to the Pope alone, even if the Pope's authority is derived from the authority "given to St. Peter when the keys were given to him,"[22] since such an authority was not given to St. Peter alone, but to the whole community." From this, Luther advocated the creation of theological seminaries that "interpret the Bible in such a way that the exact philological

---

14. Gonzalez, *The Story of Christianity: Volume II: The Reformation to the Present Day*, 47.

15. This is in reference to John 1:1, which states, "In the beginning was the Word, and the Word was with God, and the Word was God."

16. Gonzalez, *The Story of Christianity: Volume II: The Reformation to the Present Day*, 47-48.

17. Ibid.

18. Ibid.

19. Ibid., 48

20. Ibid.

21. Wace and Buchheim, eds., *First Principles of the Reformation or the Ninety-Five Theses and the Three Primary Works of Dr. Martin Luther*, 26.

22. Ibid.

application of the biblical texts to the questions [that must be asked] and which are supposed to be answered in systematic theology,"[23] even if Luther believed that what made the Bible the Word of God could not serve as a source of authority for theological and religious debate.[24]

* * *

Like Luther's doctrine of the authority of Scriptures, John Calvin (1509-1564) has a similar doctrine becoming important to the Calvinist perspective of the Bible because, "on its basis, Biblicism developed in all groups of Protestant faith [since] the Bible, for Calvin, is the law of truth."[25] Calvin's view of this law of truth is best ascertained by way of the Bible's authority, which he believed is "derived from the fact that the Bible was composed under the dictations of the Holy Spirit."[26] In this way, then, the Bible is divinely-inspired. In other words, to suggest that the Bible is divinely-inspired and composed by the Holy Spirit is to propose, when following the Calvinist perspective, that the Bible, therefore, "does not need to be supplemented and interpreted by tradition [no more than it needs to be] revised and corrected by reason."[27] To be more specific, for Calvin, the Bible, as the divinely-inspired Scriptures composed by the Holy Spirit, stands alone in its authority, justification, relevance, and purpose, all of which are inherent in it rather than being manipulated by tradition or molded by reason like Luther, Calvin does not see human tradition or human reason as the dominating factors to the Bible's authority. What this means, then, is that the Bible, as a standalone entity, consists of Scripture-consequences: inferences or deductions from scriptural statements—it is with the just and well-rounded Calvinistic interpretation of these statements that "the fundamental [Calvinistic] principles are directly and explicitly sanctioned by the Word of God."[28] One important Calvinistic principle based on the appropriation of the Word of God is the notion that the "scripture gives [the

---

23. Tillich, *A History of Christian Thought: From Judaic and Hellenistic Origins to Existentialism*, 244.

24. Gonzalez, *The Story of Christianity: Volume II: The Reformation to the Present Day*, 48.

25. Ibid., 274.

26. Ibid., 275.

27. Urban, *A Short History of Christian Thought*, 203.

28. Cunningham, *The Reformers and the Theology of the Reformation*, 529-530.

Christian] a still clearer knowledge of the truth,"[29] where the interpretation of scripture provides readings of the truth that yield understandings of "the covenant which the Lord made with Abraham"[30] as they are communicated through the Word of God. To Calvin, when considering that the Scriptures were the Word of God, the Scriptures were, in effect, infallible and "[Christians] must, therefore, take a better aim [with the Scriptures], one to which [they] are directed by the infallible guidance of Scripture"[31] —the idea of the Bible as the Word of God being infallible is in opposition to Luther, since Luther believed that the Bible being the Word of God did not necessarily make it infallible.

* * *

Calvin's conceptions of knowledge of God and knowledge of ourselves are contingent on the epistemological situation. It is through such a situation that humanity finds meaning in being human, meaning in the world in which they exist, and meaning transcendent to their human existence. All three, as meaning-makers, come to bear in the epistemological situation. I intend to define "epistemological situation" as, first, the existential awareness of human existence—it is the extent to which being human and existing as an entity is a fundamental facticity. Secondly, from that first facticity, a second facticity emerges when being human is converted into the existential awareness of the world and of other things that exist in that world—it is the degree to which being human is more than just "being," but "being-in-the-world." And finally, as a third facticity, there arises the existential awareness of "being-in-the-world" and world-hood as only part of a larger totality, one that includes transcendence—it is the notion that, though human existence is linked to world-hood, there exists objects of understanding that transcend the physical world. Carefully, I have outlined these three facticities of existence, because I believe they are critical components to Calvin's conception of the epistemological situation: a situation built on "knowing God" and "knowing ourselves" and, ultimately, how these two epistemological possibilities are inextricably linked.

---

29. Calvin, *The Institutes of the Christian Religion*, 810.
30. Ibid.
31. Ibid., 813.

Calvin makes this interrelated connection clear in Chapter 1 of the *Institutes*. In this chapter, Calvin explains this interrelatedness in the following manner:

> Nearly all the wisdom we possess, that is to say, true and sound wisdom, consists of two parts: the knowledge of God and of ourselves. But, while joined by many bonds, which one precedes and brings forth[,] the other is not easy to discern. In the first place, no one can look upon himself without immediately turning his thoughts to the contemplation of God . . .[32]

This is, of course, how *Institutes* begins. Not only does it bare some resemblance is content and focus to the Aristotle's Παντες ανθρωποι του ειδεναι ορεγονται φυσει[33] at the beginning of τον μετα τα φυσικα, but suggests that there is a distinctive epistemological situation in which humanity find itself. This situation is an existential one, since it is invested in finding meaning, not just in the self and a Heideggerian thrownness, but beyond the self and beyond that thrownness. Calvin speaks to this, especially by connecting thownness to postlapsarianism with:

> For, as a veritable world of miseries is to be found in mankind, and we are thereby despoiled of divine raiment, our shameful nakedness exposes a teeming horde of infamies. Each of us must, then, be so stung by the consciousness of his own unhappiness as to attain at least some knowledge of God. Thus, from the feeling of our own ignorance, vanity, poverty, infirmity, and—what is more—depravity and corruption, we recognize that the true light of wisdom, sound virtue, full abundance of every good, and purity of righteousness rest in the Lord alone.[34]

From there, at the end of the first section to Chapter 1, Calvin brings his discussion squarely back to the epistemological situation in the following:

> For what man in all the world would not gladly remain as he is— what man does not remain as he is—so long as he does not know himself, that is, while content with his own gifts, and either ignorant or unmindful of his own misery? Accordingly, the knowledge of ourselves not only arouses us to seek God. But also, as it were, leads us by the hand to find him.[35]

---

32. Ibid., 35.
33. *Die Metaphysik Des Aristoteles*, 1.
34. Calvin, *Institutes of the Christian Religion*, 36.
35. Ibid., 37.

As evidenced in the above, and the two previous to it, "knowledge," as a repeated term for Calvin, has a special meaning. John MacNeill, the editor of the translation from which the above excerpts appear, notes that Calvin uses the word knowledge as a stand-in for "being" or "existence." MacNeill suggests that Calvin preference for the word "knowledge" was chosen to place "emphasiz[e] the centrality of revelation in both the structure and the content of Calvin's theology."[36] Though just a footnote, the editor is highlighting something very important about Calvin's use of the term knowledge, particularly in reference to what I have often described as Calvin's epistemological situation. If, for example, Calvin considers "knowledge" as "existence," then surely what I have offered as epistemological situation is synonymous with existential situation. That is, like an existential situation, an epistemological situation—as Calvin has presented—is a "situatedness" construed through meaning-making and hermeneutics. This meaning-making must be metaphysical, not ontological—it must be concretized in God, and not concretized in human being. Calvin certainly agrees with this, and states:

> [. . .]it is certain that man never achieves a clear knowledge of himself unless he has first looked upon God's face, and then descends from contemplating him to scrutinize himself . . . we are not thus convinced if we look merely to ourselves and not also to the Lord, who is the sole standard by which this judgment must be measured.[37]

Calvin's notion of judgment, then, is extended beyond humanity's knowledge of itself, and toward God-knowledge: the latter being what Calvin calls "God's majesty." This is offered as being of chief importance to not just how knowledge of ourselves is constituted, but how humanity arrives at a knowledge of God. Clearly, as Bainton points out, the *Institutes* treat the sovereignty of God ahead of justification by faith.[38] Bainton's point is best exemplified in the following from Calvin:

> Suppose we but once begin to raise our thoughts to God, and to ponder his nature, and how completely perfect are his righteousness, wisdom, and power—the straightedge to which we must be shaped.[39]

36. Ibid., 35.
37. Ibid., 37.
38. Bainton, *The Reformation of the Sixteenth Century*, 112.
39. Calvin, *Institutes of the Christian Religion*, 38.

This "straightedge which we must be shaped" is humanity's imperfection to God's perfection, the frailty of human existence to the indestructibility of God's existence, and the impurity of human being to the "purity of God."[40] Calvin's notion of the "purity of God" is, as Bainton contends, linked to Calvin's understanding of the sovereignty of God. God's sovereignty, then, becomes a critical component of not just the epistemological situation with respect to knowledge of ourselves as the created, but in reference to knowledge of God as Creator.

* * *

Ulrich Zwingli (1484-1531) espoused a view of the Bible that was influenced by his humanist philosophy that he "regarded as an aid to the study of the Bible."[41] As a humanist and Christian, or a Christian humanist, Zwingli saw the authority of the Scriptures being "based on the call of the Renaissance: back to the sources."[42] What Zwingli wanted to go "back to" was the "source," which referred to the Bible as being the source of Christian faith.[43] In this, Zwingli dictated that the "Bible is the revelation of God."[44] This logic helped influence Zwingli's doctrine of the Spirit, which was not only something "lacking in Luther and the other Reformers [but sought to explain that] the truth is given to every individual always through the Holy Spirit, and this Spirit is present even if the word of the Bible is not present."[45] Subsequently, Zwingli advocated seeking wisdom above what is written.[46] Still, as far as Zwingli was concerned, "[Christians] are not called upon to [make] any positive affirmations as to what God can do or may do, in extending mercy to individuals among men,"[47] but, rather, adhere to certain principles are they are clearly revealed to the Christian believer

---

40. Ibid.

41. Hurst, *Short History of the Christian Church*, 234.

42. Tillich, *A History of Christian Thought: From Judaic and Hellenistic Origins to Existentialism*, 257.

43. Gonzalez, *The Story of Christianity: Volume II: The Reformation to the Present Day*, 62-63.

44. Tillich, *A History of Christian Thought: From Judaic and Hellenistic Origins to Existentialism*, 257.

45. Ibid.

46. Cunningham, *The Reformers and the Theology of the Reformation*, 221.

47. Ibid.

in Scripture.[48] In effect, Zwingli viewed the Scriptures as a means of God being able to communicate "general provisions God has made for saving [humankind] individually from their guilt and depravity."[49] As a "medium of an external revelation," Zwingli believed that the Bible impressed upon humankind's heart, by God's Spirit, "some knowledge of the only way of salvation through the Redeemer and a sacrifice"[50] as an imparted truth bound by faith in God as Judge of all the earth.[51]

Heyne through Eichhorn

In his *History of Biblical Interpretation: Volume 4* (2010), Henning Graf Reventlow discusses one of the two spheres of scholarly work for Johann Gottfried Eichhorn (1752-1821) is his research into myth. Eichhorn's research into myth and his underlying judgment about the Old Testament, as Reventlow argues, is influenced by Christian Gottlob Heyne (1722-1812). Reventlow notes Eichhorn's participation in a seminar on ancient mythology held at Gottingen by Heyne, where Eichhorn, as a student, studied Heyne's treatment of ancient poetic texts.[52] Reventlow describes Heyne's work in the following manner:

> Heyne treated ancient poetic texts, above all the poetic works of Homer and Hesiod, and he investigated the relationship between poetry and myth in classical antiquity. Previously the mythical material in these texts had been regarded simply as poetic invention, often with an allegorical intention. Heyne, however, explained it in a revolutionary new way as a typical form of expression for the childhood of humanity.[53]

In this, Reventlow sets the stage for Heyne's influence on Eichhorn. For Heyne, according to Reventlow, myths were not to be explained through allegory but, instead:

---

48. Ibid.
49. Ibid.
50. Ibid.
51. Ibid.
52. Reventlow, *History of Biblical Interpretation: Volume 4: From the Enlightenment to the Twentieth Century*, 211.
53. Ibid., 211-212.

CHAPTER 2: HERMENEUTICS BEFORE AND AFTER HEIDEGGER

> [Myths] were a necessary means of expression for the ancient period, which was characterized by the absence of knowledge, by the scarcity of the capacity for verbalization, and by the inability to disconnect oneself directly from the impressions of the senses.[54]

In this regard, then, Heyne divided myths into two groups: historical myths and philosophical myths. As Reventlow would agree, Heyne's approach to categorizing myths is essential to understanding Eichhorn's hermeneutical leanings, particularly as they are expressed in Eichhorn's *Primeval History*. But, more importantly, with Heyne in the background, Eichhorn takes a conservative perspective[55] in the work. This "conservative perspective," as such, conceived of myths either historically as depicting of historical events, or philosophically as containing speculative ethical or natural explanations.[56] It becomes possible to suggest, then, that Eichhorn's "conservatism" is the embodiment of an early hermeneutical movement in the history of interpretation. Reventlow addresses this by proposing that, along with Eichhorn's student, Johann Philipp Gabler, Eichhorn are regarded in the history of interpretation as the founders of the "mythical school." What arises from this "mythical school" is an application of Heyne's understandings of myth to the interpreting the Bible—it is conceptualizing Biblical texts as being comprised of myths similar to those of classical antiquity.

Schleiermacher's Hermeneutics

The Lutheran-Calvinistic approaches paved the way for Friedrich Schleiermacher (1768-1834) of the Eighteenth Century. For Schleiermacher, reading—albeit, interpreting Scripture—was an art and the reader assumes the role of an artist whenever they extract meaning from any given text. There is, if I may interject Gilles Deleuze (1925-1995) and Mikhail Bahktin (1895-1975), through the reader assuming the role of an artist, the sense that the act of reading is a "meaning-making" process that is situated on a creative act (Deleuze's term), or a creative activity (Bahktin's term). Though Deleuze and Bahktin do not come along until the 20th century, Schleiermacher is their forerunner. Schleiermacher's notion of the reader as artist is steeped in a sense of the creative act/activity that a reader must be gainfully employed

---

54. Ibid.
55. Ibid., 213.
56. Ibid., 212.

in, if he reader intends to honor the text as a "meaning-making" device. This means that, when the reader is engaged in the reading process, the reader is experiencing the text, where that experience of the text is predicated on what Schleiermacher calls "feeling" and "self-consciousness."

In *The Christian Faith* published in 1821-1822, Schleiermacher's conception of the church is one that is rooted in hermeneutics: the interpretation of what the Church is, what the Church should do, and how the Church should function with respect to its representation in Scripture and its role in the Christian community. Hermeneutics, then, for Schleiermacher, "feeling" and "self-consciousness" is a two-fold experience which he describes in the following manner:

> In the first place, it is everybody's experience that there are moment in which all thinking and willing retreat behind a self-consciousness of one form or another; but in the second place, [. . .] this same form of self-consciousness persists unaltered during a series of diverse acts of thinking and willing.[57]

Here, what is undoubtedly lurking behind Schleiermacher's notions of "feeling" and "self-consciousness" —though, perhaps, not so subtly—is Kant's categorical imperative to knowledge as divided into the essentialist structures of pure reason (logic), practical reason (morality), or judgment (aesthetic). This is especially the case if situating Kant and Schleiermacher historically: they were essentially contemporaries, even though only the first edition of Schleiermacher's *On Religion: Speeches to its Cultured Despisers* was published in Kant's lifetime. Nevertheless, Kant's doctrine of knowledge works in the background behind Schleiermacher's respective doctrine of knowledge, where, though Schleiermacher adopts Kant's fundamental law about knowledge being bounded by experience, Schleiermacher wholly rejects Kant's "thing-in-itself" or *Ding an sich*. Hence, Schleiermacher's elevates "feeling" and "self-consciousness," which are two very important components of his approach to hermeneutics.

As a central figure to a post-Reformation period, Schleiermacher's approach to hermeneutics was a generalized understanding of the field. In this sense, Schleiermacher views the interpretation of Scripture was predicated on a two-fold lenses: avoiding misunderstandings and discovering the author's intent. Not only is Schleiermacher concerned with the "subjectivization" of the reader's experience with a given text, but also the objectification of the

---

57. Schleiermacher, *The Christian Faith*, 7.

text itself. Schleiermacher –on opposing sides of German Idealism from Kant—is aware that "meaning and understanding" is more than just a subjective enterprise but is, by association, an objective one. It is not strictly about how a reader is doing their subjectivizing, but how they are allowing the text to do its objectifying. This goes back to the notion of "reading into" a text. To this end, Schleiermacher's post-Reformation period is not that far apart ideologically from the Reformation period's understandings of Scripture, inspiration, authority, and interpretation—in fact, I would say that Schleiermacher is concerned with the same hermeneutical concerns as the Reformers, most notably "sola scriptura" and the discernable excellence of the text.

This post-Reformation period's approach to hermeneutics directly informs the emergence of fundamentalism in America in the 19th and 20th century, particularly with respect to the "Old Princeton Theology" at Princeton Theological Seminary in the theologies of Charles Hodge (1797-1878), his son Archibald A. Hodge (1823-1886), and Benjamin B. Warfield (1851-1921). Ideologically, "Old Princeton Theology" is conservative, but its conservatism arose mainly in response to proliferation of theological liberalism at Princeton. This "theological liberalism" was a kind of "Liberal Christianity" evidenced in some of the following theologians: Adolf von Harnack (1851-1930, with the denial of the possibility of Jesus performing miracles), Walter Rauschenbusch (1861-1918, with the development of the Social Gospel movement), Rudolf Bultmann (with the concept of demythology), and Paul Tillich (with the appropriation of Heideggerian concepts and existentialism at large into the theology). Each of these figures, as did others that can be categorized under the "theological liberalism" label, infused into philosophical perspectives and contemporary scientific assumptions into their approach to hermeneutics, which, on the whole, sought to interpret Scripture from an objective point of view, decidedly setting aside the authority of Scripture in the process.

In reaction to the way in which "theological liberalism" and theologians accordingly aligned with Liberal Christianity understood the role of Scripture, "Old Princeton theology" sought to promote biblical inerrancy. The father-and-son Hodges, Warfield, and others that aligned in this regard—perhaps, as a term, "Old Princeton theology" was meant to differentiate from what might be called the "New Princeton Theology" of Liberal Christianity. To be sure, "Old Princeton theology" was a tradition of the Reformed Protestantism, specifically epitomized in John Calvin. Through an orthodox Calvinism, "Old Princeton Theology," as a hermeneutical movement, focused on the authority of the Bible and being "faithful" to the Word of God. To truly understand not only the theology of this "Old Princeton Theology," but how that theology developed into a specific hermeneutical praxis, consider Charles Hodge's *Systematic Theology* published from 1872-1873. In it, Hodge makes the following claim, which I find to be critical to understanding the hermeneutical lenses through which "Old Princeton Theology" approached biblical interpretation: "the Bible contains truths which the theologian has to collect, authenticate, arrange, and exhibit in their internal relation to each other."[58] Here, Hodge is clear: "the Bible contains truths." In effect, the Bible is a collection of facts and, when a theologian does theology—and hermeneutics itself –the theologian engages theology as a science.

Strauss and Scientific Hermeneutics

In *Hermeneutics* (2009), Anthony Thiselton suggests that David Strauss (1808-1874) was a disciple of Hegel and, as a result, this discipleship comes to bear on Strauss making a distinction between "representations" in religion and "critical concepts" in philosophy.[59] This Hegelian approach is exemplified in Strauss's *Life of Jesus* (1835-1836), where, as Thiselton argues, "[Strauss] argued that the Gospels were largely mythical, not historical."[60] From here, Thiselton cites Hans Frei's essay on Strauss as it appears in the *Nineteenth Century Religious Thought in the West*. In this, as argued through Thiselton, Frei makes the following claim about Strauss: "myths are ideas presented in the form of narrative. Miracles and the supernatural are abandoned."[61] So, for Strauss, particularly through his appropriation of Hegel, in order to truly and effectively interpret Biblical texts and the "life of Jesus," it becomes important to separate history from myth, so that the mythological elements of Biblical narrative are uncovered.

Allow me to consider how David Jasper depicts Strauss. In *A Short Introduction of Hermeneutics*, Jasper denotes that Strauss's *Life of Jesus* is the single most important book on the whole history of nineteenth-century hermeneutics and that, essentially, it embarks on "a hermeneutics of

58. Hodge, *Systematic Theology: Volume 1*, 1.
59. Thiselton, *Hermeneutics: An Introduction*, 145.
60. Ibid., 145-146.
61. Ibid., 145.

suspicion with a vengeance.⁶² As a "hermeneutics of suspicion," particularly if using Paul Ricoeur's definition of the term, Strauss's view of hermeneutics is focused on looking beyond the text. Just as Jasper suggests, Strauss's approach to biblical interpretation is one of a critical study of literary methods evident in Biblical texts and a use of sources by the Biblical authors.⁶³ In this regard, Strauss, as Jasper further argues, "wished to free the reading of Scripture entirely from all religious and dogmatic presuppositions."⁶⁴ In doing so, Jasper outlines Strauss's study of the Gospels by way of two clear principles: miracles do not happen, and all ancient, whether it is sacred or profane, should be treated alike.⁶⁵

Essentially, for Strauss, the Bible should be treated as a text, and, more importantly, as a text that must be encountered not strictly by what is in the text, but what forces come to bear on the creation of that text. This, of course, means that Strauss is, as Jasper rightly contends, "shows an impatience with the Christian history of hermeneutics of faith."⁶⁶ Because of this, Strauss, if arguing through Jasper, believes that "the task of the hermeneut is to unravel [the] primitive myth [in Biblical texts] and to discover the truth, which is accessible only by vigorous scientific inquiry."⁶⁷ As such, Strauss's *Life of Jesus* is devoted to "vigorous scientific inquiry."

But, according to Karl Barth (1886-1968), the key to understanding Strauss is not just through *Life of Jesus*, but through what I will call later-Strauss, the Strauss of 1864. In *Protestant Theology in the Nineteenth Century* (1947), Karl Barth makes the following summarization of Strauss in 1864:

> Strauss thought that there was a historical core to the 'life of Jesus,' which was shrouded in a veil of myth. With John it was a thick veil, with the Synoptics not so thick, but on the whole it was not impenetrable. It was difficult but not quite impossible to distinguish the core as such. This core consists in a human personality which made actual to a high degree the religious disposition, and to this extent the disposition of man as such. Together with others of its kind[,] this personality should be assess by us not, indeed,

---

62. David Jasper, *A Short Introduction to Hermeneutics*, 91.
63. Ibid.
64. Ibid.
65. Ibid.
66. Ibid.
67. Ibid.

as the basis, in the strict sense, for our achievement of our human destiny, but certainly as the means towards this end.⁶⁸

In this admittedly lengthy quote, I find that Barth is not limiting his understanding of Strauss to the 1835-36 version of *Life of Jesus*, but suggesting that Strauss's thought evolved in the nearly thirty years since the publication of *Life of Jesus*, culminating in a second edition. Barth's point is twofold. On one hand, by offering a view of later-Strauss, Barth is fully aware that later-Strauss differs from the Strauss of *Life of Jesus*. In this respect, Barth contends that, if Strauss had originally proposed that a mythological perspective to Biblical narrative is not all-encompassing, "[*Life of Jesus*] would definitely not have become famous, and it would not have cost its author his place at the university."⁶⁹

So, if following Barth's opinion of Strauss a bit further, not only is it evident that Barth describes Strauss as being no great theologian, but that Strauss has an ultimate goal to his mythological approach to *Life of Jesus* and other theological writing. As Barth offers in Strauss's own words, "the only aim of all my theological writing was to free me from the black folds of the cassock; and in this it succeeded perfectly."⁷⁰

Heidegger's Hermeneutics

Heidegger's Hermeneutics of "Being"

As David Jasper rightly notes in his section in *A Short Introduction to Hermeneutics* (2004), "a survey of hermeneutics cannot avoid an acknowledgment of [Heidegger's] central place in hermeneutical theory and understanding." ⁷¹ This is precisely true not only in what Heidegger offers to the field of hermeneutics, but also what hermeneutics offers towards grasping Heidegger's main philosophical preoccupation with "being." This "question of being," as it has been often argued, is an overarching theme to what Heidegger is most concerned with philosophically—"being," for Heidegger, becomes the essential Leibniz-like "monad"⁷² that is the key to encountering, recognizing, and

---

68. Barth, *Protestant Theology in the Nineteenth Century: Its Background and History*, 539-540.

69. Ibid., 540.

70. Ibid., 552.

71. Jasper, *A Short Introduction to Hermeneutics*, 104.

72. As Gottfried Leibniz describes in an essay entitled "The Principles of Philosophy,

grasping truth. In this Heideggerian sense, the question of "being" itself is, then, the essence of truth. I would argue that it is about situating "being" as a Kantian thing-in-itself,[73] so that, though "being" is out there fully-formed and *a priori*, it needs to be uncovered through methodical meaning-making strategies and working through "concealment." This latter term is Heideggerian, which I will discuss in more detail later.

For now, I want to make it clear that Heidegger's approach to hermeneutics is hyper-focused on "being," truth, and negotiating what is hidden beneath the "text"—when I say "text," I am considering the term in a more postmodern sense as something that contains epistemological value in it and, then, something that yields existential/ontological meaning. This is precisely why Jasper makes the assertion that "[Heidegger's] hermeneutics moves far beyond the business of textual interpretation."[74] What Jasper is very aptly pointing out is that Heidegger's hermeneutics is more than just about the relationship between a reader and a text, or even, for that matter, Thiselton's "two-horizons."[75] Instead, it is particularly about "being" as the ontological meaning-maker between a truth-seeker and the "truth" itself across a plane of understanding. What a truth-seeker understands and to what extent the "truth" becomes understandable suggests that Heidegger has a very specialized conception of what understanding is.

Consider Richard Palmer's *Hermeneutics* (1969), where, in his section devoted to Heidegger, he offers the following:

> Heidegger [. . .] assert[s] that all understanding is temporal, intentional, historical . . . [going] beyond previous conceptions

---

or the Monadology" in 1714, "monads" are the "true atoms of nature" and "the element of all things." The "monad" is critical to how Leibniz conceives of the truth as being either one of "reasoning" or one of "fact." In either case, truth is contingent on the monad. Leibniz, *Philosophical Essays*, 213.

73. To say that something is a "thing-in-itself" supposes, as Immanuel Kant describes, that it something that is "completely determined." This means, of course, that what we see is literally what we see, and that "what is seen" is nothing more than a universal set of elements that can "be seen" by all. Kant, *Critique of Pure Reason*, 490.

74. Jasper, *A Short Introduction to Hermeneutics*, 105.

75. I am referring to Anthony Thiselton's explication of the horizon of the reader/interpreter and the horizon of the text. These "horizons" are based on already granted meanings and intentions. So, "understanding takes place when the interpreter's horizon engage with those of the text." Thiselton, *Two Horizons: New Testament Hermeneutics and Philosophical Description with Special Reference to Heidegger, Bultmann, Gadamer, and Wittgenstein*, 17.

in seeing understanding not as a mental but as an ontological process.[76]

Allow me to explain Palmer in another way, which I hope is more helpful and explicative. The truth-seeker and the "truth" both exist in a common temporality, though they have very distinct historicities. That is to say, they share a common time in history and bring into their temporal-historical encounter of one another different histories.

Yet, there is a Husserlian intentionality[77] between the truth-seeker and the "truth"—the truth-seeker is naturally-oriented towards grasping the "truth" as much as the "truth" is naturally-oriented towards being graspable. In this sense, the "truth," before it is grasped, is strictly metaphysical, since it exists, as Kant would likely argue, as a "transcendental idea."[78] Heidegger's "being" makes "truth" ontological, since as Palmer points out, this "ontological process" is not "a study of conscious or unconscious processes, but as disclosure of what is real for man."[79] I find that the two terms "disclosure" and "real" become very important to the meaning of Heideggerian hermeneutics, particularly if taking careful consideration of what Palmer means when he suggests that "Heidegger is concerned with the hermeneutical process by which being can be brought to light."[80] This is, of course, not just the key to Heidegger's hermeneutics in the "early Heidegger" denoted by *Being and Time*, but also "later Heidegger" dedicated to issues of language.

Just as Palmer proposes, *Being and Time* is, indeed, "the soil out of which the later thought [of Heidegger] grows."[81] This sort of insight makes it possible to understand the connection that later Heideggerian thought makes between "being" and language and, then, the proposition that Heidegger makes in *On the Way to Language*: "language is the house of Being."[82]

---

76. Palmer, *Hermeneutics*, 140.

77. I would describe this with the following: the ability for a subjective being to recognize their "intented-ness" towards what Husserl calls an "intentional object" to the point that that "intentional object" becomes the epistemological ultimacy of a subjective being. See Husserl, *The Crisis of European Sciences and Transcendental Phenomenology: An Introduction to Phenomenological Philosophy*, 85.

78. Kant, *Critique of Pure Reason*, 315.

79. Palmer, *Hermeneutics*, 140.

80. Ibid., 141.

81. Ibid.

82. Heidegger, *On the Way to Language*, 63.

But, this "being," though it is "housed" in language, is not readily accessible and must be, consequently, "uncovered" due to what Heidegger calls "concealment." This term "concealment" is a post-Being and Time term that is essential to Heidegger's *Contributions to Philosophy*.[83]

Rather than going too far into *On the Way to Language* and *Contributions to Philosophy*, I would argue that Heidegger's hermeneutics is grounded on the notion of "concealment." For Heidegger, the hermeneutical process has one main goal: grasping "being," uncovering the truth and negotiating concealment, so that truth becomes, in Heidegger's view, "unsheltered."

On the other side of what Heidegger is doing is considering that the truth is "sheltered" and that any truth-seeker must recognize this crucial fact as a component of the hermeneutical process. What Heidegger is operating upon is Plato's "Allegory of the Cave" as it is expressed most notably in *The Republic* by Socrates. Here, as Heidegger appropriates in hermeneutics, the truth is about grasping "The Forms"—it is about finding the "being" that is housed in the language, teasing the truth out of "The Forms" that are expressed in language and, thereby, "coming out of the cave." In this regard, then, all "truth" is "concealed," and becomes the ultimate imperative of the truth-seeker to not only conceive of "The Forms," but to do so in order to fully embrace to the real world, its truth inherent in the Sun, and the totality of existential reality by freeing oneself from the Cave.

Heidegger's Hermeneutics of "Unconcealment"

In the introduction to *Parmenides*, Heidegger always makes his intentions clear, and those intentions revolve around providing what he calls a "preparatory meditation" on the name and the word "aletheia" and its corresponding "counter-essence." This "meditation," of course, is an examination of "aletheia" from its Greek roots, where Heidegger begins his investigation by carefully considering two critical Greek thinkers. For Heidegger, Parmenides and Heraclitus are two Greek thinkers that, as contemporaries in the decades between 540 and 460, were concerned with "thinking the true" –that is, as Heidegger explains: "to experience the true in its essence and, in such essential experience, to know the truth of what is true."[84]

---

83. Heidegger, *Contributions to Philosophy*, 232.
84. Heidegger, *Parmenides*, 1.

The notion of "thinking true" in the thought of two pre-Socratic thinkers—Parmenides and Heraclitus—has, as Heidegger contends, never been "affected" by "the passing of the years and centuries."[85] One reason for this, as Heidegger proceeds to argue, is that "what is thought in [their] thinking is precisely historical, preceding and thereby anticipating all successive history."[86] In effect, the degree to which this kind of thinking "precedes and determines all history" makes it possible to call the thought of Parmenides and Heraclitus "the beginning"—the thinking of these two thinkers denotes them as "primordial thinkers."

In order to access the thought of these primordial thinkers and subvert the "intention to reflect today on the thinking of Parmenides and Heraclitus" through doubts and objections, Heidegger suggests that we must embark on the task of "think[ing] the thoughts that both [of] these thinkers have thought."[87] Such a task is unavoidable. To be sure, the unavoidable requirement involves "attending to the words of these thinkers."[88] In this regard, Heidegger turns to Parmenides, whose words have the linguistic form of verses that "seem to be a poem."[89] But, the "poem" of Parmenides presents a "philosophical doctrine"—it can be best characterized as a "doctrinal poem" or a "didactic "poem" functioning as a teaching device in very much the same vein as the *Didache, or Teaching of the Twelve Apostles* from the 2nd century.

Perhaps, just as an early Christian followed the *Didache* text, Heidegger proposes that we must follow Parmenides' text, since it is "the most secure way to learn what is said and thought in the words of Parmenides. Even in following the text, Heidegger concedes that, despite the interpretation, neither the translation nor the clarification of the text "carries much weight so long as what is thought in the word of Parmenides does not itself address us."[90] What this means, then, for Heidegger, is that everything—how we follow the text—depends on our paying heed to the claim arising out of the thoughtful word."[91] This is the only way for us to pay heed to the claim and know the dictum. The relationship between heeding and knowing

85. Ibid.
86. Ibid.
87. Ibid., 2.
88. Ibid., 3.
89. Ibid.
90. Ibid.
91. Ibid.

CHAPTER 2: HERMENEUTICS BEFORE AND AFTER HEIDEGGER

concerns the being in its ground—essential knowing, or heedfulness, is a retreat "in face of Being [so that] in retreating we see and we perceive essentially more."[92] This is what Heidegger calls "thoughtful heedfulness," which especially comes to bear on his exegesis of lines 22-32 from a fragment of a Parmenides poem—specifically, exegetical work on lines 22, 25, 30, and 32. The lines that Heidegger highlights tell of a goddess who greets the thinker Parmenides as he arrives at her home in the course of his travels. The goddess' greeting is accompanied by an announcement of the revelations she has in store for the thinker as he goes his way. Consequently, Heidegger contends that "everything the thinker says in the subsequent fragments of the 'didactic poem' is the word of this goddess"—not only does Heidegger arrive as the proposition that the goddess is the goddess 'truth,' but "the truth—itself—is the goddess."[93]

The connection that Heidegger makes between the goddess and "truth" has implications not just in translating the Greek "aletheia," but also the "conflictual" character of "unconcealness" as "concealment." The implications call for, as Heidegger offers, a "fourfold directive" for translating the word "aletheia." The first two directives pertain to changing the emphasis in the word "unconcealness" with the intent of recognizing, once extracting "un," "unconcealness" points to "concealness." This, of course, directly leads into the third directive as outlined in Part One: what Heidegger calls the "realm of the opposition between "aletheia" and "lethe" in the history of Being. In Part Two, Heidegger discusses the fourth directive as "the open and free space of the clearing of Being"[94]—this fourth directive is particularly predicated on the insufficiency of "unconcealness," from which Heidegger arrives at the following: "aletheia is the essence of the true: the truth [and] truth dwells in everything that comes to presence; it is the essence of all essence: essentiality."[95]

---

92. Ibid., 4.
93. Ibid., 5.
94. Ibid., 131-163.
95. Ibid.

Theological Hermeneutics "After" Heidegger

Existential Hermeneutics: Macquarrie, Bultmann, Tillich, Rahner

David Jasper makes the following assertion about Bultmann's notion of "myth," which is undoubtedly an important place to begin when thinking about Bultmann's hermeneutics and the preoccupations that shape his hermeneutics:

> Myths are anything but old legends or mere stories and fables. Myths, rather, are expressions of human being in the world [where] we all live within their terms, and they are changing all the time as culture and society changes.[96]

This is a very important point to start when discussing Bultmann, particularly in light of the fact, as Jasper rightly notes, Bultmann, having learned from Martin Heidegger, defines "human being in the world, or human existence, as authentic and inauthentic.[97] In a sense, Bultmann's concept of "demythologization" is Heideggerian, since, because it is so focused on taking the "myth" out of interpretation and compartmentalizing "kerygma,"[98] is intent on approaching interpretation as an existential kind of hermeneutics.

I believe that a very helpful way to understand Bultmann's demythologization is along the two rather analogous approaches of Paul Tillich and John Macquarrie. The Tillich and Macquarrie approaches reflect—as does Bultmann with his demythologization—the sense that the authentication of human existence comes through careful consideration of both temporal and spatial limitations as well as the power of personal experience to shape "being."

For Tillich, whose theology is just as influenced by Heidegger as Bultmann's is, human existence comes into being as a result of "being thrown"[99]

---

96. Jasper, *A Short Introduction to Hermeneutics*, 102.

97. Ibid., 103.

98. Thiselton makes this distinction in *The Two Horizons*, where Thiselton argues that Bultmann's notion of the "Christ myth" revolved around the traditional elements of the "kerygma," which, in turn, allowed the notion of "myth" to arise. Thiselton, *The Two Horizons: New Testament Hermeneutics and Philosophical Description with Special Reference to Heidegger, Bultmann, Gadamer, and Wittgenstein*, 222.

99. This is a Heideggerian term that is used in a variety of ways: "thrown-ness," "being-thrown-towards-death," "thrown-ness into the there," and "being thrown through abandonment." "Thrown-ness into existence" is one of these ways. See Heidegger, *Being*

into existence. From this, Tillich asserts, in brief, that humanity is encased in an existential predicament, where it must seek authentic existence through conceiving and grasping the concept of God and God's "Being." Now, Macquarrie is operating from much the same Heideggerian-influenced perspective, suggesting that the fulfillment of human selfhood is contingent on "Being." Macquarrie goes a bit further and more explicitly than Tillich—though I think Tillich would agree by way of his notion of New Being[100]—and asserts that the historical symbol of Jesus has "ontological import" of personal existential ramifications, which "gives to our minds the fullest disclosure of the mystery of Being that we can receive.[101] What becomes essential about Macquarrie's and Tillich's sense of human existence in reference to God's existence is that humanity must be concerned with the present, the here and now. In other words, humanity cannot authenticate its existence by historicizing Jesus, but, instead, through applying ontological-existential meaning what Christ is and what Christ does –the theory and praxis, respectively—to fully understand what human existence is and what God's Being is. Here is where Bultmann's argument lies: the sense that humanity must tease out meaning through the reinterpretation and demythologization of Scripture, in order to apply that meaning experientially to our current, contemporary lived situation. What this means, furthermore, is that humanity's encounter with Scripture must be delineated along two lines: the historical event and the personal event. The latter is the most important, as I am sure Bultmann would agree, since the personal event—the individualized experience—opens the possibility for the greatest amount of meaning to be uncovered through the immanence of the event.[102]

In Tillich's *Systematic Theology Volume 2: Existence and the Christ* (1957), in a section entitled "The Marks of Man's Estrangement and the Concept of Sin," we can make note of the following assertion that Tillich makes at the very beginning of the selection: "The state of existence is the state of estrangement. Man is estranged from the ground of his being, from other beings, and from himself."[103] The first thing I would like to do, is

---

and Time, 321.

100. Tillich, *Systematic Theology Volume 2: Existence and The Christ*, 119.

101. Macquarrie, *Principles of Christian Theology*, 272.

102. I am thinking, here, of Gilles Deleuze's noton of the "immanent event" as an event that humans bring their lived experiences into and become changed by that event after the encounter.

103. Tillich, *Systematic Theology Vol. 2: Existence and the Christ*, 44.

unpack what Tillich means by the "ground of being," then use what I can unpack as a way of possibly understanding what I would contend is at the heart of his notion about existence equating to estrangement.

Tillich's use of "being" can be surmised in two very distinct ways: what he refers to as "the ground of being" and what I will call "being after the fact." These are two very different notions of existence. I would argue, then, that the former is a state that we exist in prior to being born into this world, while the latter is focused exclusively on the state of reality that we live in once we are aware of our humanity. In other words, we exist on two different levels that I will term as "pre-mortem" and "post-mortem" states of existence. To keep from going too far afield with these terms, I will describe them simply as "pre-birth" and "post-birth," both of which are construed in relation to human mortality and the connectedness of temporality. As Kierkegaard would likely agree, human existence is a sickness unto death.[104]

At any rate, what Tillich is asserting and what I am proposing are similar—there is something that fundamentally changes what it means "to be" once that "being" becomes "human existence." Human existence is not "being" in the metaphysical sense, or, as Tillich points out, "the ground of being." Instead, human existence is a state of "being" that is always ontological interconnected to all the physical trappings of being human. So, essentially, there is existence and then there is human existence. The first, perhaps, is more pure than the second, since the second is one that has been corrupted by the messiness of human existence, the facticity of the existential situation we inevitably find ourselves in, and our phenomenological and epistemological awareness of the limitations that human life bears upon us. These limitations can include two very prominent sociologically restrictive constructions: race and gender. Of course, Tillich is not observing race and gender as limitations, but he is, however, concerned with certain sociological restrictions that human existence holds. In Tillich's case, "estrangement" is a kind of sociological restriction, even if it cannot be defined as a man-made construction. It is, frankly, not placed upon us by societal norms or institutional-hierarchal structures, or anything else created through power relations—which are very much at the ideological crux of the concepts of race and gender as they are respectively embodied in racism, prejudice, and sexism—but is placed upon us by the fact that we exist as humans.

Our "being," in this regard, comes into actuality by being "estranged," where we harbor an existential conflict within ourselves and with others

---

104. See Kierkegaard's *Sickness Unto Death* (1849).

due to this "estrangement." To exist as a human being, therefore, means to existence as a result of conflict centered in knowing that we are estranged. This conflict occurs not just through the fact that we are born into a world of sin, but that that sin is, in turn, carried forward as a concept through our own sinfulness. Sin becomes a part of our humanity and human nature, and is inextricably linked to our "being" and how that "being" is translated into our spatial and temporal perceptions of the world's "being." Our sinfulness becomes linked to our sense of self, or selfhood, to the point that, as Tillich rightly notes, "man as he exists is not what he essentially is and ought to be."[105]

In my view, Tillich is touching on the notion that once we know we exist and can meaningfully interpret what we "know" of our existence as strictly a human enterprise, we come to the realization that our humanity is not the way, as Tillich suggests, we "ought to be." I take this to mean that humanity's sinfulness greatly diminishes our existence precisely because our humanity is connected to the physical: to live in the flesh is to live in a constant state of negotiating our sinfulness with the ideality of what we "ought to be." To that end, there is another conflict that develops into an existential conundrum: the fact that we exist in human reality puts any pre-human ideality out of reach. Essentially, being steeped in our human reality of sin greatly diminishes any meaningful conception we can ever have of pre-human ideality—I find that this is personified in Tillich's conception of "sin," but, particularly, "sin" as the impetus for how Tillich describes "estrangement."

What becomes diminished through this "estrangement," I would argue, is the essence of our existence, the purity of what it means to exist at a metaphysical level before we come into contact with the world and, as a result, become ontologically situated in our human existence. This ontological estrangement from the metaphysical forces humanity to perpetually seek "The Other." Not only does Tillich agree with this by ascertaining that "man[kind]'s hostility to God proves indisputably that [mankind] belongs to [God]," but that, if I may argue a bit further, human existence is always trying to qualify and self-validate itself in relation to God's divine existence. The "estrangement," as Tillich notes, that occurs in the human-God dialectic is something that human existence attempts to bridge, since God, as "The Other," becomes, if applying another Tillich idea, our ultimate concern.

---

105. Tillich, *Systematic Theology Vol. 2: Existence and the Christ*, 45.

In light of Tillich's specific argument about estrangement, Rahner is also concerned with the "ground" of human being. I find that Rahner is keenly aware of onto-theology, not just Kantian, but Heideggerian—the sense that "being" and "Being" are inextricably linked through issues of ontological value, existential meaning, and theological ramifications. Like Heidegger specifically, Rahner seems to be operating under the assumption that the connectedness of being and Being is as much an ontological concern as it is a theological one.[106]

But, of course, Rahner offers some very important nuances that deviate from Heidegger, Kant, and Tillich. Rather than being concerned with seeking outwardly for the ground of humanity's being, Rahner focuses the seeking inwardly –I would argue that Rahner conceives of this ground as being intrinsic, not extrinsic. That is, in order to "transcend" the finitude of Tillich's human existential predicament, Rahner suggests that the human "spirit" is the "ground." But, more importantly, if taking Rahner a bit further, it is possible to suggest that the facticity of humanity's "spiritual" side is contingent on having been "grounded" in God's "Being," even if there is some sense of estrangement evident in what is "grounded.

Though there is "estrangement" in Tillich's view, that estrangement is not one where humanity's being is mutually exclusive from God's Being. Instead, regardless of estrangement, God is within us. In other words, I would argue that what Rahner is precisely articulating—that is to say, through the notion that God "willed" the spiritual nature of humanity within humanity—is that the "transcendental nature of humanity" is what makes it possible for God to "self-communicate" God's "Being" in the form of Jesus's humanity.

As Rahner suggests, the way that this "self-communication" occurs is through, as I have interjected with Kant, a transcendental dialectic. Here, with the transcendental dialectic, it is possible to argue that Rahner's self-communication is based on the situatedness between two that share a dialectic with one another. Specifically, in regard to what Rahner proposes as "communication" between humanity and God's "Being"—of course, through the form of Jesus's humanity –the Kantian transcendental dialectic is one that is between humanity's being and God's "Being," or, as "being-Being" dialectic.

The association between humanity's "being" and God's "Being" is much more than just a connectedness shared through existence. Rahner would

---

106. Heidegger, *Identity and Difference*, 59.

likely agree with this, since it seems that his notion of self-communication is more than just a communicative connectedness. Yet, I think it is prudent to begin here, in order to understand, on some fundamental level, the plane of reality that "being" and "Being" share, to some degree.

To begin here requires simply, at least in terms of the man-God relationship, that "being" is human being and "Being" is divine existence. I want to make that distinction clear first, particularly with respect to how Rahner appropriates God's existence in relation to humanity's. It is safe to say, then, that Rahner, along with Macquarrie and Tillich, and even Bultmann to a lesser degree, are placing a distinction between two existences: the human and the divine, or, respectively, "being" and "Being." The connectedness between "being" and "Being," in this regard, is inextricably linked within the "being-Being" dialectic.

In other words, to superficially connect "being" to "Being" along the lines of "how" they exist is strictly about considering them as only two existing entities. To that end, it is about mainly reflecting on human existence and divine existence, respectively, as differing states of existing reality. I would argue that this is one of the chief concerns of Macquarrie, Tillich, Bultmann, and Rahner alike. I would even go so far as to assert that any fundamental connectedness between "being" and "Being" situates both within two means of living, or two perspectives of situatedness: one grounded on materiality and physicality, the other conceptualized through ideality and transcendence. I do concede, more directly, that such a distinction is necessary and immensely important, particularly as an ideological touchstone for much of what it means to the connectedness of "being-Being"—though I am lending credence to describing "being" and "Being" as separate senses of situatedness that are situated in two very different existing realities, we must only start here in formulating an argument, where making a point to denote the differences, or even confliction, inherent in the two is not enough.

The being-Being "relation" is, in fact, a dialectical construction. It is not strictly dialectical in the Kantian/Fichtean or Hegelian models.[107] It is certainly a "relation" in only the loosest sense of the word, not defined by the thesis-antithesis arrangement no more than it is by the abstract-negation. In either regard, there is, as I find it, an implied supposition of conflict, where "being" and "Being" become points of diversion separating human epistemology into two epistemologies. Yet, I do not find a conflict,

---

107. The Kantian and Fichtean models of dialectics are defined as thesis-antithesis-synthesis, while Hegel uses the abstract-negation-concrete approach.

or divergence, between "being" and "Being" apparent in their "relation." I see the term "relation" problematic. It limits "being" as such and "Being" as such by setting up the two through opposition, through their positionalities and situatedness relative to one another, and through implying their dissimilarity across situated difference. When using "relation," there is, inherent in that word's definition, something that I would call an epistemological reduction[108] occurring—the reduction of "being" and "Being" through separate sets of knowledge of their individual situatedness with the intent of bringing about a disconnectedness between the two.

Even if taking into consideration that Haim Gordon defines "relation" in the *Dictionary of Existentialism* (1999) as a concept of human existence or the nature of a being that stresses specific relations for self-realization,[109] it is possible to conceive of "relation" as a "relationship," since I would define "relationship" as a condition of "relations." But, even "relationship," I would argue, poses certain problems in the being-Being dialectic. I find that, if operating under Gordon's definition, "relations" open up the potentiality of "self-realization." What Gordon seems to be suggesting, then, is that a "relation," or the "relations," between the "natures" of two beings allows each to recognize the other as a "nature" of being and, in turn, "self-realize" their own "nature" of being. In other words, beings "self-realize" their "nature" through recognizing the "nature" of other beings. To that end, it is safe to describe that what Gordon is asserting is that beings have relationships and, through those relationships, present a two-directional self-realization process: one on account of one being, the other on account of the other being.

This is not the way that "being" and "Being" encounter one another across what I would call a plane of understanding. I use "encounter" in place of "interact," since I believe that "interact" does not truly articulate the positionalities and situatedness evident between humanity's "being" and God's "Being." As Rahner would likely agree, "transcendental" is about positionalities and situatedness and, furthermore, is concerned

---

108. Here, this an adaptation of Edmund Husserl's "phenomenological reduction" as he uses it in Ideas Part I. Husserl asserts that any phenomenological reduction has the intent of limiting the universality of something, so that that "something" can be better understood or comprehended. Husserl, *Ideas Pertaining to a Pure Phenomenology and to a Phenomenological Philosophy*, 60-62.

109. These relations are necessary conditions or constitutive elements for realizing a dimension of humanity. Gordon, ed., *Dictionary of Existentialism*, 397.

CHAPTER 2: HERMENEUTICS BEFORE AND AFTER HEIDEGGER

with the extent which "being" and "Being" encounter one another by way of an interaction.

Of course, there is no true "interaction," at least when defining what occurs with respect to how "being" might come to refer to another "being," and vice versa. So, for me, "interaction" is limited to "beings" that exist in same sphere of existence, sharing certain materiality and physicality, having the ability to objectify one another as a "being," and summating that mutual objectivity within time and space. Such an objectification, within the way I would describe "interaction," is about an exchange of knowledge—it is about having an epistemological awareness between "beings" that does not necessarily require any higher phenomenological contemplation. What is there is "there." What a "being" sees in another "being" is self-referential.

This self-reference is unachievable between "being" and "Being," since, as I have already argued to some extent, the former is a material object of understanding and the latter is a transcendent object of understanding. Unlike what can be said of "being" and "being," there is no direct epistemological exchange between "being" and "Being"[110] where it becomes only possible to say that humanity's "being" is as self-realized to God's "Being" as God's "Being" is to humanity's "being." The issue is with self-realization: the affirmation or validation of "being" through an objective reality. While it is possible for "being" to self-realize its "being-ness" in reference to "Being," the same cannot be said of "Being." That is because "Being" is the agent of self-realization—the fact that "Being" is "Being" means that it is always the point of reference and needs no self-realization. Yet, as the agent of self-realization, "Being" and its "Being-ness" is relative to the finite capacity of "being" to understand that God's "Being" transcends that finitude—this means that "being" can only encounter "Being" as such, and cannot, therefore, interact with God's "Being" in God's totality.

The encounter between "being" and "Being" is through the "relatedness" between them. I intend to assert, then, that "relatedness" best describes the being-Being encounter. This will be extremely important to what "being" means to "Being," and vice versa. This does not occur as a "relation," or through "relations," but, instead, by a kind of relatedness, where "being" and "Being" relate. What I am offering, as a major point of argument, is that "relate" more accurately articulates the extent to which "being"

110. This is in contrast to the direct epistemological exchange that occurs between "being" and "being." What I mean, particularly, is that "being" cannot know all there is to know about "Being" in a direct manner, through the use of perception and senses, but can, to some extent, attain epistemology from "being."

and "Being" encounter one another across a plane of understanding so that "being" can relate to "Being."

So, my intent, then, is to suppress "relation" and "relations" in order to offer "relate." In effect, rather than suggesting that "being" and "Being" have a "relation" or embody "relations," I would argue that they "relate" to another and how they "relate" becomes essentially communal. When considering humanity's "being" and God's "Being," or truly understanding human existence and divine existence, what must be taken into consideration, if using the term "relate," is that an interplay occurs between the two: they mutually affect one another in a Platonic sense.[111] This is, of course, an interplay that is skewed more on behalf of "being" than "Being," since "being" will find that it is grounded in "Being," and "Being" is the ground for all beings.

The interplay that I am describing is ultimately more than how "being" relates to "Being," but how ontology relates to theology. While ontology is the study of being,[112] theology is the study of "The Divine" and divinely revealed truths.[113] If I may put it another way, both ontology and theology, as they come to bear on the existential hermeneutics of Macquarrie, Rahner, Tillich, and Bultmann, examine "being-ness" in the physical and transcendent, respectively. So, I can offer the following: ontology is concerned with "being," theology is focused on "Being," and, finally, onto-theology, as existential hermeneutics, is centered with the "being-ness" inherent in the dialectical structure of "being-Being."

Philosophical Hermeneutics "After" Heidegger

Gadamer and Dialectical Hermeneutics

As we move further and rather relentlessly through the history of hermeneutics and into what we can consider as philosophical hermeneutics—though, by "philosophical," we are still working through theological concerns—we find that Hans Gadamer is an immensely (and undeniably) important figure in modern hermeneutics. Much of Gadamer's own concept

---

111. In the *Sophist* dialogue, Plato explains "being" as anything which possesses any sort of power to affect another, or to be affected by another, if only for a single moment, however trifling the cause and however slight the effect. To that end, it has real existence. The definition of being, then, is simply power. Hamilton and Cairns, eds., *The Collected Dialogues of Plato*, 957-1017.

112. Honderich, ed. *The Oxford Guide to Philosophy*, 670.

113. Macgregor, *Dictionary of Religion and Philosophy*, 609.

CHAPTER 2: HERMENEUTICS BEFORE AND AFTER HEIDEGGER

of hermeneutics is influenced by Heidegger, especially since Gadamer was once Heidegger's student. So, I would like to start with Heidegger for a moment, particularly as a way to ground Gadamer's approach to hermeneutics. That is to say, perhaps, that Gadamer's hermeneutics is, in fact, Heideggerian, not just in theory but praxis. I would argue that Gadamer purposefully carries forward in his view of hermeneutics something that preoccupied Heidegger's philosophy:[114] the notion of "Being" and the sense that "Being" is beyond ontology and, more specifically, metaphysics to the extent that "Being" is grounded in everything.

As David Jasper asserts about Heidegger in *A Short History of Hermeneutics*, "Heidegger's whole life was devoted to exploring the coherence of "Being" and the connectedness of all things."[115] This "coherence" and "connectedness" is predicated, in part, on the degree to which "all things" have "Being" as their ultimate—albeit "telos"—point of universality. It is here, as Jasper seems to agree, that we can find something Heideggerian in Gadamer's "emphasizing the universality of hermeneutics."[116] What occurs in this universality, just as Jasper rightly argues, is the degree to which the universality of hermeneutics is based on the interdependence of "truth" and "method."

As deeply influenced as Gadamer was by Heidegger, which Jasper aptly notes, Gadamer's *Truth and Method* is more than just a Heideggerian approach to hermeneutics. Such an assessment would be a bit short-sighted. What concerns Gadamer about "truth" and method" is, as I mentioned, an interdependence between the two, where they always remain in dialogue with one another. This dialogue, essentially, is structured around a "plane of understanding" between two "objects of understanding." The former term is Heideggerian through concept of "Dasein," while the latter is Kantian since it refers to the way in which objects are objected through synthetic unity.[117] I

---

114. Most notably his later work, which involved returning to Aristotle and Plato and, for better or worse, considering the original Greek of the terms "being," "ontos," "logos," and "meta" to name a few.

115. Jasper, *A Short Introduction to Hermeneutics*, 106.

116. Ibid.

117. For Immanuel Kant, an "object of understanding" is something that is represented, or objectified, prior to all experience. This means an object of understanding is an "*a priori*" concept when filtered through rigorous experiential objectification processes. According to Kant, "indicate the synthetic unity which alone makes possible an empirical knowledge of objects." Kant, *Critique of Pure Reason*, 315.

offer these two terms as a means to understand the following assertion that Jasper makes about Gadamer's use of the terms "truth" and "method":

> [Gadamer's] dialogue between the claims of "truth" on the one hand and the processes of "method" on the other –a return to ... a familiar pattern in hermeneutical thinking as it exists between an absolute demand (whether God or Dasein) and the relentless, systematic application of methods and processes.[118]

The "truth-method" dialogue that Jasper describes is one that is dialectical. While "truth" is, as Jasper suggests, an absolute demand," the manner in which "truth" discloses itself out of a Heideggerian concealment[119] is heavily dependent on the "relentless, systematic application of methods and processes." I would argue that Gadamer's notions of "truth" and "method," as they owe a debt to Heidegger, are articulating something undeniably and inevitably Platonic. It is the extent to which the "truth," as Plato offers through Socrates, is something that cannot be bestowed through pouring knowledge into the soul, but is only accessible by physically orienting the body in the right direction.[120] Such a sentiment is evident in Plato's "Allegory of the Cave," which, through Heidegger, is about grasping truth.[121] I only say this to suggest that Gadamer's sense of truth is the same as Heidegger's and, for that matter, Plato's. Gadamer's notion of "truth" is pivotal to how he constructs "method." The degree to which Gadamer chooses to examine the connectedness between "truth" and "method" is through phenomenologically bracketting[122] them and, according to Richard Palmer in *Hermeneutics*:

> [Gadamer's] examination of the hermeneutical experience by criticizing the prevailing concept of experience, which he finds too much oriented towards knowing as a perceptual act and knowledge as a body of conceptual data.[123]

---

118. Jasper, *A Short Introduction to Hermeneutics*, 106.

119. Heidegger, *Contributions to Philosophy*, 232.

120. Plato also offers the explanation of "truth" as something that needs to be prepared in a methodical or procedural way, since, for Socrates, truth is like pearls laid before swine. See Plato's *Republic*, Books 1 and 2.

121. The truth is about grasping "The Forms" –it is about finding the "being" that is housed in the language, teasing the truth out of "The Forms" that are expressed in language and, thereby, "coming out of the cave."

122. Palmer, *Hermeneutics*, 194.

123. Ibid.

CHAPTER 2: HERMENEUTICS BEFORE AND AFTER HEIDEGGER

As Palmer further notes, Gadamer's experience is "carefully enunciated" not just as a historical concept but a dialectical one. Just as Gilles Deleuze does with his concept of the "immanent event,"[124] Gadamer does not base "experience," as Palmer argues, as "simply a stream of perceptions but a happening, an event, an encounter."[125] Here, what becomes all the more evident about Gadamer's notion of experience is that it is not particularly Heideggerian, or even Kantian, but, as Palmer rightly argues, much more in line with Georg W. F. Hegel.

In Hegel's *Phenomenology of Spirit* (1807), "experience" is essential to all dialectic relationships. For Hegel, particularly through the "lordship and bondsman" relation across two self-consciousnesses, these dialectical relationships develop between the "relation of the self-conscious individuals [where it] is such that they prove themselves and each other through a life-and-death struggle."[126] In this sense, Gadamer would likely agree about hermeneutics: it is a life-and-death struggle between "truth" and "method" —it is, in fact, a struggle between the shifting horizons of truth in the text and the "method" that the reader takes towards "meaning-making."

What this means, then, is that "method" that a reader applies to the reading of a text and their individualized "meaning-making" processes influence that reader's "experience" of the text as "truth." This is particularly important when understand how Plato describes "The Forms," but also, and more significant, the extent to which The Cave encompasses individualized meaning, even though it is a limited and restricted meaning. For Gadamer, then, as with Plato, it is essential for anyone interpreting their surroundings to do so diligently and pragmatically, since what seems to be there might not be what is "truly there." The meaning-making process, as I have described it, is about infusing the experience into what is being made into meaning, and, therefore, committing to that truth. To commit to this truth, as such, means, if understanding the limitations placed upon the person that is in The Cave, recognizing the individualized meaning in the chains that chain one to the floor, and the "meaning" in the Wall towards which the eyes stare, and the extent to which what is projected upon that Wall is merely a secondhand representation of what truth "is."

---

124. Deleuze, *Immanence: Essays on a Life*, 31.
125. Palmer, *Hermeneutics*, 194-195.
126. Hegel, *Phenomenology of Spirit*, 113-114.

Foucault and the Hermeneutics of the Subject

In the Forward to the English edition of *The Order of Things* (1966), Michel Foucault (1926-1984) proposes a question that will fuel the trajectory of this work, and that question is the following: "what if empirical knowledge, at a given time and in a given culture, did possess a well-defined regularity?"[127] What ultimately undergirds this question is the notion that this "regularity" is predicated on what Foucault refers to as "the laws of a certain code of knowledge."[128] Not only does this offer the possibility of conceiving knowledge as being structured by a "certain code" that is governed by specific "laws," but also grasping and explaining ways of knowing metahistorically. To do this, Foucault contends that such an approach to knowledge must employ a comparative study, rather than a symptomatological one. As he suggests, a comparative study is concerned with the assessing a definite number of elements "side by side," which he outlines in this manner: "the knowledge of living beings, the knowledge of the laws of language, and the knowledge of economic facts."[129] These elements are, then, related to the "philosophical discourse that was contemporary with them during a period extending from the seventeenth to the nineteenth century." While the elements he respectively outlines are natural history, grammar, and the economy, the period that is chiefly focused upon extends across the Renaissance, Classicism, and Historicism. Associated with each of the aforementioned periods and elements are naturalists, grammarians, and economists, all of which are dedicated to "employ[ing] the same rules to define the objects proper to their own study, to form their concepts, to build their theories."[130] What does this relatedness mean?

For Foucault, it reveals what he calls a "positive unconscious of knowledge"—it is the notion that, despite the epistemological objective, there remains a system through which all epistemological "discovery" must operate. In this system of knowing, Foucault concedes to three underlying problems: the problem of change (changes that occur on different levels proceeding at the same pace, obeying the same laws), the problem of causality (a problem that have been put to this side in this work), and the problem of the subject (conditions of existence). Despite the connotations that may be apparent in

---

127. Foucault, *The Order of Things*, ix.
128. Ibid.
129. Ibid., x.
130. Ibid., xi.

this system of knowing, Foucault is careful to assert that he is not embarking on a structural analysis that makes use of methods, concepts, or key terms, even if it is dependent on conditions and rules. To be clear, Foucault is not systematizing knowledge, but merely concentrating on revealing how "knowing" functions through comparative analysis.

In the subsequent Preface, Foucault is also careful to argue that he is not concerned with "describ[ing] the progress of knowledge towards objectivity."[131] Instead, he is attempting to analyse the "pure experience of order" and its "modes of being," which are linked to the following lines of inquiry: "language as it has been spoken, natural creatures as they have been perceived and grouped together, and exchanges as they have been practi[c]ed."[132] Through these lines of epistemological inquiry, culture is a manifestation of the "existence of order" and the "modalities of that order" predicated on laws of economic exchanges, the constraints of living beings, and the sequence and representative value of words. Under an overarching "existence of order," Foucault uses a rather detailed analysis of Velazquez's "Las Meninas" to suggest that the painting puts forth a "classical representation, and the definition of the space it opens up to us."[133] This representation "opens up to us" epistemological assumptions that undergird what is epistemologically acceptable. Foucault utilizes "Las Meninas" as a "techne" to consider how "ways of knowing" are represented through speaking, classifying, and exchanging, which are respectively linked to natural history, grammar, and economics.[134]

By 1981-1982, when Foucault delivers his lectures at the Collége de France, entitled The Hermeneutics of the Spirit, the "hermeneutics" we find in *The Order of Things* is broadened, particularly in light of the four volumes that make up *The History of Sexuality* (1976, 1984, 1984, 2018) and *Discipline and Punish* (1975), both of which also make use of hermeneutics to interpret the body has interpolated respectively through sexuality and prison structures.

---

131. Ibid., xv-xxiv.
132. Ibid.
133. Ibid.
134. Ibid.

Derrida and "Deconstruction"

The hermeneutics of Jacques Derrida (1930-2004), as David Jasper appropriately puts it, is a more contemporary hermeneutics that gestures "towards the postmodern."[135] Essentially, Derrida's hermeneutics is moving in a very different direction, which, as Jasper rightly proposes, is "entirely interdisciplinary."[136] That means, of course, that Derrida's notion of hermeneutics is one that involves applying a hermeneutical lens to various fields of inquiry.

Aside from theological implications, Derrida's hermeneutics is particularly important in the field of literature through what is interchangeably known as literary or critical theory. Literary/critical theory is about critiquing literary texts with a specific perspective, such as feminist, Marxist, reader-response or reception theory, structuralist, post-structuralist, historicist, and so on. Each of these perspectives interprets a literary text in a highly specialized way, so that a reader can assess to what extent "meaning" can be teased from a literary text for further "beneath the surface" analysis.

That is to say, all literature specialists approach a text by, first, paying carefully attention to the structure of the language appropriated. From there, consideration is placed on the way in which that language is appropriated as a facilitator of meaning, then, the registers of meaning that that text is capable of expressing to the reader as that "meaning" becomes filtered through and molded by a reader's understanding of the historical, cultural, and societal contexts from which text arises. To this end, the text is categorized by its ability to answer *who*, *what*, *why*, and *how* questions—these are not just limited to the text itself, but, frankly, extended to all the outside forces that bring the text into being, such as its authorship and historicity. This is precisely what Derrida is arguing against: the belief that, in order to derive meaning from a text, "meaning" has nothing to do with authorship or historicity.

Though Derrida is immensely interesting and influential to postmodern and postcolonial theories at large, his theory remains elusive and misunderstood. One reason for this, I believe, is because the central text to Derridian thought, *Of Grammatology* (1967), is very dense and technical in its original French and, at turns, even more convoluted in Spivak's translation. If moving beyond the superficial, another reason is due to the

---

135. Ibid.
136. Jasper, *A Short Introduction to Hermeneutics*, 112.

CHAPTER 2: HERMENEUTICS BEFORE AND AFTER HEIDEGGER

very distinct lines that Derrida makes between the following components of a text: signifier/signified, totality/ideality, and inscriptions/signs. Such distinctions can be found in the following passage from *Of Grammatology*:

> The idea of the [text] is the idea of a totality, finite or infinite, of the signifier; this totality of the signifier cannot be a totality, unless a totality constituted by the signified preexists it, supervises its inscriptions and its signs, and is independent of it in its ideality.[137]

Here, Derrida is, as Jasper asserts, breaking down the essentialist categories of the text due to "notions of relativity and a suspicion of paradox."[138] But, more importantly, Derrida is pushing back against all the literary conventions that normally go into how a text is perceived and understood. On one hand, Derrida is certainly not all that happy with the signifier/signified of Ferdinand de Saussure's *Course on General Linguistics* (1916), since Saussure's use of the sign, in Saussure's own words, "reduces [language] to its elements."[139] This reduction is based on the difference between the "signifier" and the "signified." Derrida, on the other hand, is very much aware of the ideological hold that Saussure has had on modern linguistics, and uses Saussure's notion of difference in his own appropriation of the term "différance." Anthony Thiselton recognizes this connection quite well in *Hermeneutics*.[140] So, if turning back to Derrida, Derrida uses Saussure to formulate a specific notion of what he calls the "written signifier," which Derrida argues in the following way:

> The written signifier is always technical and representative. It has no constitutive meaning. This derivation is the very origin of the notion of the 'signifier.' The notion of the sign always implies within itself the distinction between signifier and signified, even if Saussure argues, they are distinguished simply as the two faces of one and the same leaf.[141]

When Derrida considers that the written signifier "has no constitutive meaning," he is suggesting that "meaning" in a text is independent of its authorship and historicity. The text constitutes itself, in other words.

---

137. Derrida, *Of Grammatology*, 18.
138. Jasper, *A Short Introduction to Hermeneutics*, 112.
139. Saussure, *Course in General Linguistics*, 65.
140. Thiselton, *Hermeneutics: An Introduction*, 332-333.
141. Derrida, *Of Grammatology*, 11.

I find that Derrida is treading in the same territory as the likes of Roland Barthes (1915-1980) and Michel Foucault, both of whom argued that, in brief, once a text comes into being, the author loses being.[142] As Barthes put it more blatantly, the life of the text is the death of the author.[143] But, Derrida takes Barthes and Foucault a bit further with his appropriation of deconstruction, which, as Jasper describes, is "the critical overturning of all structures and hierarchies on which we have built beliefs and systems in culture."[144] So, simply acknowledging the existence of an author, even by proposing the author's death as Barthes does, offers a structure and hierarchy: there exists an omnipresent text-author dialectic, where the author is an essentialist category applied to the text.

For Derrida, the "text" must be "deconstructed" beyond its "essentialist categories" in order to uncover more implicit layers of meaning –Derrida is concerned with "meaning" that, I would argue, is somehow limited or restricted due to the essentialist structures through which meaning is scaffolded and delineated.[145] The chief task of Derrida is to overthrow any essentialist structures applied to a text, particularly structures that have been historically constituted as far back as Aristotle's *Categories* and *Poetics*. Through Derrida, "a text" becomes a standalone structure that is capable of extending meaning through an epistemological value that does not require the author or anything else beyond the text itself. I find that this is the key to understanding Derrida: the text is a kind of living, existing entity that transcends contextualization and history, as well as rank and order. As Derrida famously—or, perhaps infamously—argues, "there is nothing outside of the text."[146] Many critics have taken Derrida to task for this statement, since, even in its simplicity and "deconstructionist" approach, makes certain implicit propositional concessions that are unavoidable. Such a statement itself opens a contextualization and history to his own method, which Derrida argues against—particularly in interviews given towards the end of his life—and leads him to passionately resist the term "deconstruction" all together.

---

142. While Barthes argued for the "death of the author," Foucault questions the existence of the author with an essay entitled "What is an Author?"

143. One of Roland Barthes most important essays on this matter is entitled "Death of the Author."

144. Jasper, *A Short Introduction to Hermeneutics*, 113.

145. Derrida, *Of Grammatology*, 158.

146. Ibid.

CHAPTER 2: HERMENEUTICS BEFORE AND AFTER HEIDEGGER

* * *

Derrida's "Structure, Sign, and Play in the Discourse of the Human Sciences" (1966) is not only concerned with changing the manner of discourse in human sciences, but it is also deeply invested in completely destroying underlying assumptions and implied structures inherent in structuralism. To be sure, Derrida's aim in this essay is to reconsider what has become known as structuralism, particularly the kind found in Levi-Strauss's nature/culture binaries. Though Levi-Strauss was a cultural anthropologist, the connections he made between nature and culture have become critical to structuralism as a discipline, one that is built upon the ever-presence of structures. This is at the core of the discourse of the human sciences, which is precisely what Derrida is focused on. But, more importantly, Derrida's task is not just an attack on Claude Levi-Strauss (1908-2009), but on the whole of structuralism. That means, then, a reconsideration of Foucault's structuralist approach in *The Order of Things*, as well as a rethinking of Heidegger's notion of being as based on a primordial understanding of "Being" and, even Plato's Forms. Granted, though these may not be explicit in Derrida's essay, it is certainly in the background to Derrida's overall metaphysical understanding of what structuralism is—Foucault, Heidegger, and Plato are important representative figures, by which Derrida constructs his own semiotic discipline that has come to known as deconstruction.

Of course, "deconstruction" is not a term that Derrida uses in this essay, nor is it a term he would have been comfortable subscribing to. Surely, his method is, if anything, "deconstructionist," since, above all, it encounters structuralism as something that must be deconstructed. That is, structuralism is grounded by inherent structures. In Derrida's view, these structures are problematic and constrictive, since meaning should not be structural or narrowed at all. It is this sentiment that directly confronts Foucault's archaeology of knowledge, but more poignantly, Heidegger and Plato.

Common in Heidegger's notion of being and Plato's Forms is the transcendental signifier: a signifier that is a fixed frame of reference that always has a referred meaning to something signified. In Heidegger, "being" is oriented towards "Being" through an onto-theological relationship—this relationship is predicated on the structural imperative of Dasein. In Plato, the "Forms" contain a structural imperative, one that, as we see in *The Republic*, becomes the means by which a society is structured, organized, and ordered in terms of who can perceive those "Forms." In both Heidegger and Plato, and even Foucault, there is the sense that certain ontological structures lend the possibility for metaphysical structures, especially in relation to a definite center from which everything that is ontological is delineated. This "center" is what Derrida is arguing against. His argument is that there should a reconsideration of the role that the "center" plays in the structure. As Derrida proposes, "the function of the center was not only to orient, balance, and organize the structure [. . .] but above all to make sure that the organizing principle of the structure would limit what we might call the *play* of the structure."[147]

"Play," as Derrida has coins it, is analogous to tolerance or give. That is, "the play of the structure" is the tolerance/give of the structure. This is decidedly arguing against the notion that a structure is complete in itself and that referred meaning—for example, between the signified and a transcendental signifier—is a closed-ended, absolutist endeavor. The completeness of the structure and referred meaning, as Derrida points out, is in the form of presence: the identity of a thing as it is. This identity, as it were, is grounded on a center and this concept of center lies in the possibility of "play." What we see from the identity of a thing, as a form of presence, is the direct result of "play" predicated on a system of differences. In effect, "play" makes both presence and absence possible, since presence cannot be as it is without absence.[148] Because of this, Derrida argues that "there is also the tension between play and presence [since] play is the disruption of presence."[149] In this regard, then, Derrida comes to the conclusion that: "Being must be conceived as presence or absence on the basis of the possibility of play and not the other way around."[150]

* * *

An important means of entry into *Of Grammatology* (1967) is through Spivak's "Translator's Preface" where Spivak asserts that Heidegger describes Nietzsche as the last metaphysician of the West. To be sure, Spivak is drawing a lineage from Heidegger to Nietzsche, with Heidegger becoming the next generation metaphysician following Nietzsche—something that

---

147. Derrida, "Structure, Sign, and Play in the Discourse of the Human Sciences," 278.
148. Ibid., 292.
149. Ibid.
150. Ibid.

is of particular importance when considering that Heidegger, as Spivak rightly argues, is a "philosopher of that special nostalgia for the original word."[151] Here, it is with the original word, or so to speak, that Heidegger is situated between Derrida and Nietzsche and, thusly, the possibility of concluding that Derrida is also a metaphysician. Such a claim holds true not only with Heidegger's critique of Nietzsche's asking the question of being without questioning the questioning itself, but with Derrida's treatment of Heidegger that ultimately seeks to further destroy Heidegger's destruction of metaphysics. If remaining faithful to the "destruction" that Derrida seeks, labeling him a metaphysician will prove just as problematic as describing his task and method in *Of Grammatology* as overwhelmingly the destruction of metaphysics.

It is at this point of entry that we find Derrida's "special nostalgia for the original word" based on a different extrapolation of what the "original word" is. Clearly, Derrida's "original word" is at the very core of his determination of being and, as a result, critical to how he wishes to destroy metaphysics further than Heidegger, or even Nietzsche, for that matter.

Like Heidegger, Derrida finds inherent and fundamental problems in the western intellectual tradition as it pertains to the history of being. But, the key move that Derrida makes—a move that is situated from an epistemological space, or gap in Heideggerian thought—is against binary oppositions that are set up between speech and writing. In a Heideggerian manner reminiscent of *Being and Time*, Derrida picks Plato and the philosophical tradition that develops from Platonic thought as a necessary beginning point that can be carried forward to the linguistic work of Ferdinand de Saussure. Over the course of this period, Derrida charts the history of writing centralized on the assumption that writing is considered as a derivative of speech. As a result, what arises from this assumption is the pervading notion that speech is closer to the truth than writing—that is, speech is a more accurate manifestation of meaning and representation. This notion, as such, contains an intersectionality between issues of certitude (in a Kantian sense), representation (as Foucault conceived of a classical way of knowing), and auto-affection (as certainty that comes from oneself, or as Foucault suggests, self-gratification).

Whether taken collectively or individually, each is an επιστημη that, when construed through writing, turns writing into, as Derrida argues, a dangerous supplement. What makes writing "dangerous" and

---

151. Derrida, *Of Grammatology*, xxxiii.

"supplemental" is that it is not natural, and is merely a representation of what it isn't. Writing acts as a "sign" which Charles Peirce ascribes three references in the following manner: a sign "to" some thought which interprets it, a sign "for" some object to which in that thought it is equivalent, and a sign "in" some respect or quality, which brings it into connection with its object.[152] This becomes an important backdrop to Spivak's assertion that "'writing' so envisaged is on the brink of becoming a unique signifier, and Jacques Derrida's chief care."[153] But, more importantly, when considering Peirce and, then Saussure's work with the "sign" through linguistic structuralism, Derrida offers Saussure's sentiment that "language and writing are two distinct systems of signs; the second exists for the sole purpose of representing the first."[154] With special emphasis added to *exists for the sole purpose of representing*," Derrida is chiefly concerned with the relationship between language and writing, situating that relatedness or connectedness by way of writing in the narrow sense (after speech) and writing in the general sense (before speech). By considering writing as two distinct systems of speech, the former is the dangerous supplement, since it contains irreconcilable contradictions, and hidden "there-ness."

Ricoeur, Hermeneutics of Suspicion, Hermeneutics of Faith, and the "Wall"

Hermeneutics of suspicion and hermeneutics of faith, by the theoretical definitions of Paul Ricoeur (1913-2005), are respectively associated with approaches to interpreting meaning "beyond" the text or "within" it. In this regard, as the John Thompson's introduction to Ricoeur's *Hermenetiucs and the Human Sciences* (1981), hermeneutics of faith is one of restoration that is "animated by faith, by a willingness to listen to it, and [...] a respect for the symbol as a revelation of the sacred."[155] In contrast, Thompson describes Ricoeur's hermeneutics of suspicion as "the demystification of a meaning presented to the interpreter in the form of a disguise."[156] Thompson's assertions about the role that "faith" and "suspicion" play in hermeneutics

---

152. Peirce, "Some Consequences of Four Incapacities" in *Philosophical Writings of Peirce*, 233.

153. Derrida, *Of Grammatology*, lxxx.

154. Ibid., 30.

155. Ricoeur, *Hermeneutics and the Human Sciences*, 6.

156. Ibid.

not only suggest that interpretation can either be approached by searching "within" the text or looking "beyond" the text, but that, in either hermeneutical approach, what becomes interpreted can greatly differ, even if the ground for that interpretation is the same. This means of interpreting is essential to how I intend to use Ricoeur's terms. So, rather than use "hermeneutics of faith" and "hermeneutics of suspicion" in the way that Ricoeur does towards the text, I intend to use them in a more specialized way –my intent is to appropriate those terms towards existence. In this way, instead of referring to the hermeneutics of a text, as Ricoeur does, I would call my appropriation "hermeneutics of existence." As such, there is a hermeneutical process that must be engaged in when interpreting existence into "Existence" –this, of course, is used in much the same manner as Ricoeur utilizes a hermeneutical process to interpret a text.

In some sense, I would argue that "Existence"—note the capitalization here—as an object of understanding, acts as a text. "Existence," as a text, contains elements and components that produce meaning from its totality but, at the same time, provides individualized meaning in its particulars. I would describe this as Platonic hermeneutics, since, as Plato suggests about the "Forms," any hermeneutics of existence is a relative endeavor that is limited by experience. This is how the Platonic "Wall" comes to bear in a hermeneutics of existence: it is the possibility that, though experience has a certain epistemological and phenomenological value in it, "meaning" is not made solely on those things but, instead, on an existential value beyond the experiential.

Deleuze and Guattari's Hermeneutics of Rhizomes and Plateaus

In the introduction to *A Thousand Plateaus* (1980), Gilles Deleuze (1925-1995) and Felix Guattari (1930-1992) summarize the "principal characteristics" of a rhizome as the following: "[. . .]connects any point to any other point, and its traits of the same nature; it brings into play very different regimes of signs, and even nonsign states."[157] Based on how Deleuze and Guattari describe, the rhizome—if it "connects any point to another point"—seems to relate itself to "any point," while positioning itself as something capable of being a relation between points. The rhizome is, first and foremost, positioned and situated between points in what can be best explained in a Kierkegaardian manner, especially as a Kierkegaardian "self"

---

157. Deleuze and Guattari, *A Thousand Plateaus*, 3-25.

in *The Sickness Unto Death*, which is "a relation that relates itself to itself, or is the relation's relating itself to itself in the relation . . . "[158]

What this means, more importantly, is that a rhizome—if I can continue to liken it to a Kierkegaardian "self"—is an entity that is both a passive and active participant in a dialectic. A rhizome is, in fact, seemingly in a position of power and powerlessness, as it "connects any point to any other point." To be clear, if Deleuze and Guattari view the rhizome as an entity—it must be, of course, be some kind of entity, rather than a thing, or even an object—that, through its dialectical relationship with "points," becomes a *"techne"* connecting those points, and, in the end, contains an existential character of "traits [that] are not necessarily linked to traits of the same nature" as those of the points that it connects in the dialectic.

If a rhizome is an existential dialectical entity that connects and categorizes "points"—it both forges a relatedness and differences between "points." It is in this latter way that the rhizome "brings into play very different regimes of signs and even nonsign states." Are these "different regimes of signs" based on an existential difference on either dialectical side created and sustained by rhizomes? In other words, does the fact that there are "different regimes of signs" suggest that rhizomes have a connectedness with the "different regimes of signs" on one hand, and on the other, a disconnectedness with them? If considering this connectedness and disconnectedness, it would seem that—especially if interpreting the summarization Deleuze and Guattari give—that rhizomes have analytic possibilities similar to Heidegger's *Dasein*.

In brief, Heidegger contends in *Being and Time* that *Dasein*—though generally defined in the German as "human existence," but modified narrowly by Heidegger to mean "being there" with "da-" standing for "there" and "sein" for "being—is an existential entity with "analytic possibilities." Like Heidegger's *Dasein*, the rhizome is at the metaphysical center of what is ontologically possible—it is, just as Heidegger conceives of *Dasein*, an entity that translates "being" from the metaphysical into the ontological. I am defining "the metaphysical" and "the ontological" in a specialized way, situating the former at the core of what makes the latter possible. In this sense, the ontological, or the ontics represents how "being" stands out from the metaphysical, or metaphysics—"being-in-the-world," for instance, is

---

158. Kierkegaard, *The Sickness Unto Death: A Christian Psychological Exposition for Upbulidng and Awakening*, 1.

CHAPTER 2: HERMENEUTICS BEFORE AND AFTER HEIDEGGER

"being" that has "ek-sistence."[159] With this existential formula in mind, Deleuze and Guattari's rhizome has *Dasein*-like analytic possibilities that "brings into play very different regimes of signs, and even nonsign states"—the degree to which this is even possible can be derived directly from what can "ek-sist" as an extension of a rhizome's being.

The analytic possibilities of the rhizome liberates and confines "being." Just as the rhizome "brings into play very different regimes of signs," it also prevents—or conditions against, perhaps—possibilities that yield no true existential value. The degree to which the rhizome allows there to be "very different regimes of signs" on one hand, and on the other, "nonsign states" means that the rhizome is a hermeneutical entity rooted in the free exchange of signs. That is to say, the exchange of signs are only as "free" as the rhizome deems analytically-possible, particularly in the broader scope of translating "the metaphysical" into "the ontological"—what comes "into play," so to speak, is a Derridean-like structure that has metaphysics as a starting point, but is ultimately oriented towards ontics. This stands to reason why the rhizome has "traits [that] are not necessarily linked to traits of the same nature"—when *the metaphysics of the rhizome* is oriented towards *the ontics of the rhizome*, the "traits" of the rhizome seem to assume the quality of a Platonic Form, a quality that is "not necessarily linked" to what results from quantification. This not only makes the rhizome analytic (in terms of allowing a Heidegger-like "clearing" for quantifiable possibilities), but also hermeneutic (in terms of what gets interpreted, how it gets interpreted, and why)—the difference is made clear in the following:

> The rhizome is reducible neither to the One nor the multiple. It is not the One that becomes Two or even directly three, four, five, etc. It is not multiple derived from the One, or to which One is added . . . It is composed not of units but of dimensions, or rather directions in motion. It has neither beginning nor end, but always a middle (milieu) from which it grows and which it overspills. It constitutes linear multiplicities.[160]

These "linear multiplicities" are, as Deleuze and Guattari argue, plateaus. Not only is "a rhizome [. . .] made of plateaus," but, like rhizomes, "a plateau is always in the middle, not at the beginning or the end."[161]

---

159. The term "ek-sistence" is expressed more fully and explicitly in Heidegger's "Letter on Humanism" than it is in *Being and Time*.

160. Deleuze and Guattari, *A Thousand Plateaus*, 3-25.

161. Ibid.

With this in mind, if rhizome have a *Dasein*-like function, plateaus do as well, because they are "always in the middle, not at the beginning or the end." What this means, then, is that the relationship between the rhizome and plateaus is dialectic, since they are connected, on one hand, by the analytic possibilities that exist in the rhizome and, on the other, the degrees by which a plateau can "ek-sist." But what remains unclear is which is more dependent on the other—do plateaus "ek-sist" strictly because of the rhizome's being, or is the only way a rhizome can fulfill its being inextricably linked to the analytic possibilities of plateaus brought into the Heideggerian clearing.

Rhetoric, Language, and Heidegger: Dialogues on Hermeneutics

Bertrand Russell's "Logical Atomism" and Heidegger's "Being"

What immediately stands out from *Logical Atomism* (1918) by Bertrand Russell (1872-1970) is the need to reduce "what is there" to what "is." In other words, Russell is chiefly concerned with distinguishing between "there-ness" and "is-ness," particularly as Heideggerian terms. The connection between Heideggerian and Russellian "there-ness" and "is-ness" is critical to understanding Russell's "logical atomism."

If "there-ness" is exemplified by what can be experienced as "the ontological," then "is-ness" is "the metaphysical"—that is, the former is something that, if furthering Heidegger a bit here, is in *the clearing*, has been unconcealed as "aletheia," and can be accessed as "what is there." But, the latter—"the metaphysical," as such—is something that "is," especially in the purest sense of what "is" is. So, if applying Heidegger's "there-ness" and "is-ness" to Russell's "logical atomism," I find that he is working from the same philosophical presuppositions—his "logical atomism" is logical in the Heideggerian sense that something "what is there" can be logically reduced to a basic, atomic structure.

To be clear, even when drawing a philosophical parallel between Heidegger and Russell, aligning Heideggerian and Russellian understanding of "a basic, atomic structure" can be problematic. One problem, of course, lies in the degree to which Heideggerian "being" can be imposed on Russell's concept of "atomic." In that regard, though it is surely possible to argue that both are founded on a metaphysical conceptualization of "is-ness," it may be more difficult to contend that Russell's "atomic" is an expression of "being."

Russell never uses the term "being" in his "Logical Atomism" article, nor would it be likely that Russell would have even been concerned with addressing Heideggerian "being" at all. Russell's "atomic" is more mathematical than it is philosophical. Surely, there is an existential need in Russell to make meaning out of "what is there," but that need is strictly logical. That is to say, Russell sets forth the task of working within the system of metaphysics, rather than destroying it, the latter of which Heidegger is mainly arguing for. Rather than calling for a destruction of metaphysics—the main task of Heidegger's *Being and Time*, for instance—Russell's "atomism" adheres to certain pre-established standards about a Carnap-esque logical structure of the world. Russell's approach to "logical atomism" is certainly more Platonic than Heidegger's, particularly if it can be said that Heidegger was not a Platonic and, in fact, insisted that the history of the western philosophical tradition since Plato has incorrectly conceived of, grasped, and explained what "being" is. Again, though "being" is not explicit in Russell's mathematical vocabulary, "atomism" is undeniably a stand-in for "being."

If, as Russell argues, "my own logic is atomic," then his "atomism" is the logical endpoint of interpreting ontological structures, or the Platonic "whole," of metaphysical structures, or Platonic "parts." Russell's "logic," to this extent, is situated towards the "atomic," as parts of the whole. These "parts" and "the whole" are mathematical structures—for example, "parts" make up "the whole," just as much as "the whole" can be reduced to the summation of its "parts." What such an expression seems to lead to is a description of the whole as a unity of its parts. It is precisely this expression that Russell pushes back against, since he argues, instead, that "in place of 'unities' [. . .] I prefer to speak of 'facts.'" Russell's unease with "unity" and his preference of the term "fact" is a mathematical decision. That decision, as such, is similar to Wittgenstein in *Tractatus Logico-Philosophicus*. Like Wittgenstein, Russell's idea of a fact is grounded in an analytical understanding of "what is there"—Russell is undoubtedly arguing that facts make up "what is there." A fact, in the singular, lends itself to a string of facts, and those facticities make up "there-ness." Of course, Heidegger is also concerned with facts and facticity, since Heidegger's own "being" is a factical, or ontical—either term for Heidegger denotes the metaphysical imperative placed on "the ontological" as something that must be reduced.

Like Heidegger, Russell sees "facts" as things that must be logically analyzed and logically synthesized. For Russell, "the business of philosophy [. . .] is essentially that of logical analysis, followed by logical synthesis." What this means, then, is that, according to Russell, philosophy must take up the task of analyzing what has been synthesized, in order to logically parse out the "parts" from "the whole."

If I were to go no further than this with Russell, it would appear that Russell is in agreement with Heidegger, especially if it can be agreed that Heidegger's "being" is a fact and that "Dasein" is the vehicle through which facts are synthesized. But, of course, any Heideggerian approach to understanding a fact is mainly philosophical-existential, and it is clear that Russell's approach is more philosophical-mathematical. So, is there a difference here? I believe that there is a difference. Though it may be possible to situate Russell as a pseudo-Heideggerian, this kind of label would be inappropriate. Russell is not Heideggerian in the narrow sense, even if it is possible to propose such a claim in the general sense.

But, what ties Russell's "atomism" to Heidegger's "being" is the meaning-making that both have respectively argued—like Heidegger, Russell's notion of the "atomic" is one that is rooted in relations, relatedness, and relationships, particularly the degree to which a fact, in itself, is always related to another fact and, in that relation, meaning is made both dialectically and comprehensively. If taking Russell to this length, though it may be difficult to label Russell a Heideggerian, it is certainly possible to label him as an existentialist precisely and largely in the vein of Kierkegaard.

Donald Davidson's "Epistemology Externalized" and Heidegger's Unconcealment

As the title of article suggests, Donald Davidson (1917-2003) suggests that knowledge—as in epistemology—is grounded on "the external." That is to say, when we say we know an object of understanding, we are really referring to that object's externalism, rather than our own subjectivity of it. For Davidson, subjectivity is a myth, since, "if we think we have a thought or sensation, there is a strong presumption that we are right."[162] Davidson believes that this "presumption" leads us to believing that "what we know" begins in our subjectivity—perhaps as Immanuel Kant proposes in his

---

162. Davidson, "Epistemology Externalized," 193.

Three *Critiques* of reason.[163] Not only does Davidson disagree with this "presumption" about knowledge, but his notion that epistemology is "externalized" employs a Heideggerian-like task of deconstructing the way we think about the meaning of knowledge.[164]

Of course, I am not implying that Davidson is a Heideggerian. To be sure, any such suggestion would prove problematic, even if I am only situating Davidson's concept of "external knowledge" within the realm of later Heidegger. However, Davidson is undoubtedly—though it is probably difficult to pin down Davidson's intentions—utilizing a Heideggerian method to approach "what knowledge is." What Davidson is chiefly concerned with is "what knowledge is" in a foundational sense, or in terms of the "unconcealment" of knowledge. When I say "unconcealment," I am referring to Heidegger's ἀλήθεια, or the extent to which something can be-in-the-sense-of-the-true,[165] unhidden, and unmasked as it already is. In other words, Davidson's understanding of "what knowledge is" is an understanding that is predicated on "unconcealing" precisely "what knowledge is." Through a Heideggerian lens this means: disclosing the *being* of knowledge, as what it really is. This becomes especially important if considering Davidson's Heideggerian-like "task" as:

> [. . .]supplying a foundation for the rest of knowledge, particularly, of course, for our knowledge of the 'external world' and of the minds of others. Such knowledge stands in need of a foundation, it is thought, precisely because there is no presumption that our beliefs about the world or the minds of others are true.[166]

For Davidson, our beliefs "about the world or the minds of others" are unreliable and our presumptions only further conceal, hide, or mask our experience of objects of understanding. This is because subjectivity mythologizes "what knowledge is"—the myth of the subjective leads the epistemological situation away from "what knowledge is," and not towards ἀλήθεια.

163. Immanuel Kant's *Critique of Pure Reason*, *Critique of Practical Reason*, and the *Critique of Judgment*.

164. I believe there is an analogous strain here, particularly if it is possible to suggest that Quine's way of thinking about the meaning of knowledge echoes Heidegger's approach in the First Introduction to thinking about the meaning of *Being*. Heidegger, *Being and Time*, 1.

165. I have adapted this term from Franz Brentano's "being in the sense of the true," which directly influences Heidegger's ἀλήθεια. See Brentano, *The Theory of Categories*, 18; 21.

166. Davidson, "Epistemology Externalized," 193.

When we assert that what we know of an object of understanding begins with our subjectivity, Davidson believes we are simply giving an account of how we know, instead of providing a foundation for knowledge itself. Just as Heidegger's task is to overcome the metaphysics of *being*, Davidson is invested in the task over overcoming the metaphysics of knowledge.

Moreover, as Heidegger uses Plato as a point of opposition to deconstruct the metaphysics of *being*, Davidson similarly uses W. V. Quine (1908-2000) to deconstruct the metaphysics of knowledge—in light of Heidegger's Plato, Davidson's Quine has misdirected the question to be asked and inaugurated a problem in the answer presented. Davidson points to this problem in Quine's notion that epistemology is naturalized. In Davidson's view, Quine is internalizing knowledge and, in turn, mythologizing subjectivity. Davidson's stance is clear, arguing that: "I do not accept Quine's account of the nature of knowledge, which is essentially first person and Cartesian."[167] Davidson furthers this argument, then, with concluding that "[Quine's] account of how we came by this knowledge is [. . .] just the kind of account that has traditionally been taken to constitute an attempt at justification."[168] What remains missing in Quine, according to Davidson, is justification, as well as describing "what knowledge is." But also, Davidson believes that Quine misses the following:

> [. . .]the distinction between describing and justifying, between an empirical account of the genesis of knowledge and a statement of the norms belief must satisfy to count as knowledge[. . .].[169]

Here, Davidson contends that Quine's naturalized epistemology is "a fairly conventional form of empiricism."[170] Because of this, Davidson finds that he is more a naturalized epistemologist than Quine.[171] Partly, this is due to Davidson's understanding that "we must come to the direct exposures that anchor thought and language to the world."[172]

What this stands to suggest is that Davidson believes that, because he views knowledge as externalized, to know an object of understanding

---

167. Ibid., 194.
168. Ibid.
169. Ibid.
170. Ibid.
171. Ibid.
172. Ibid., 197.

means having a "direct exposure" to it. That means, then, as a naturalized epistemologist, Davidson recognizes that knowledge—to be clear, "what knowledge is," as an object of understanding—must be accessed in the clearing of *unconcealment*. Like Heidegger, Davidson's approach to "what knowledge is" is based on a conceptualization of ἀλήθεια as that which "anchor[s] thought and language to the world."

CHAPTER 3: THEOLOGIZING ON HEIDEGGER'S TERMS

WHEN CONSIDERING THE RELATIONSHIP between Heidegger and theology as undoubtedly and predominantly about Heidegger's role in theology, it becomes prudent to grapple with Heidegger's philosophizing in itself. What that means, then, is we must work through what Heidegger philosophizes as a means of conceptualizing what his theologizing is. We know, of course, that Heidegger's philosophizing and theologizing are explicated through his interpretations of Augustine, Aquinas, and Luther, as much as theologizing, in itself, from a philosophical standpoint directly influences what Macquarrie, Bultmann, Tillich, and Rahner all do as theologians. From this, in light Heidegger's influences on theology proper through specific theologians, it is important to know more about Heidegger's philosophizing and how this philosophizing lends itelf to what can be meant by Heidegger's theologizing. To do so, if we are to theologize on Heidegger's terms, we must adequately work through what is generally philosophized in the terminology appearing in *Plato's Sophist* (Winter 1924/1925), *Being and Time* (1927), *The Fundamental Concepts of Metaphysics* (Winter 1929/1930) and "Letter on Humanism" (1946), as four key texts that lay a general foundation for how Heidegger theologizes more broadly.

Plato's Sophist (Winter 1924/1925)

Before discussing Heidegger's *Plato's Sophist*, it is prudent to, first, provide a (brief) discussion of the *Sophist* dialogue in a general sense, with respect to Plato, and, secondly, in a narrow sense, as a way of understanding what Heidegger considers as important about this text, especially with regard to Heidegger's opening reference to it in *Being and Time*.

As Heidegger was certainly aware, *Sophist* is a continuation of the *Theaetetus* dialogue, in order to interrogate the question of how knowledge is to be defined, Socrates leaves his main interlocutor Theaetetus without much of an answer. After taking Theaetetus through three possible understandings of knowledge: perception, justified belief/true judgment, and an explanation with a justified belief/true judgment, Socrates arrives at the conclusion that knowledge is neither of the three possibilities. In what is supposed to occur the next day, *Sophist* begins with Socrates playing a minor role, and Theaetetus engaged with another interlocutor: "the stranger from Elea." It can be said, perhaps, that this "stranger" can be viewed as a literary stand-in for Parmenidean thought, not just an individual that happens to come from Parmenides's hometown. Moreover, even, it could be argued that "the stranger" could be Parmenides himself, impersonated by Plato. Nevertheless, I do not intend to make an argument on this. Instead, I wish to focus on the interaction between "the stranger" and Theaetetus, which involves a discussion focused on defining a sophist in relation to a "philosopher" and a "statesman." Heidegger would likely deem this as *the meaning of the question of sophistry*.

As a means of arriving at that *meaning*, it is suggested that the sophist presents Heidegger's entities as "non-being" and "non-being" as "being" (or entities). What results in this, then, is a thoroughgoing discussion of the meaning of "being" and "non-being," as espoused by Parmenides, as inextricably linked to "sameness" and "difference"—this is explained with special care in juxtaposition to two other pre-Socratics (or Heidegger's primordial thinkers): Empedocles and Heraclitus, in order to define sophistry.

For Heidegger, this "definition" of sophistry does not necessary define anything. The interrelatedness of "non-being," "being," "sameness," and "difference" begins at a point of misinterpretation/misunderstanding about *the meaning of the question of Being*. In other words, certain interpretations/understandings about *the meaning of Being* as a "question" that are not fulfilled with the interrelatedness of "non-being," "being," "sameness," and "difference," but rather, makes *the meaning of Being* a "question" that is further obscure, when *Being* is something that is taken for granted. Heidegger notes this in the reference to *Sophist* in *Being and Time*, pointing out the extent to which *Being* is forgotten.

But, this reference is not so much an indictment of Parmenides—since, for Heidegger, in his *Parmenides* lecture, Parmenides is a primordial thinker thinking an authentic kind of thought—but is a criticism of Plato in particular. To be sure, Heidegger seems to suggest that Plato only uses "the stranger"—whether or not he is Parmenides notwithstanding—in a way that is ultimately disingenuous to Parmenidean thought, using it as a platform to think a thought that is inauthentic thinking about *the meaning of the question of Being*. It is safe to say, then, that Heidegger may see "the stranger" more as a mouthpiece for Plato's thinking about *Being* (i.e. as what has been argued about Socrates' role in the dialogues), and not a fair representation of Parmenides. More importantly, it may be fair to propose that this, at least in part, is a grounding component of Heidegger's approach to Plato, and Heidegger's assertion that Plato has not "concretely" worked out *the meaning of the question of Being*—no more than Plato has "concretely" worked the meaning of the question of sophistry in *Sophist*.

Finally, this brings me to Heidegger's *Plato's Sophist*, a lecture course given in the winter semester of 1924-1925 at Marburg, just before the publication of *Being and Time*, and Heidegger's leaving for Freiburg to assume Husserl's Philosophy Chair. It would seem, of course, that Heidegger would begin *Plato's Sophist* in much the same manner as *Being and Time*: highlighting what Plato missed about *the meaning of the question of Being*. Heidegger, instead, suggests that the theme of the *Being* of beings must be accessed by way of "knowledge" and "aletheia." Not only does this critique *Sophist* and its explanation of "being" and "non-being," but Heidegger positions both as not in opposition, but in conjunction with one another, predicated on "aletheia" and *Dasein*—this, again, suggests that Plato does not understand *the meaning of the question of Being* as that which is relegated/regulated by "aletheia" and *Dasein*, and not by negation, sameness, and difference (as offered from the mouth of "the stranger").

The significance of "aletheia" and *Dasein* is not directly addressed with respect to *Sophist*, but is accessed "as a point of departure" with Aristotle and his *Nicomachean Ethics* and *Metaphysics*. It is not so much a "departure" as much as it is a way into Plato's understanding of *Being*, in effect, *qua* Aristotle—that is to say, through Aristotle, as Heidegger seemingly suggests, the roles of ethics and knowledge intersect and convolute the authenticity of understanding the meaning of the question of *Being*, to the extent that certain ethics and knowledge place Being in concealment ("*lethe*").

For Heidegger's "Introductory Part," by way of Aristotle, we can better articulate *the meaning of Being* through *the meaning of "aletheuein"*—it has five modes to it: "*logos echon*," "*episteme*," "*techne*," "*phronesis*," and "*sophia*," with "*aletheuein*" as the ground of research into *Being*. Thereafter, in what announces itself as "The Main Part," Heidegger presents some introductory remarks about *Sophist* (in much the same manner as I have done at the opening of this paper), proceeding carefully in a straightforward line-by-line exegesis up to Line 236c. After this point, at Line 236e, Heidegger denotes the introduction of an ontological discussion about "the Being of non-being," or "*pseudos logos*" as an ontological problematic.

What is "problematic," here, is the contradictoriness of "*pseudos logos*"—in this, Heidegger identifies difficulties in the individual concepts of *being* and *non-being*, with special attention given to ancient and contemporary doctrines about "on," both of which play significant roles in *Sophist*. That is to say, the difficulties in the "meaning" of being and the "meaning" of non-being rests in the "meaning" of Platonic ontology that simply does not reckon with—or even wrestle with—*Being* concretely, with "on." In both cases, Heidegger differentiates the use of "on," in order to set up a summary of the theses about "on," with respect to the phenomenon of knowledge. What this means, I would argue, is that Heidegger believes that Plato's ontology in *Sophist*—centered on "being" and "non-being"—is not an authentic ontology without working out *the meaning of Being* through *the meaning of aletheuein*, as the ground of research into *Being*. Plato's "research into Being," being sure to qualify it with quotes as a means of highlighting its inauthenticity—does not engage in a thinking that thinks the kind of thought necessary to disclose *the meaning of Being* in its *Dasein*-most-ness, in reference to *the meaning of aletheuein*.

Being and Time (1927)

Being and Time begins very appropriately with a critical assessment of Plato's *Sophist*, which seems poised to position Heidegger's investigation in the same investigative lineage as Plato. By pointing out Plato's own admission that the expression of Being—both conceptually and functionally—has been forgotten and misunderstood, Heidegger's approach to "being" becomes seemingly one of recovery or even reconciliation with the question of meaning of the being.

As with Plato, Heidegger is aware of the elusiveness of not just the practicality of *Being*, but the overarching theory that proceeds the term. So, Heidegger's first task is to re-conceptualize *Being* by finding a way to appropriately ask: what is *Being*? In particular, how has this "what-ness" been misunderstood This task is critical to Heidegger's approach to *Being*, since Heidegger argues that the question of *Being* has not been asked correctly—that is to say, concretely—and this, in turn, has led to the term's elusiveness for Plato. If, as Plato confirms, Heidegger suggests that we must rethink the kind of thought (i.e. as Heidegger argues in his *Parmenides* lecture) necessary to ask the question of *Being* the right way. To do so, this means setting aside the tradition of *Being*—as it has been forgotten and misunderstood—in order to, as Heidegger argues, "reawaken an understanding for the meaning of [the question of the meaning of Being]." In doing so, Heidegger believes that the way to offer the "meaning" of the question of *Being* is to destroy how this meaning has been disseminated by traditional ontology post-Plato—the question of *Being*, as such, has its "meaning" incorrectly conceptualized by the tradition of ontology, to the extent that what *Being* is (i.e. its metaphysics), consequently, becomes a question left woefully unanswered in its traditional interpretation. Because of this, Heidegger sets the "provisional aim" of *Being and Time* towards an understanding the meaning of the question of *Being* by "the possible horizon" of the "Interpretation of time."

Before suggesting what this "Interpretation of time" as a "possible horizon" for understanding *Being* would look like, Heidegger calls for some "introductory remarks" situated on the "exposition of the question of the meaning of Being." Such an "exposition" attempts to avoid "dogma" that "declares" the question itself—of the meaning of *Being*—"superfluous" on one hand, and on the other, "sanctions its complete neglect." But more importantly, since *Being* is "rooted in ancient ontology," there are certain categorical imperatives (of ontology) that Heidegger highlights as three "presuppositions": 1.) that *Being* is "the most universal concept," 2.) that *Being* is "indefinable," and 3.) that *Being* is "of all concepts the one that is self-evident."[1]

In light of these "prejudices," as Heidegger calls them, the question of *Being* not only "lacks an answer, but that question itself is obscure and without direction." What this means, then, is that there must be a "formal structure of the question of Being" constructed around an inquiry based on three interrogative elements: *that which is asked about, that which is interrogated*, and *that which is to be found out by asking*.[2] For Heidegger, these "constitutive factors" reveal, through inquiry, that "the meaning of Being must already be made available to us in some way"—in other words, by formulating this inquiry into question about *Being*, what is required, then, is an explanation of "how Being is looked at, how its meaning is to be understood and conceptually grasped."[3] As a result, Heidegger suggests that "it requires

1. Heidegger, *Being and Time*, 21-35.
2. Ibid.
3. Ibid.

CHAPTER 3: THEOLOGIZING ON HEIDEGGER'S TERMS

us to prepare the way for choosing the right entity . . . and to work out the genuine way of access to it"—this entity, as the inquirer, is "transparent in his own Being," because "the very asking of [the question of *Being*] is [this] entity's mode of Being."[4] This entity that Heidegger contends "gets its essential character from what is inquired about Being" is the entity "which each of us is himself and which includes inquiring as one of the possibilities of its Being": this entity is denoted by the term "Dasein," fundamentally grounded on ontological and ontical priorities.

The *ontological priority* of the question of *Being* as the extent to which "Being is always the Being of an entity" through the totality of entities in conjunction with the ontical priority of the question of Being as the degree to which *Dasein* "always understands itself in terms of its existence" illustrates *Dasein*'s ontico-ontological priority, as it shapes Heidegger's analytic of *Dasein*. By way of this analytic, *Dasein*'s *essentia* resides in its ability "to be," while the means by which we can speak of it (at all) underscores its *existentia*—the latter, for Heidegger, is a "mine-ness" denoted as "presence-at-hand," by which "entities are grasped in their Being."[5]

But, what lies more primitively to "presence-at-hand" is "ready-to-hand," or the average, "everydayness" of *Dasein*—it is a use-value of entities "in the world."[6] *Dasein*, then, allows entities to have *Being* "in the world"—when *Being* is "in the world," it is translated beyond the "is-ness" of its everydayness and towards an "in-ness" extended in "the world." Additionally, "*Being*-in-the-world" opens a possibility for "worldhood," which, if one more carefully considers the original German, could be better represented as "worldliness." Heidegger recognizes that Being-in-the-world is a "unitary phenomenon" composed of "in-the-world," the every-case-ness of the way in which an entity is, and "Being-in" as such—all of which becomes facticities of *Dasein*.

* * *

Following Heidegger's "Introduction," which is meant to set up his theoretical approach to *Being and Time*, Heidegger presents the term "Dasein." This special term not only has implications in the original German as "being-there," but contains particular resonance as "human being." In

4. Ibid.
5. Ibid.
6. Ibid.

both cases, *Dasein* construes human existence through "being-ness," and it is that "being-ness" that constitutes the "there-ness" of *human being*. It is this "there-ness," or the "Da-" of *Dasein* that becomes essential not just to Heidegger's necessity, structure, and priority of *the question of Being*, but is decidedly pivotal to how Heidegger wishes to approach the two-fold task of working out this question. As we have learned in the "Introduction," this two-fold task, in part, seeks to destroy the history of ontology by providing, upon entering Part 1, an interpretation of *Dasein* along two "analytic" fronts of inquiry: in terms of temporality, and the extent to which an explication of time lends a transcendental horizon for *the question of Being*. This "explication," however, requires, for Heidegger, providing the theme for the analytic of *Dasein* and presenting "Being-in-the-world" as the "basic state" of *Dasein* itself. To be sure, Heidegger defines this "basic state"—that is, in terms of what *Being-in-the-world* means as a unitary phenomenon—as "in-the-world," what I would term as the *every-case-ness* of the way in which an entity is, and "Being-in" as such.

In revisiting these constitutive elements grounding how Heidegger conceives of *Being-in-the-world* (as I have mentioned at the close of the previous paper), a critical step forward for Heidegger involves prefacing that the "in" in *Being-in-the-world* is not an inside-ness. In other words, if we consider this inside-ness as how *Dasein* is "in" the world, we become victim to a Cartesian subject-object understanding of the world as an enumeration of things— Heidegger's intention, then, is to describe the phenomenon of world (the idea of the worldhood of the world/*Welt*) by avoiding and critiquing the intentionality of subjects towards objects. Heidegger contends that this sort of intentionality between subjects and objects is rooted in traditional ontology, rooted in Cartesian metaphysics, and furthered in Husserl's phenomenology, especially if, as Husserl argues in *Cartesian Meditations* (1929), the Cartesian way is "the prototype for philosophical reflection."[7] Yet, Heidegger would argue that Husserl's "philosophical reflection" is "always confined to entities [to the point that] it is ontical."[8] This indictment recognizes that Cartesian-Husserlian "reflection" reflects on entities themselves. More importantly, Heidegger's indictment of Descartes/Husserl suggests that both provide "a phenomenological description of the "world" [that] mean[s] to exhibit the Being of those entities which are present-at-hand within the world, and to fix it in

---

7. Husserl, *Cartesian Meditations*, 1.
8. Heidegger, *Being and Time*, 91.

CHAPTER 3: THEOLOGIZING ON HEIDEGGER'S TERMS

concepts which are categorical."[9] Consequently, Heidegger considers the Cartesian-Husserlian definition of the "world" as *res extensa*—the extension, or extendedness of substances in terms of the accessibility of their attributes and the degree to which, Heidegger argues, that "every substance has some distinctive property from which the essence of the substantiality of that definite substance can be read off."[10] This kind of thinking, then, comes to bear on Cartesian spatiality.

Because of this, Heidegger embarks on a rethinking of spatiality and arriving at an understanding of how *Dasein* is "in" the world, or *Dasein*'s worldhood itself—for Heidegger, it is "the sense that [*Dasein*] deals with entities encountered within-the-world, and does so concernfully and with familiarity."[11] If spatiality, then, has a belonging-ness to Dasein, that belongingness, if you will, is, as Heidegger ascertains, only possible "because of this Being-in."[12] From here, Heidegger suggests that "spatiality shows the characters of *de-severance* and *directionality*."[13]—the latter becomes contingent on the former, where, through *Dasein* essential de-severance, "[Dasein] lets any entity be encountered close by as the entity which it is."[14] To say that there is a close-by-ness between *Dasein* and the possibility for an encountered entity to be as it is means recognizing *Dasein*'s spatiality. That is, it means recognizing, as Heidegger does, that space is not in the subject, nor is the world in space [but] space is rather "in" the world in so far as space has been disclosed by that Being-in-the-world which is constitutive for Dasein."[15]

Engagement with the world—in terms of worldhood and spatiality—comes to bear on "Being-with" (solicitude) and "Being-one's-Self" ("who") as the extension of *Being* into "the world" as Being-for-self and Being-for-others. Here, we enter Chapter 4, where Heidegger offers an approach to the existential question of the "who" of *Dasein*—this who-ness is answered through how *Dasein* is absorbed in the world, and the manner in which "certain structures of Dasein are equiprimordial with Being-in-the-world:

---

9. Ibid., 91.
10. Ibid., 122.
11. Ibid., 138.
12. Ibid.
13. Ibid.
14. Ibid., 139.
15. Ibid., 146.

Being-with and *Dasein-with*."[16] This lends "the mode of everyday Being-one's-self,"[17] which "enables us to see" the subject of everydayness as "the they." Yet, the who-ness of *Dasein* is relegated to "I" as its essential characteristic, "one which must be interpreted existentially,"[18] through Chapter 5's "Being-in as such" and the existential constitution of the "There" by way of *Dasein*'s "state-of-mind" after finding itself in its "thrownness."[19]

* * *

Upon entering Chapter 5 of Division One, particularly after establishing the basic state of *Dasein* as "being-in-the-world," Heidegger contends that "our first aim is to bring into relief phenomenally the unitary primordial structure of *Dasein*'s *Being*, in terms of which its possibilities and the ways for it 'to be' are ontologically determined."[20] What Heidegger's "first aim" is, then, is to address what "being-there" means, which, as he proposes, is just as much predicated on "being-ness" as it is on "there-ness." In the former, "being-there" must a clearing for itself, since its *Being* is its most immediate issue. Because of this, for the latter, the "there-ness" of *Dasein* is unfolded in its situation—being-there" must be situated, first, through an understanding of "da" as a conceptualization of both "here" and "there."

The German "*Da*" of *Dasein* does not differentiate "here" from "there," but, rather, expresses the duality of there-ness, as "there-ness" is unconcealed in the clearing. To consider what the "there-ness" of *Dasein* is means considering the way in which "being-there" "is" in the world—Heidegger's argues that "care" is the fundamental functionality of *Dasein* as "being-in as such."[21]

The notion of "being-in as such" is contingent on the activity of understanding, especially as a means to grasp the possible and be aware of a world of possibilities. "Being-there" as understanding is a "state of mind" that is constituted by three basic traits: mood, understanding and interpretation, and speech acts/discourse. All of these traits are grounded in "fallen-ness"—it is the extent to which *fallen-ness* ("*verfallenheit*"), or "thrownness"

16. Ibid., 149.
17. Ibid.
18. Ibid., 152.
19. Ibid.
20. Ibid., 169.
21. Ibid., 223.

is, as Heidegger offers, neither an unfinished fact, nor a settled Fact.[22] This notion of falling is the essential "as-structure" (fundamental ontological) of *Dasein* itself, particularly if grasping *Dasein*, its "being-ness" and "there-ness" in light of everydayness.

In effect, the possibility of *Dasein* as "being-in-the-world" is ontologically construed through the intersectionality of truth ("aletheia," or "unconcealment" in *Parmenides*), care, and reality. This intersectionality meets at the notion of anxiety—this approach to anxiety itself is, on one hand, an extension of Soren Kierkegaard's concept of anxiety (in *Concept of Anxiety*, 1844) as subjective and objective in relation to original sin, and on the other, interpreted as a kind of anguish by Jean-Paul Sartre towards the possibility of nothingness positioning itself between the Self and temporality (in *Being and Nothingness*, 1943). For Heidegger, however, anxiety—or *angst*—"provides the phenomenal basis for explicitly grasping *Dasein*'s primordial totality of Being."[23] Totality is the key word here. Heidegger's aim is to conceive of Being as a totality—that is, Being of the totality—that brings about a structural whole—in itself, to proceed in this manner means proceeding towards "care" as a reinterpretation of Husserl's concept of "intentionality." Another way to consider "care" is as "concern" or, as Paul Tillich denotes in his Heideggerian-influenced *Systematic Theology*, as humanity's "ultimate concern."

Nevertheless, "care" is an immensely important ontological term with respect to unifying "being-there" as a structural whole of relations and intersectionality that consists of "thrownness" (in the past tense) and "fallenness" (in the present tense). But, in order to conceptualize the meaning of "care," we must contend with temporality—in this regard, "care" is grounded in temporality. The meaning of *Being*, as a structural whole, is confronted by temporality, especially truth, care, and reality—it is the sense that reality poses a problem of *Being* just as much as truth becomes equally problematic when derived from an external world that may not be definitively proved. That is, as Heidegger puts it, though *Being* may not be explained through entities, particularly because this *Reality*—as an ontological problem—is possible only in the understanding of Being.

So, essentially, "Reality" is an ontological problem—particularly as a traditional ontological problem—when *Reality* consists of the *Being* of entities present-at-hand within-the-world to the point that, as Heidegger

22. Ibid.
23. Ibid., 227.

concludes, "entities *within-the-world* are ontologically conceivable only if the phenomenon of within-the-world-ness has been clarified."[24] To say that entities are "conceivable" means that they are meaning-making constructions and, then, have an ability to disclose "a truth" about themselves in disclosedness. With this in mind, as Heidegger rightly asserts, "Being does indeed go together with truth."[25] In following this, *Dasein* is in the truth (aletheia)—Heidegger highlights this with four essential tenets: disclosedness in general, thrownness, projection, and falling. What these essentialist tenets do is constitute the "Being of truth" as fundamentally about *Dasein*—*Dasein* is about disclosedness as it occurs within temporality. The intersectionality of truth (aletheia), care (Tillich's "ultimate concern"), and reality unfolds in Heidegger's discussion of "authenticity" in Division Two's Chapters 2-4 as the "potentiality-for-Being-one's-Self." Or, "Self" as selfhood. For Heidegger, selfhood arises through *Dasein* as the character of conscience as a "call" and the role of guilt and a connectedness with care's ontological meaning in temporality—but, also, the explication of selfhood through the temporality of disclosedness and everydayness.

* * *

Division 2 of *Being and Time* begins with the header entitled "Dasein and Temporality," announcing "the outcome of the preparatory fundamental analysis of Dasein," which is oriented towards "the task of a primordial existential interpretation of [Dasein]."[26] What follows, though, is a brief review—or recapitulation—of the landscape of Division I, culminating in "[an] understanding of Being which lies in care; that is to say, it must be possible to define the meaning of Being."[27] From here, Heidegger raises the following question: "But is the phenomenon of care one in which the most primordial existential-ontological state of Dasein is disclosed?" The answer to this question is seemingly *no*—if we can say that care is a state in which *Being* lies, we are not speaking of *Being* at its "most primordial existential-ontological state of Dasein" at all. Essentially, care does not disclose *Dasein* at its most primordial, since care is, as Paul Tillich adopts the term in the 3-volume *Systematic Theology*, "our ultimate concern." For Tillich,

24. Ibid., 228.
25. Ibid., 256.
26. Ibid., 274.
27. Ibid., 273.

the primordiality of *Dasein* lies in "Kairos" (or "event") and what can be described as a basis for *Being* in "Reason"—"our ultimate concern," then, is with *Being* in "Reason" through "thrown-ness," and yet, "our ultimate concern" is not with primordiality, or the level at which *primordial being* is unconcealed as/in/through "aletheia." This, of course, falls in line with Heidegger's assertion that "the Being of Truth is connected primordially with Dasein."[28] So, if unconcealment (i.e. the goddess "truth" in Heidegger's *Parmenides*, Winter 1942/1943) does not primordially disclose *Being* through the phenomenon of care, Heidegger is right to question if "the structural manifoldness which lies in [care ever presents] us with the primordial totality of factical Dasein's Being."[29] The answer is certainly *no*, as well—"care" (or "our ultimate concern") is always in terms of Reality, readiness-to-hand, and presence-at-hand with, as Heidegger proposes, "entities with a character other than that of Dasein."[30] This brings Heidegger to a final question: "has our investigation up to this point ever brought Dasein into view *as a whole*?"—to which the answer is still indubitably no.[31] The phenomenon of care does not "[bring] Dasein into view as a whole"—only *the primordial existential-ontological state of Dasein* can do so.

In beginning Division 2, Heidegger's task is to "[bring] Dasein into view as a whole," especially if, as Heidegger implies, we are not "entitled to the claim that in characterizing Dasein ontologically *qua* care we have given a *primordial* Interpretation of this entity."[32] Are we not, however, still "entitled" to something unavoidable in the characterization of *Dasein* ontologically *qua* care? Not only is Tillich "ultimate concern" unavoidable, but the same can be said of Rudolf Bultmann's "myth" (i.e. the goal of demythologizing)—like Heidegger, both acknowledge that the characterization of *Dasein* only goes so far *qua* care, if this kind of interpretation is nothing more than an ontological investigation (note: a lower case "I" in both cases). To be sure, Heidegger is aware that "ontological investigation is a possible kind of interpreting [. . .] as the working-out and appropriation of an understanding."[33] Heidegger continues to assert that "every interpretation

---

28. Ibid., 274.
29. Ibid., 273.
30. Ibid.
31. Ibid.
32. Ibid., 274.
33. Ibid., 275.

has its fore-having, its fore-sight, and its fore-conception."[34]—all of which can be certainly viewed as elements of Gadamer's fore-structure of understanding in *Truth and Method* (1960). Essentially, "every interpretation" arises out of a hermeneutical situation, as "the totality of [fore-having, fore-sight, and fore-conception as] 'presuppositions.'"[35] With these, what makes such situations *hermeneutical*—such as with Descartes *cogito ergo sum* and the opening of Calvin's *Institutes of the Christian Religion* as knowledge of God versus knowledge of ourselves—is that "presuppositions" only abridge *Dasein* in ontological investigation. But, for a hermeneutical situation to consider *Dasein*'s primordiality—by which, in the more accurate words of Derrida in *Of Grammatology*, "there is no outside text"[36]—Heidegger argues that "it must first have brought to light existentially the Being of Dasein in its possibilities of *authenticity* and *totality*."[37]

After discussing in Part Two's Chapter 1 the possibility of *Dasein*'s being-a-whole in terms of *Being*-towards-Death (i.e. striking a tenor of *Angst* similar to Kierkegaard's *Sickness Unto Death*), Heidegger outlines, in Chapter 2, "an authentic potentiality-for-Being for Dasein, which will be attested in its existentiell possibility by Dasein itself"[38]—this occurs by way of (the call of) conscience as a disclosedness of Dasein's basic state "constituted by state-of-mind, understanding, falling, and discourse."[39] Chapter 3 takes a "methodological step" from Chapter 2 to "the laying-bare of temporality as a phenomenon" towards approaching temporality as the ontological meaning of care—this brings about a discussion of the hermeneutical situation to interpret the meaning of the Being of care and care's constitutive elements of existentality, facticity, and fallenness. While, in Chapter 4, Heidegger ties temporality to everydayness by providing a temporal Interpretation the disclosedness of *Dasein*'s basic state, Chapter 5 ties temporality to historicality, in order to assess *Dasein*'s historicality. Heidegger's Chapter 6, then, goes further, tying temporality to "within-time-ness," offering an existential-temporal analytic of *Dasein*, but only provides the unanswered: "Does *time* itself manifest itself as the horizon of *Being*?"[40]

34. Ibid.
35. Ibid.
36. Derrida, *Of Grammatology*, 163.
37. Heidegger, *Being and Time*, 276.
38. Ibid., 312.
39. Ibid., 314.
40. Ibid., 488.

CHAPTER 3: THEOLOGIZING ON HEIDEGGER'S TERMS

The Fundamental Concepts of Metaphysics (Winter 1929/1930)

In *The Fundamental Concepts of Metaphysics: World, Finitude, Solitude*—delivered in the Winter 1929/1930 as a lecture course at Freiburg—after embarking on a contemporary "preliminary appraisal" of philosophy and metaphysics that sets up "the task of the course and its fundamental orientation,"[41] Heidegger proceeds to awaken "a fundamental attunement" as his task, which is indicated by an orientations towards "a concealed fundamental attunement in our contemporary Dasein."[42] However, before considering this—what kind of relationship exists between "fundamental attunement" and "contemporary Dasein"—Heidegger's "preliminary appraisal" becomes an important starting point that, in part, "detours towards determining the essence of philosophy."[43]

To be sure, though Heidegger states that this "preliminary appraisal" is a "detour," this is a bit misleading. More accurately, he is taking a "pathmark"—a *Holzwege*—situating the task of the course itself by providing a fundamental orientation grounded in "the essence of philosophy," in order to trace a route that will become a new path. Heidegger understands this "essence" as not just rooted in metaphysics, but also in "the unavoidability of looking metaphysics in the face."[44] The intersectionality of "essence" and "unavoidability" suggests, then, that philosophy and metaphysics share a fundamentality as "philosophy/metaphysics." In this fundamentality, Heidegger considers the "essence"/"unavoidability" in the "incomparability" of *philosophy/metaphysics* as "neither science, nor the proclamation of a worldview."[45] But also, this "incomparability" is with art and religion, particularly since any such comparison "does not mean identity,"[46] if the *essence/unavoidability* of *philosophy/metaphysics* is rooted in identity itself. Up to this point, Heidegger has viewed science, art, and religion as possible ways to avoid *philosophy/metaphysics*. In offering "one final way out" through "the

---

41. Heidegger, *Fundamental Concepts of Metaphysics*, 1.
42. Ibid., ix.
43. Ibid., 1.
44. Ibid.
45. Ibid.
46. Ibid., 3.

147

realm of history": as "a historical orientation [where] we shall straightaway obtain information about [philosophy as] metaphysics."[47]

This, then, becomes not only significant to understanding the "task" of his *Fundamental Concepts*, but becomes critical to interpreting the relationship between *Fundamental Concepts* and *Being and Time*. When considering what Heidegger argues in *Being and Time* about destroying the history of ontology, it is interesting that he never explicitly mentions "ontology" in *Fundamental Concepts*—his focus on metaphysics in his "preliminary remarks" suggests, I would argue, that the "task" of *Fundamental Concepts of Metaphysics* is theoretically positioned as an extension of the destruction of traditional ontology in *Being and Time*. In other words, the extent to which Heidegger defines the *unavoidability* of metaphysics and the *essence* of philosophy by merging metaphysics/philosophy in terms of an *essence/unavoidability* is the byproduct of Heidegger's (Heideggerian) ontology. Indeed, if *Being and Time* can be described, by Heidegger, as an analytic of *Dasein*, *Fundamental Concepts of Metaphysics*, subsequently, can be explained as another analytic of *Dasein*: an analytic devoted to *Dasein* as the intersectionality between world (i.e. everydayness), finitude (i.e. temporality), and solitude (i.e. mood).

Perhaps with *Being and Time* in mind—that is, the destruction of the history of ontology by constructing an *essence/unavoidability* of *philosophy/metaphysics*—Heidegger concludes that "[through] all these attempts to characterize metaphysics by way of detours"—or, again, what can be called *pathmarks*—"have we not gained anything in doing so? Yes and no. We have not gained a definition or anything like that."[48] This is because, for Heidegger, philosophy must be determined "from out of itself"—this means that, when translating metaphysics by philosophy (and philosophy by metaphysics), there arises the need to "withdrawal" metaphysics, as philosophizing and "human activity into "the obscurity of the essence of man" and, then, the recognition of "homesickness as the fundamental attunement of philosophizing and the question concerning world, finitude, individuation."[49] At this point, Heidegger arrives at "the stage of a preliminary appraisal [and] this appraisal is meant to bring the task of the course closer to us, and at the same time to clarify our *overall*

---

47. Ibid.
48. Ibid., 4.
49. Ibid., 5.

orientation."⁵⁰ This "orientation" is based on metaphysical thinking as comprehensive thinking—similarly argued in Heidegger's lecture, *What is Called Thinking?* (in Summer 1951 and 1952)—as a way of "dealing with the whole and gripping existence through and through."⁵¹ "Metaphysical/comprehensive thinking" as *metaphysics/philosophy* "is a questioning in which we inquire into beings as a whole, and inquire in such a way that in so doing we ourselves, the questioners, are thereby also included in the question, placed into question.⁵²

What this means for Heidegger is that there arises, through *metaphysical/comprehensive thinking*, an ambiguity in philosophy—this ambiguity affects "the truth in philosophy," to the extent that "the truth of philosophizing is in part rooted in the fate of Dasein."⁵³ But, more importantly, the presence of ambiguity in "philosophy/philosophizing" requires what Heidegger outlines as the justification of the characterization of comprehensive questioning concerning world, finitude, and individuation as metaphysics—to do this, in Chapter 3 of the "Preliminary Appraisal," Heidegger proceeds to examine the origin and history of the word "metaphysics," which takes an interrogative path through Aristotle's "physis," Thomas Aquinas's metaphysics, and Franz Suarez's modern metaphysics, as contributors to the perpetuation of a traditional concept of metaphysics. Consequently, what metaphysics has become traditionally influence what metaphysics is, since *metaphysical/comprehensive thinking* and *metaphysics/philosophy* are "gripped" by a metaphysical questioning—according to Heidegger, "these questions arise in their necessity and possibility *from out of a fundamental attunement*, and seek to preserve them in their independence and unambiguousness."⁵⁴

Upon entering Part One, *metaphysical/comprehensive thinking*, *metaphysics/philosophy*, and "metaphysical questioning" are pivotal to how "our fundamental task now consists in awakening a fundamental attunement in our philosophizing."⁵⁵ Heidegger announces, in turn, "coming preliminary understanding about the significance of awakening a fundamental

50. Ibid., 8.
51. Ibid.
52. Ibid., 9.
53. Ibid., 19.
54. Ibid., 57.
55. Ibid., 59.

attunement"⁵⁶ constituted on a two-fold relationship of attunement between "being-there" and "not-being-there": 1.) as a relatedness that cannot be dependent on making a distinction between consciousness and unconsciousness, and 2.) as a relatedness that is grounded on man's being as being-there and being-away, or being absent. Through this two-fold relationship, Heidegger argues that "an attunement is to be awakened, [to the extent that] this means that it is there and not there."⁵⁷ Certainly, Heidegger recognizes that this "attunement" in *being-there* and *not-being-there* also "has to do with the innermost essence of man's being, with his Dasein."⁵⁸ What this means, in a narrower sense, is that *attunement*, as Heidegger particularly conceives of it, "belongs to the being of man"⁵⁹—more importantly, Heidegger describes this attunement, in its most fundamental manner and in a positive terms, carries with/through it "[a] *fundamental way in which Dasein is as Dasein.*"⁶⁰

Though Heidegger sees this as a "provisional characterization of the phenomenon of attunement," he takes time to interpret the meaning of the phenomenon of attunement against an "awakening" of the phenomenon through recognizing "Dasein as Dasein is always already attuned in its very grounds,"⁶¹ especially if *our contemporary situation*, as defined by Heidegger, is pervaded by *fundamental attunement*. The way in which this *fundamental attunement* "pervades" our contemporary situation through an "awakening attunement" becomes predicated on "[the] manner and means of grasping Da-sein with respect to the specific 'way' in which it is, of grasping Da-sein as Da-sein."⁶² This separation of *Dasein* into the hyphenated *Da-sein* denotes a highlighting of the "*Da-*" ("there-ness") element over and distinctively to "*Sein*" (*Being*)—in particular, what connects the "there" of *Being* to *Being* itself is a *fundamental attunement* and it (that is, the *fundamental attunement* itself) allows *Dasein* to function as it always already is as *Da-sein*. Heidegger seems to suggest this, by proposing that the "awakening" of a fundamental attunement "let[s] Da-sein be as it is, or can be, as Da-sein."⁶³ Not only is

56. Ibid.
57. Ibid., 63.
58. Ibid.
59. Ibid.
60. Ibid., 67.
61. Ibid., 68.
62. Ibid.
63. Ibid.

CHAPTER 3: THEOLOGIZING ON HEIDEGGER'S TERMS

it critical, in a general sense, to awaken a fundamental attunement, but it is especially critical, in a narrow sense of how our contemporary situation pervades *Dasein*, to determine, according to Heidegger, "*which* attunement we are to awaken or let become wakeful in us."[64] Here, Heidegger emphasizes "which" by asking some of the following questions—specifically as a means to clarify the meaning of the question of *which*—1.) how can an "attunement pervade *us* fundamentally," 2.) who is the "*us*" that we are referring to, as in "what do we mean here in referring to *us*," and 3.) when we say "*us*," in what situation does us occurs and how are we to demarcate and delimit this [contemporary] situation?"[65]

In Chapter 1 of Part 1, after attempting to answer the aforementioned questions through four interpretations of our contemporary situation (Oswald Spengler, Ludwig Klages, Max Scheler, and Leopold Ziegler) and the Nietzschean source of those interpretations, Heidegger views profound boredom "as the concealed fundamental attunement of the interpretations of our situation provided by the philosophy of culture."[66] Nevertheless, Heidegger finds that the means by which such a philosophy of culture interprets our contemporary "fails to *take hold of us* or even *grip us*."[67] In effect, any interpretation along this line—by a philosophy of culture—is mistaken about our contemporary situation, since it, according to Heidegger, ultimately, "unties us from ourselves in imparting us in a role in world history."[68] Because of this, Heidegger suggests that we must "seek a role for ourselves"—because, we have, in turn, "become bored with ourselves."[69] What, exactly, does Heidegger mean by "becom[ing] bored with ourselves," if we can say that this is disclosed in *boredom*?

Perhaps, *boredom*, as a condition of "ourselves," is a state-of-mind, a mood of *Dasein*, If viewed this way, it becomes apparent that, through the mood of *Dasein*, the concept of *boredom* is a constitutive state-of-mind: *boredom* is a category of mood (i.e. anxiety), which is the grounding of our contemporary situation as a hermeneutical situation. The extent to which *boredom* becomes a *profound boredom* is rooted in this "situation"—contemporary and/or hermeneutical—as it comes to bear on "seek[ing] a role

64. Ibid., 69.
65. Ibid.
66. Ibid., 74.
67. Ibid., 75.
68. Ibid., 77.
69. Ibid.

for ourselves" and what I would call *the meaning of the fundamental attunement of Dasein* as-it-is, or can-be, as-Da-sein. This brings Heidegger to the following question: "*Do things ultimately stand in such a way with us that a profound boredom draws back and forth like a silent fog in the abysses of Dasein?*"[70] In other words, if the fundamental attunement of *Dasein*, too, "draws back and forth like a silent fog," what makes *Dasein* as-it-is, or can-be, as *Da-sein* is in the constitution of "the abysses of Dasein"—that is, what can be considered as the fundamental in-ness of "the abysses" that give rise, disclose, summon, or unconceal forms of boredom individually predicated on its manifestations of *attunement*.

In Chapters 2, 3, and 4, Heidegger outlines three forms of boredom respectively as "becoming bored by something," "being bored with something," and "profound boredom as 'it is boring for one.'" Each of these forms of boredom are, according to Heidegger, characterized with respect to individual relationships with temporality—more specifically, though, in each of these forms of boredom, temporality exhibits a specific (or special) character that makes each form of boredom in a narrow sense and, then, more generally, makes each significant to the overall *fundamental attunement of Dasein* "as it is, or can-be, as Da-sein." Heidegger poses the questionableness of boredom in terms of "awakening [the] fundamental attunement [of *Dasein*] as letting it be awake, [and] as guarding against it falling sleep."[71] This is announced in the title of Section 19, and suggests that this first form of boredom is foundational to the other two—that is to say, if we can assume that Heidegger begins with this first form as a means of building upon it the other two, not just as other manifestations (or forms) of boredom, but as oscillations of boredom. This makes Heidegger's assertion about the *fundamental attunement of Dasein* "draw[ing] back and forth like a silent fog" grounded in an understanding of the oscillation of boredom.[72] In this back-and-forth-ness, the *attunement of Dasein* is measured by the temporality of that back-and-forth-ness.

The "questionableness" of this back-and-forth-ness is in the degree to which we can determine if the attunement of Dasein "pervades us or not."[73] What this means, then, as Heidegger argues, is that the need to escape boredom in a general sense—that is, more frankly, to not be bored, or become

70. Ibid.
71. Ibid., 78.
72. Ibid., 79.
73. Ibid.

trapped in a state of boredom and so forth—does not truly happen authentically in the situations in which boredom is confronted, because there remains, for us, a not-knowing and not-being-acquainted with the essence of boredom ultimately tied "to the way in which we are, to our situation."[74]

Boredom itself—as the essence of boredom—is so inextricably linked to our situations that there is: 1.) no way to actually escape it as an authentic act of resistance, and 2.) since it is relegated/regulated by time, difficult to know when boredom "pervades" us in its own authenticity. In Chapter 5, Heidegger builds on the three forms of boredom by reconsidering the meaning of the question of *profound boredom as the fundamental attunement of Dasein* to critique a specific "being left empty" and a specific "being held in limbo," which, taken together as "the most extreme demand on Dasein," lead into "*help*[ing] *bring to word* that which Dasein wishes to speak about in this fundamental attunement."[75]

Not only does is this word something that "addresses us and summons us to action and to being [but also] we are to understand this word, i.e., *to project the truth of fundamental attunement upon this essential content.*"[76] This word—upon which "[the] essential content" has the truth of fundamental attunement projected—becomes part and parcel of the manner in which *metaphysical questioning* is developed from the attunement of *profound boredom*. This word is "world"—and by way of metaphysical questioning, we must ask: *what is world?* Not only does "*world*" and "*what is world?*" both arise respectively as *metaphysical/comprehensive thinking* and *metaphysical* (comprehensive) *questioning*, but both, as centerpieces of Part II, disclose the "as a whole"-ness, when *as-a-whole* "manifests itself in profound boredom, as world."[77]

For Heidegger, since *profound boredom* in our contemporary *Dasein* contains a fundamental attunement to it, the profoundness—or the profundity itself—of boredom solicits a kind of questioning (*metaphysical questioning*, that is) that revolves around world, individuation, and finitude, but is rooted essentially/fundamentally in the essence of time. To arrive at this specific kind of questioning, we must take, first, "what it is that this profound boredom properly and really gives us to question"[78]—Heidegger's

74. Ibid.
75. Ibid.
76. Ibid.
77. Ibid., 169.
78. Ibid., 170.

"profound boredom" is at the intersection of the relationship/relatedness of world, individuation, and finitude. From this, Heidegger proposes we ask about the "necessity" of this relationship/relatedness "between expanse and extremity, between horizon and moment of vision, between world and individuation, and why does it arise?"—when the "it" we are speaking of is profound boredom.[79]

As a result, Heidegger concludes that "the fundamental attunement of boredom is rooted in the temporality of Dasein [and] the *temporality of Dasein* and thus the *essence of time* itself is the *root of these three questions* which in themselves, in their own peculiar unity and connection, express the fundamental question of metaphysics."[80] Heidegger furthers this by suggesting that this—the rooted-ness of questions concerning world, individuation, and finitude in the fundamentality of the question of metaphysics—"is what we have called the *question concerning being: Being and Time*."[81]

"Letter on Humanism" (December 1946)

In its unfinished form, *Being and Time* only argues two of the three sections of Part One and is, for the most part, constructed around posing the question of the meaning of *Being* and situating *Dasein* as the means by which that fundamental question—and the problem of metaphysics by large—can be explicated. The *question of the meaning of Being*—the meaning of it and the extent to which it must be asked in a way it has not been asked before—is never completed answered, and the full extent to which Heidegger intended to figure the relationship between time and *Being*, Kant, Descartes, and Aristotle into that possible answer is largely unclear. It is possible, however, to form a semblance of an answer from four Freiburg lectures Heidegger gave from 1925 and 1927.[82] Because these lectures were not published in Heidegger's lifetime, *Being and Time* remains ripe with significant unanswered questions and hermeneutical openings in its Part Two, all of which present problems not just to what *Being and Time* proposes and where it attempts

---

79. Ibid.
80. Ibid., 173.
81. Ibid.
82. These lectures include: *The Basic Problems of Phenomenology, Logic: The Question of Truth, The History of the Concept of Time*, and *Kant and the Problem of Metaphysics*.

to go, but how the work was received and interpreted in post-World War II France by Jean-Paul Sartre.

The manner in which Sartre interpreted *Being and Time* figures into Sartre's development of his distinct school of existentialism. Though directly influenced by *Being and Time*, Sartre's *Being and Nothingness* (1943) offers a deeply ontological investigation of *being*, making use of Husserl's method of phenomenology.[83] Sartre's investigation into "being," though just as phenomenological as Heidegger's *Being and Time*—is more concerned with reversing the Platonic metaphysical assertion that "essence precedes existence" and setting up an ontological conflict between human *being* and "negation."[84] Sartre's concern with *being* is a direct concern with how *being* becomes a uniquely human problem. In this regard, *being*, as Sartre conceives of it, is a humanistic concern, which becomes a predominant theme to his distinct anthropocentric form of existentialism. This is more explicitly expressed in Sartre's "Existentialism is a Humanism" (1946), whereby *existence precedes essence* not only becomes inextricably linked to Sartre's brand of existentialism and his centralization of "human being," but is extended ideologically to the "existentialism" of Heidegger's *Being and Time*. Here, I have placed "existentialism" in scare quotes, because tying Heidegger to Sartre's existentialism—or what might be more accurately called French existentialism[85]—is problematic, since Heidegger himself disagreed with this connection and argued that Sartre misread *Being and Time*. What was exactly misread? I would argue that Sartre's reading of *Being and Time* does not take into account Heidegger's wish to *destrukt* the ontologies of Kant, Descartes, and Aristotle.

Sartre's appropriation of *existence precedes essence* and the need to tie it to humanism, in particular, completely ignores what Heidegger intended to do in *Being and Time*. I want to consider this, first, in terms of how Heidegger understands *existence* and *essence*. Not only does Sartre's sequential use of *existence* and *essence* fundamentally misread Heidegger's notions of the terms under the overarching term of "being-thrown" into the world—also termed as "thrown-ness"—as a way to suggest that *existence* and *essence* are not sequential entities with separate lines of origin.

83. Edmund Husserl's "phenomenology" was influential to Sartre, particularly after Husserl presented lectures in Paris in 1929, which were published in 1931.

84. Sartre's use of "negation" seems to align with Hegel's, though it may be possible to argue against this.

85. A "French" form, which is different from the German version, and even from the Kierkegaardian version.

Existence and *essence* are inextricably linked, which Sartre does, to some extent, acknowledge (as does Plato), but, in terms of temporality, one does not "precede" the other. Heidegger's "being-thrown" recognizes that *essence*, by way of *Dasein*, "has in each case already been delivered over to existence, and it constantly so remains."[86] In my view, Heidegger is denoting a kind of entanglement between *existence* and *essence* that has so much more temporal consequence than simply conceding that the two are inextricably linked or have an existential relationship. I consider the term "entanglement" as Karen Barad uses it in *Meeting the Universe Halfway* (2007), and I would contend, then, Heidegger conceives of *existence* and *essence* similarly to Barad's "mattering," so that *existence* can be considered as "matter" and *essence* as "meaning." In other words, for Heidegger, *existence* is no more dependent on *essence* (in the Sartrean model) as *essence* is on *existence* (in the Platonic model).

The *existence-essence* inseparability goes part and parcel with Heidegger's reproach of humanism in general and, in particular, Sartre's perpetuation of the separation of *existence* and *essence* through existential humanism. Though Heidegger traces the problem of humanism to Plato and the subsequent history of ontology that requires *destruktion*, the fact that Heidegger highlights the ontologies of Kant, Descartes, and Aristotle means that these three have exponentially skewed things away from *the question of the meaning of Being*. Yet, I would argue that Descartes figures more central to Heidegger's *destruktion* than the other two, since Heidegger's phenomenological method of *destruktion*—which is most notably apparent in the inseparability of *existence* and *essence*—according to Heidegger in *Being and Time*, depends on:

> The ontological foundation of Descartes' '*cogito sum*,' and how the medieval ontology has been taken over into the problematic of the '*res cogitans.*'[87]

As an "ontological foundation," the Cartesian *cogito*—more accurate as *cogito ergo sum* than *cogito sum*—sets up a dualism, separating the acts of thinking from existing, and *essence* from *existence* respectively.

This distinction rests in the Cartesian use of "*ergo*" in *cogito ergo sum*, which I believe operates analogously to "precedes" in the Platonic *essence precedes existence*. Heidegger seems to make note of this, but also

---

86. Heidegger, "Letter on Humanism," 321.
87. Heidegger, *Being and Time*, 64.

rightly recognizes that "medieval ontology has been taken over" by Descartes *cogito ergo sum*. Although I find it unclear what Heidegger means by "medieval ontology,"[88] Descartes definitely introduces a phenomenological problem with his *cogito*—this problem is rooted in two phenomenologies on either side of the *ergo*. Modern ontology, as Heidegger cites in *The Basic Problems of Phenomenology* lecture (Summer 1927), appropriates *cogito ergo sum* to differentiate between *res extensa* (being of nature) and *res cogitans* (being of mind) under ways of being—the former aligns with *existence*, and the latter with *essence*.[89]

I would argue that, for Heidegger, the "problematic"—or *die Problematik*—of the *res cogitans* is not exclusively in the purposeful separation of it from *res extensa*, but, through a critique of Sartre's humanistic assertion of *existence precedes essence*, the impulse to define *res extensa* and *res cogitans* as different substances: the former physical (or material), the latter non-physical (non-material). Sartre's humanism, in particular, situates the two as different materialities, so that the materiality of the former "precedes" the (non)materiality of the latter—I see important to Heidegger's critique of Sartre's humanism as a misreading of *Being and Time*.

Heidegger's critique of Sartre's misreading is indicated in a more full-throated manner in "Letter on Humanism" (1946), as a direct response to a letter from one of Sartre's followers, Jean Braufret. Heidegger's "Letter" distances himself from Sartre's existentialism philosophically and, more importantly, questions humanism in particular because, according to Heidegger, "every humanism is either grounded in a metaphysics or is itself made to be the ground of one."[90] Heidegger criticizes Sartre's pronouncement of *existence precedes essence* for not escaping metaphysics—if we are to assume that Sartre is as interested in *destrukting* metaphysics as Heidegger (though I doubt Sartre's intentions are Heideggerian)—even if it attempts to reverse Platonic metaphysics by offering a reversal of the *essence-existence* metaphysical statement. To this extent, Heidegger contends that "the reversal of a metaphysical statement remains a metaphysical statement [and] with it, [Sartre] stays with metaphysics in oblivion of the

---

88. In my view, "medieval ontology" is a very broad term, which could describe various kind of ontologies from about the 5th Century CE to the late 14th Century CE, including Aquinas up through Duns Scotus.

89. Heidegger, *The Basic Problems of Phenomenology*, 122-125.

90. Heidegger, "Letter on Humanism," 225.

truth of Being."[91] Not only does Heidegger suggest that Sartre's handling of metaphysics "happens clumsily enough," but he argues that *Being and Time* is in opposition humanism.[92] To this end, Heidegger suggests that:

> [...]this opposition does not mean that such thinking aligns itself against the humane and advocates the inhuman, that it promotes the inhumane and deprecates the dignity of man. Humanism is opposed because it does not set the *humanitas* of man high enough. Of course, the essential worth of man does not consist in his being the substance of beings, as the 'Subject' among them[...].[93]

Here, Heidegger's explanation of his opposition is riddled with contradictions, each of which must be addressed individually before attempting to construct what it is about humanism he actually opposes. To be sure, this "opposition" is undoubtedly aligned with a kind of meta-metaphysical idea that is not humanism—that is, Sartre's humanism, and more specifically, Sartre's *existence precedes essence*. Yet, even though Heidegger opposes Sartrean humanism, he makes concessions, which seem to serve the purpose of suggesting that he does agree with some aspects of Sartre's overall conceptualization of humanism—for Heidegger, to be "against the humane" or advocate "the inhuman" seems unimaginable, and any promotion of "the inhumane" and deprecation of the "dignity of man" become unethical non-negotiables. To this end, Heidegger is certainly on board with Sartrean humanism, but only up to a point, and this point of diversion is very important to how Heidegger chooses to define humanism.

Clearly, Heidegger is careful to argue that his "opposition," as exemplified in *Being and Time*, is not "align[ing] itself against the humane and advocates the inhuman," by implying that he is just as much concerned with "the human" (and the humane) as Sartre. The centering of "the human" is, in particular, a kind of metaphysics that Heidegger is ultimately unwilling to completely eliminate—even if Heidegger disagrees with Sartre's *existence precedes essence*, his concern with the relationship between "existence" and "essence" remains a significant strand in his "opposition" to Sartrean humanism.

To what exactly is Heidegger in "opposition"?

Such a question does not yield a straightforward answer, because Heidegger's "opposition" to Sartre seems muddled and contradictory—but,

91. Ibid., 232.
92. Ibid., 233.
93. Ibid., 233-234.

perhaps, not quite as muddled as Heidegger's opposition to Platonic thought. To this end, any understanding of Heidegger's "opposition" is situated in his notions of "the humane," "the inhuman," and "the human," all of which must be unavoidably excavated from how he defines the existence-essence relationship. It is apparent that Heidegger does view *existence* and *essence* as having a meaning-making relationship that is inseparable and dialectic—but how does this relationship work?

From here, the key question that must be asked is this: how does Heidegger conceive of an *existence-essence* relationship, if he is in opposition to Sartre's formula as much as he is opposed to the Platonic formula?

One way to begin to answer this question involves focusing on, as aforementioned, comparing Heidegger's notions of *existence* and *essence* to Karen Barad's notion of "mattering" in *Meeting the Universe Halfway*—that is, even if one does not "precede" the other, *existence* and *essence* are two kinds of matter, two modes of materality. However, Heidegger only uses the term "matter" three times in *Being and Time*, only one of which is even remotely in Baradian ballpark. Though *Being and Time* does use "materiality," Heidegger views it as a superficial, ontological hurdle that must be cleared since "the entities which we encounter in concern are proximally hidden."[94] This lack of discussing "matter" and "materiality" is because, I would argue, Heidegger's phenomenological method in *Being and Time* wishes to avoid all issues of natural science—which is representative of the Continental philosophical tradition as a whole—but, through largely critiquing Sartre's humanism based on *existence precedes essence* in "Letter on Humanism," Heidegger's "opposition" unwillingly leads him into new territory that is indebted to Sartre.

To be sure, Heidegger does seem to be share Sartre's notion of "the dignity of man" and the need to resist deprecating that "dignity." Where Heidegger diverges from Sartre is with what "the dignity of man" should look like, particularly if that "dignity" is related to "thrownness"—I would argue that "thrownness" presents a challenge to "the dignity of man." More importantly, even though "thrownness" is the simultaneous "thrownness" of *existence* and *essence* in the world, Heidegger qualifies this with the suggestion that "the essential worth of man does not consist in his being the substance of beings." Rather, Heidegger believes that Sartre does "not set the *humanitas* of man high enough." But, what does Heidegger mean by "*humanitas*"? This notion of "*humanitas*" is crucial, when considering

---

94. Heidegger, *Being and Time*, 96.

Heidegger's understanding of humanism as a that which must be ventured beyond—"*humanitas*," as Heidegger uses it, becomes a term that, on one hand, liberates his approach to what I will call "(post)humanism" but, on the other, confines that approach to the same metaphysical baggage (of metaphysics itself) for which he criticizes Sartre (and the whole Western philosophical tradition since Plato).

CONCLUSION: THEOLOGIZING PRIMORDIALITY THROUGH HEIDEGGER

THE NOTION OF THE "primordial," or what exists fundamentally before *the meaning of being* is "the question" of what Heidegger's ultimate concern. *The question of the meaning of being*, as a point of inquiry, is unmistakably oriented towards locating what exists meaningfully and in a way that must be, in itself, located in something other than metaphysics or humanism. "Primordiality," or the state of what is primordial, is about existence, but it is about a kind of existence that cannot necessarily be philosophized, even though philosophizing is always-already the beginning point. If "primordiality" is only philosophized, it becomes impossible to truly confront it in its authenticity and in its unconcealedness, since the existence of things that we more readily grasp are collectively nothing more than a concealment of what cannot be grasped or conceived primordially. For Heidegger, the problem here—what can be thought of as *the problem of the question of the meaning of being*—is that the framework by which thinking about existence builds itself is based on the forgetfulness of being, as well as what is inauthentically presented through metaphysics and humanism.

At this point, when thinking about *the question of the meaning of being*, this becomes merely a philosophizing about "being"—it becomes a philosophizing that does little to unconceal what is primordial to "being." This kind of thinking about *the question of the meaning of being* is unable to problematize what is being thought into *the problem of the question of the meaning of being*, since what lies primordally to "being" remains concealed by what is believed to be known about the meaning of being. It is only with this in mind, by recognizing that *the problem of the question of the meaning of being* never poses the most appropriate question and never makes being meaningful, it stands to reason that it becomes all the more necessary to theologize about primordialty, rather than philosophizing.

The relationship between Heidegger and theology, when viewed through the theologies of Macquarrie, Bultmann, Tillich, and Rahner, can be predicated on theologizing primordiality. That is to say, if Heidegger's concern with *the question of the meaning of being* is about problematizing what we know about being, what can be made meaningful about being, and how we can come to even ask about being at all, what ultimately brings philosophizing in contact with theologizing is precisely what brings "being" in contact with "Being"—it is about not exclusively focusing on "being" but orienting ourselves toward "Being." The problem in this is not just about the limitations inherent in philosophizing alone, but it is also the limitations in theologizing alone. To be concerned with *the problem of the question of the meaning of being* means not compartmentalizing what we do when philosophize about human existence and separating that from we do when we theologize about God's existence. Because of the latter, in itself, is a point of primordiality, what we are solely philosophizing never fully grasps the meaning of human existence any more than what we are solely theologizing fully grasps the meaning of God's existence through the constituency of human existence.

To theologize primordiality means simultaneously philosophizing about "being" and "Being" while theologizing about "being" and "Being," so that what is philosophized unconceals the meaning of "being" and what is theologized unconceals the meaning of "Being." And yet, because the meanings of "being" and "Being" remain epistemologically and phemoenologically slippery, a stand-in is required for what primordiality is and can represent itself as, so the epistemological and phenomenological dimensions align into the concrete meaningfully.

In *Heideggerian Theologies* (2018), I provided a four-fold framework attuned to the Wesleyan Quadrilateral in terms of how Macquarrie, Bultmann, Tillich, and Rahner respectively theologize primordiality through Heidegger. In doing so, while in keeping in mind more broadly the relationship between Heidegger and theology, and considering more specifically what is left undone in *Being and Time*, the ways with which Macquarrie, Bultmann, Tillich, and Rahner respectively theologize primordiality through Heidegger all attempt to venture into decidedly theological territory Heidegger previously halted at the very boundaries of the philosophical. I intend to relitigate these matters, by either amending or revising how Macquarrie, Bultmann, Tillich, and Rahner take Heidegger further than strictly the philosophical in *Being and Time* and into the theokogical, such that each of them theologizes the primordial, which never fully materializes as Heidegger intended it to in *Being and Time*.

CONCLUSION: THEOLOGIZING PRIMORDIALITY THROUGH HEIDEGGER

As unfinished as *Being and Time* is as a means of philosophizing about "being," and as often as Heidegger theologizes "Being" across the decade before *Being and Time* and up to the mid-1960s, it becomes possible to see that Heidegger fundamentally contributes to the making of modern and even postmodern theology. We may ask, then, if we can extend to Heidegger the role of a "theologian"—not just with all the seminars, lecture courses, and talks in which he addresses theological concerns and theological thinkers, but also with the pedagogical hold he unmistakeably has on the theologizing of Macquarrie, Bultmann, Tillich, and Rahner.

I am aware that to even ask if Heidegger is a "theologian"—which is left unexpressed in *Heideggerian Theologies*—presents unavoidable problems that prevent welcoming Heidegger to the fold of theology and the development of the theological mind. These problems are duly noted. These problems do not abound in, for example, what is thought of Hegel and of Kierkegaard, and the extent to which both are as welcomed as makers of the philosophical mind as they are of the theological mind. However, Heidegger's status is more difficult to determine, more problematic to express, and more tenable to contextualize—through a determination, an expression, and a contextualization of how Macquarrie, Bultmann, Tillich, and Rahner respectively theologize primordiality, Heidegger's role in theology becomes clearer, insomuch as primordiality is at the very core of the relationship between Heidegger and theology.

For Macquarrie, what resides at the very core of the relationship between Heidegger and theology is scripture, which Macquarrie confronts, through existential theology, as an ontical stand-in for what is situated primordially to scripture. I have previously explained Macquarrie's concerns in the following way:

> Macquarrie's pathmark in existential theology searches for λόγος in scripture—this venture pursues a *Heideggerian pathmark* of "logos" as an object of primordiality. Through Macquarrie's existential theology of scripture, *what we talk about* must be translated from its ontic state into what it already is as *primordial being*—that is, *what [scripture] is*. Macquarrie's λόγος is "linguistical-existential," since *what language is* gets to *what being is*, at its most primordial [so that] λόγος, as a *Dasein*-like analytical possibility, makes meaning out of *what we talk about* in order to *unconceal* what language is as ἀλήθεια.[1]

---

1. Woodson, *Heideggerian Theologies*, 52-53.

The "linguistical-existential" is what allows Macquarrie to translate the ontics of scripture into the primordiality of λόγος, so how we initially confront *what language is* becomes the means by which we recognize *what being is* in scripture as the *unconcealment* (or ἀλήθεια) of the *primordial being* of λόγος.

For Bultmann, resides at the very core of the relationship between Heidegger and theology is tradition, which Bultmann confronts, through existential theology, as an ontical stand-in for what is situated primordially to tradition. I have previously explained Bultmann's concerns in the following way:

> Bultmann's pathmark in existential theology is focused on κηρυγμα in tradition. The demythologization program that Bultmann undertakes is a venture that pursues a *Heideggerian pathmark* of κηρυγμα as an object of primordiality. In this regard, Bultmann's demythologizing task—what I have referred to as an existential theology of tradition—is concerned with isolating κηρυγμα by utilizing the "historical-existential." To do this, Bultmann's [demythologizing] deconstructs what tradition does, or how tradition operates, at the ontic level, in order to disclose what tradition is as ἀλήθεια.²

The "historical-existential" is what allows Bultmann to translate the ontics of tradition into the primordiality of κηρυγμα, so how we initially confront *what tradition is* becomes the means by which we recognize *what being is* in tradition as the *unconcealment* (or ἀλήθεια) of the *primordial being* of κηρυγμα.

For Tillich, what resides at the very core of the relationship between Heidegger and theology is reason, which Tillich confronts, through existential theology, as an ontical stand-in for what is situated primordially to reason. I have previously explained Tillich's concerns in the following way:

> Tillich's pathmark in existential theology is devoted to καιρος in reason—this venture pursues a *Heideggerian pathmark* of "kairos" as an object of primordiality. As the primordiality of *being*, καιρος discloses *what being is* on the way to ἀλήθεια. That is to say, καιρος is what *being* looks like when it is in a state of primordiality and, then, opens the possibility for *unconcealment*, or ἀλήθεια—in effect, primordial *being*, once disclosed, makes it possible for *being* to be *unconcealed* as what it already is. By way of Tillich's *Heideggerian pathmark*, the "rational-existential" venture he takes attempts to

2. Ibid., 89.

CONCLUSION: THEOLOGIZING PRIMORDIALITY THROUGH HEIDEGGER

translate "what being has become," or *being* in its ontic state into *what being is*, or the primordiality of *being* on the way to ἀλήθεια.³

The "rational-existential" is what allows Tillich to translate the ontics of reason into the primordiality of καιρος, so how we initially confront *what reason is* becomes the means by which we recognize *what being is* in reason as the *unconcealment* (or ἀλήθεια) of the *primordial being* of καιρος.

For Rahner, what resides at the very core of the relationship between Heidegger and theology is experience, which Rahner confronts, through existential theology, as an ontic stand-in for what is situated primordially to experience. I have previously explained Rahner's concerns in the following way

> Rahner's pathmark in existential theology searches for χάρις in experience—this venture pursues a *Heideggerian pathmark* of "grace" as a supernatural object of the primordiality of experience. Through Rahner's existential theology of experience, *what is experienced* must be translated from its ontic state into what it already is as *primordial being*—meaning, as the existential embodiment of *what experience is*.[. . .] Rahner's χάρις is related to the "experiential-existential" as one of its *Dasein*-like analytical possibilities. [. . .] when utilizing a *Heideggerian lens*, χάρις is a particular, conditional, and affective *Dasein*-like entity by which humanity pre-apprehends the ontics of experience (our existence) and unmasks primordial being toward ἀλήθεια.⁴

The "experiential-existential" is what allows Rahner to translate the ontics of experience into the primordiality of χάρις, so how we initially confront *what experience is* becomes the means by which we recognize *what being is* in experience as the *unconcealment* (or ἀλήθεια) of the *primordial being* of χάρις.

When viewed collectively, let us, for a moment, consider what is meant by scripture, tradition, reason, and experience. In my view, because scripture, tradition, reason, and experience, as an epistemological four-fold, and history are so inextricable, the meanings of the two concepts merge. We might ask: which of the two comes first? That is, does history dictate what the epistemological four-fold is, or does the epistemological four-fold define history? Worded this way, we find that such a question—nevermind the structure—is immensely difficult to answer. We know that the epistemological four-fold of

3. Ibid., 116.
4. Ibid., 148.

scripture, tradition, reason, and experience show us what history is, just as we know that history is explicated in what is brought forth collectively from scripture, tradition, reason, and experience. Yet, because of the conenctedness scripture, tradition, reason, and experience and this epistemological four-fold's inter-dependence, it becomes all the more impossible to know what is primordial to any of the four, what *primordial being* is with respect to any of them, and the extent to which we can even locate *what being is* as standing over and beyond any of them.

What must be understood is that there is an existential interplay between the epsistemological four-fold and history. This interplay, as existential as it is, suggests that the meaning of history is determined by the epsistemological four-fold in the same way that the meaning of the epsistemological four-fold is determined by history. This occurs by necessity, since we cannot do witout either. For that matter, we cannot do without the interplay between the two. Even if history has a tendency to mythologize the epsistemological four-fold and, likewise, the epsistemological four-fold mythologizes history, this sort of mythology is how the temporal and temporality express themselves. In short, when we address the notion of time itself, we are always-already confined to the parameters of history and the epsistemological four-fold, so that whatever is understood about the meaning of being is undoubtedly articulated by what history and the epsistemological four-fold tells us about temporality.

Essentially, history and the epsistemological four-fold act as stand-ins for temporality—they become the only thing by which we can concretize what temporality means. Because of this, we rely on history and the epsistemological four-fold —as devoted as we are to *the question of the meaning of being*, that question is both asked and answered witnin the contexts of history and the epsistemological four-fold, such that it is always-already beheld by mythology. Indeed, *the meaning of being* becomes so mythological that, upon proposing *the question of the meaning of being*, we are ultimately questioning the relationship between history and the epsistemological four-fold, questioning how "being" is located between the two, and questioning how they function as necessary, unavoidable stand-ins for temporality.

There remains an inordinate amount of problems in the interplay between history and the epsistemological four-fold. There are, in fact, too many problems to adjudicate between the two, if our intent, so far, is to further and more adequately conceptualize temporality—in particular, our focus will be on "what temporality is," without the demands of history or the epistemological four-fold. It is on this point, in an effort, to properly understand the meaning of history in relation to the meaning of the epsistemological four-fold that we define *primordial being* and *what being is* with *what temporality is*.

As such, *what temporality is* becomes the "temporal-existential," which I hope will make the role of temporality more evident, particularly in a way that is not as obvious in its earlier articulation in *Heideggerian Theologies*. Here, the articulation of "temporal-existential" makes note of temporality's primoriality to history and the epistemological four-fold and how, at the same time, temporality itself remains a stand-in for what is not yet disclosed in the temporal.

In focusing more narrowly on the meaning of "the temporal" rather than the meaning of the epistemological four-fold, it is possible to bridge the difference between the interplay of history and the collective understanding of scripture, tradition, reason, and experience. The *temporal-existential* is what makes history and the epistemological four-fold possible, to the extent that temporality itself has history and the epistemological four-fold as its constituents—this is precisely so, due to the fact that temporality can only represent itself in the world through what is represented respectively by history and the epistemological four-fold. Still, as much as temporality finds history and the epistemological four-fold as its stand-in, the reverse is not true—neither history nor the epistemological four-fold is temporality, since temporality is situated primordially to history and the epistemological four-fold.

As term makes explicit, Macquarrie, Bultmann, Tillich, and Rahner engage in an existential pursuit of temporality as a pursuit of primordialty. Just as history and the epistemological four-fold are necessary and unavoidable stand-ins for temporality, temporality, too, is a necessary and unavoidable stand-ins for Macquarrie's λόγος, Builtmann's κηρυγμα, Tillich's καιρος, and Rahner's χάρις—it is only by unconcealing each in its primordiality that temporality is properly understood as that which conceals each and distances us from *primordial being* and *what being is*.

To do this, Macquarrie, Bultmann, Tillich, and Rahner all provide programs deconstruct what history does and what happens with their individual concerns with the epistemological four-fold, or how hisrory and the epistemological four-fold operate at the ontic level, in order to disclose *what temporality is* as ἀλήθεια. This deconstruction—if thought of in the sense of Derrida—is about unmasking primordiality of temporality. To do so means to deconstruct history and the epsistemological four-fold, in order to respectively unmask the primordiality of λόγος, the primordiality of κηρυγμα, the primordiality of καιρος, and the primordiality of χάρις, tsince both hisrory and the epsistemological four-fold have *concealed* each in ληθε. The underlying intent, then, is to conceptualize *what being is* in *unconcealment,* or as άληθεια—that is, respectively conceptualizing λόγος in scripture, κηρυγμα in tradition, καιρος in reason, and χάρις in experience as the primordiality of temporality embodied in the *temporal-existential.*

APPENDIX A: THE HEIDEGGER PROBLEM

THE ONGOING CONVERSATION ABOUT Heidegger's personal involvement with the Nazi Party and the extent to which Heidegger's philosophy can be interpreted by that ideological affiliation has found new life recently, particularly with the 2014 publication of the *Black Notebooks* (in German as *Schwarze Hefte*).

These personal diaries, written mainly from 1931-1941, detail Heidegger's private thoughts, which most notably include entries espousing Nazi ideologies and profound anti-Semitism. From them, significant questions arise about what kind of relationship can be made between Heidegger the man and Heidegger's philosophy—inherent in this, then, is a need to read Heidegger's philosophy through the *Black Notebooks*, and use the personal diaries to suggest that there is Nazi ideology within Heidegger's philosophy. This connection has presented a new field of research into Heidegger, by which the history of his Nazi involvement has become central to Heideggerian philosophical studies in general, when, before the publication of the *Black Notebooks*, Heidegger's Nazism has been mainly marginalized, gnostic, and separated from mainstream work with Heidegger—any strand of philosophical study into Heidegger's Nazism, historically speaking, has not been taken seriously, even though the *Black Notebooks* have existed since 1931, his Nazism itself has been widely-known since his public allegiance with National Socialism in 1933—as "political ideology," as Julian Young suggests in *Heidegger, Philosophy, Nazism*(1997)—as the newly elected rector of the University of Freiburg, and the denazification hearing held shortly after World War II in 1949 classified Heidegger as a "Nazi follower" (*Mitläufer*). In the decades since, two occasions have proven significant to establishing a relationship between Heidegger's philosophy and his Nazism: the 1989 publication of Victor Farías' *Heidegger and Nazism* and the 2009 publication of Emmanuel Faye's *Heidegger: The Introduction of Nazism into Philosophy in Light of the Unpublished Seminars of 1933-1935*—in both cases, the authors have approached the Heidegger's philosophy-Nazism relationship by, in effect, suggesting that there should be no distinction between them and, moreover, Heidegger's philosophy should be considered as the work of a "Nazi ideologist." Yet, in opposition to this, another line of thought maintains that there should be a clear separation between Heidegger as a philosopher and Heidegger's Nazism, whereby, through such a distinction, the latter must be interpreted as a "political interlude," and should not contaminate Heidegger's philosophy.

What makes the publication of the *Black Notebooks* so interesting, on one hand, and significant, on the other, is that it forces us to think about Heidegger differently and, by extension, read his work from a newfound perspective—within this, there lies the impetus to compare Heidegger's anti-Semitism in the *Black Notebooks*, particularly as a means of shedding new light on a possible ideology that lay hidden Heidegger's philosophy, such as in *Being and Time*. To this end, the *Black Notebooks* demonstrate two essential questions that must be posed about Heidegger's involvement with the Nazi Party: was it just, as Gadamer argues, a "political interlude," or was Heidegger, as argued by Farías and Faye and a "Nazi ideologist"?

In effect, in asking either question, both are merely leading questions that guide a more important, pivotal question: does Heidegger's relationship with Nazism matter when understanding the philosophy in *Being and Time*, and, by extension, determining the work's significance (1927)?

My main contention is that Heidegger's involvement with Nazism does not matter and, furthermore, should not be held as a way to read and interpret Heidegger's philosophy, not just as it is in *Being and Time*, but with respect to his philosophical corpus. Of course, to read Heidegger's philosophy separately from Heidegger's involvement with Nazism requires what I will call a "pragmatic-limited" hermeneutical lens—that is, it pragmatically reads Heidegger through a lens limited to his philosophy and resists synthesizing Heidegger's Nazism into that reading. This kind of reading—this sort of hermeneutical lens—must first consider *Being and Time* outside the realm of historical conjecture, or the need to fill in gaps with what is not explicitly there. To this end, by taking a *pragmatic-limited* position, I intend on situating *Being and Time* as stand-alone text, which must not be subjected to and intertwined with Heidegger's personal moral failings. What that means, then, is assuming a "pragmatic" approach to reading *Being and Time*, which limits that reading to the book's historical context, as well as narrowing any hermeneutical lens to a strictly philosophical interpretation that remains decidedly ahistorical.

APPENDIX A: THE HEIDEGGER PROBLEM

The Question Itself: Does Heidegger's Nazism Matter?

This is not a simple question, since the facts necessary to answer that question are quite complex, subject to interpretation, and dependent on making hard choices between the personal and public, between what the *Black Notebooks* express and what is not expressed in *Being and Time*—the question, then, becomes quite difficult, not just because of the ramifications any possible answer has to the various philosophers, theologians, thinkers, and theorists rooted in a variety of discipline directly influenced by Heidegger's thought, but because of the ultimate meaning behind the question. This meaning is grounded in the historical readings that must be given to the *Black Notebooks* and *Being and Time*, particularly as relatively contemporary writings, but also as works that must not be considered as companion pieces. But, more importantly, the meaning of the question—if we first begin with how we should ask such a question and what assumptions undoubtedly follow it—is if a clear distinction can be made between Heidegger's philosophy as represented mainly in *Being and Time* and Heidegger's Nazism as documented in the *Black Notebooks*, or if the two must be mutually exclusive. To do the former—to read the two against one another—is to commit a kind of hermeneutical violence against *Being and Time* that uses the *Black Notebooks* as a means of ethically decoding Heidegger's philosophical system. If this approach wins out in the end, not only will the *Black Notebooks* be abused, but *Being and Time* will be unnecessarily used to further that abuse—and become discredited. I would argue that any engagement in both becomes rather unfortunate and greatly undermines any serious consideration of Heidegger's philosophy and his relationship with Nazism—the former espousing a certain ideology, and the latter arguing for a particular ideology.

To be clear, Heidegger's alignment with Nazi ideology forces a careful, more critical reassessment of the ideology behind *Being and Time*, in particular. That is to say, a philosophical analysis of *Being and Time* must remain "philosophical" and not become a referent to the *Black Notebooks*. What remains unclear, however, is to what extent Heidegger was a member—in effect, was he an active or passive participant—and if his degree of membership can be infused with *Being and Time*—meaning, does Heidegger's membership somehow disqualify, or minimize the importance of Heidegger as a philosopher? For the first question, we must clarify the meaning of "active" and "passive," since Heidegger was, indeed, a card-carrying member of Nazi Party for years, up until the end of the World War

II—however, he did not attend meetings. The second question, then, invites us to consider how much significance must be placed on Heidegger's role in the Nazi Party and if, to this end, that role should have disqualifying weight upon how we understand Heidegger's importance to modern philosophy and, to a greater extent, to the history of philosophy on the whole.

I have, frankly, only addressed the difficulties of the question, when there are more important ramifications involved. Though the difficulties are important, particularly as a way to actually enter the ongoing conversation, to map its complexity, and to effectively situate ourselves, there are undeniably ramifications to how we answer the questions: Does Heidegger's Nazism matter?

Heidegger's Nazism matters because, on one level, the *Black Notebooks* and what they mean to Heidegger fundamentally changes how we encounter the man behind *Being and Time*. On a more meaningful level, if we are ready to assume that Heidegger was, in fact, as anti-Semitic as his diary entries, then it colors how we read his philosophy—we read *Being and Time*, then, for any of the subtlest references that might underscore Heidegger's racism towards Jews and, more generally, a Nazi ideology that abhors all races other than the Nazi and National Socialism's definition of a pure race. I do not wish to argue that Heidegger was not anti-Semitic—his entries in the *Black Notebooks* only valid this. There is really no way to explain it away. I also do not wish to claim that Heidegger's racist entries do not matter—they do matter, because they present a picture of the man that is, at best, unflattering, and, at worst, depressingly disappointing.

My intent is not to split hairs here about whether or not Heidegger was a bad person—rather, in my view, Heidegger was not particularly a good person and had a lot of moral failings (the least of which being that he was an adulterer that cheated on his wife with a student), but should unblemished goodness be a prerequisite for reading and studying a philosopher? I would say no. Precisely because, as contemporary thinkers, we should not be compelled to cross-pollinate a philosopher's private life with that philosopher's publications. If we were compelled to do so, we would have to eliminate a lot of authors, theorists, and the like from serious academic study and ban them contemporary scholarly endeavors. Is this not hasty and narrow-minded? Should the concern, with any thinker, be more about the thought itself and not about the thinker themselves? Sure, there is quite a narrow line here, when we read Heidegger, and when the *Black Notebooks* give us a kind of insight that makes complete objectivity almost impossible. But, what good would come from condemning *Being and Time* for the sins of *the Black Notebooks*? We must let the former stand on its own, in its own right, and not weigh it down with the latter. As scholars, do we not always adjudicate between a writer/thinker's published works and unearthed private writings that paint problematic pictures of that writer/thinker, especially when those published works have such far-reaching influence and consequence? Then, this should be so with Heidegger—even if he was a despicable human being (to which I would agree), particularly because he aligned himself with the same National Socialist movement that sought to wipe an entire race of people off the face of the Earth, and specifically if that alignment is worthy of our disdain (to which I would also agree), this does not mean that his philosophical thought is unworthy of our critique and investigation. At any rate, it is because of all of Heidegger's failings that we should read his philosophy as in *Being and Time*, and not disqualify or minimize that work's importance.

Four Assumptions about *Being and Time*

I do not believe Heidegger's Nazi involvement disqualifies or minimizes Heidegger's importance, since *Being and Time*, in particular, should be interpreted separately from Heidegger's relationship with Nazism, because of four very essential reasons: 1.) *Being and Time* was written (and published) six years before Heidegger publicly aligned himself with National Socialism, 2.) Heidegger's philosophy (particularly in *Being and Time*) does not explicitly express Nazi ideology, 3.) Heidegger's conceptualization of *being* lacks any explication ontological explication of race or the body, and 4.) Heidegger aligned himself with National Socialism (and Nazism) through his Rectorate of Freiburg more out of survival rather than necessity.

I have chosen the above assumptions, since none of them would prove to be controversial and, for their better judgements, should be essential places to begin any fruitful conversation about the relationship between Heidegger and Nazism, and where his philosophy (and the entirety of his corpus, for that matter) fits into that overarching relationship. Yet, I am aware that concerns certainly will arise, questioning why such things should be decided in advance. In other words, rather than telegraph the direction of argumentation, why do I not allow arguments about Heidegger's Nazism to be made using any sort of evidence, and then let those arguments naturally lend their own credence, rather than have them predetermined, as I have done? Such objections are important, and definitely worth addressing. In truth, trying to make arguments about Heidegger's Nazism is problematic—there are not only problems with what evidence should be used, and which should not, but, also, what evidence is most likely to build consensus, and which will not. Are we not, then, talking about warrants? Does this mean, too, that any line of argumentation should follow a logical, ethical, reasonable train of inquiry that presents best of all possible conditions where agreement can be reached and cultivated?

To do this, it means considering—and quite carefully—what evidence best illustrates those conditions. Evidence is critical, and evidence must have certain realistic elements tied to them—evidence must be able to stand on its own, and not be riddled with agenda, innuendo, and ideology. What that means, accordingly, is that, if we are to have a constructive conversation about Heidegger's Nazism and how his philosophy fits into that relationship, we must predetermine—before beginning—which evidence best brings us together and, conversely, which evidence only creates division. To this end, I would argue that the four "essential reasons" I have offered provide the best evidence to wade through the water of this murky Heidegger issue—each of them, in my view, focus particularly on *Being and Time*, since it was Heidegger's only published work and is certainly the most important work in Heidegger *Gesamtausgabe*. The reasons are as follows: 1.) *Being and Time* was written (and published) six years before Heidegger publicly aligned himself with National Socialism, 2.) Heidegger's philosophy (particularly in *Being and Time*) does not explicitly express Nazi ideology, 3.) Heidegger's conceptualization of *being* lacks any explication ontological explication of race, ethics, or the body, 4.) Heidegger aligned himself with National Socialism (and Nazism), precisely due to his role as Rectorate of Freiburg, more out of survival rather than belief.

Though I am entering this conversation in the aftermath of the 2014 publication of Heidegger's *Black Notebooks*—which represent Volumes 94-96 of Heidegger's Collected Works (*Gesamtausgabe*)—what has been ultimately ignited by these private diaries is essentially a new wave of the debate about Heidegger's Nazism, originating on May 27, 1933.

In 1933, only six years after the publication of his career-making, philosophical masterpiece *Being and Time*, Heidegger was appointed Rector of the University of Freiburg and delivered his "inaugural speech" ("*Rektoratsrede*") entitled "The Self-Assertion of the German Universities." The speech is an important starting point because, as the author of *Being and Time*, Heidegger marks "the beginning of a movement from which there can be no turning back," initiating a public association between his philosophy and National Socialism ("*Nationalsozialismus*"). After only a year, Heidegger resigned as Rector, effectively ending his public alignment with Nazism. Though it is unclear what degree of involvement Heidegger had with the Nazi Party from his 1934 Rectorate resignation to the end of World War II, the denazification hearing held shortly after World War II classified Heidegger as a "Nazi follower" (*Mitläufer*) in 1949, and subsequently banned him from teaching until 1951. Thereafter, the ban was lifted and, though Heidegger was allowed emeritus status from Freiburg in 1953, he was never allowed to regain his Freiburg professorship. With all these facts in tow, to both professional and personal ruin, Heidegger never expressed contrition or any meaningful regret for his Nazi involvement, and died in 1976 with significant lingering questions remaining unanswered. Because of this, the manner in which answers are reached becomes the entry point into a larger conversation about Heidegger and Nazism—this larger conversation revolves around how Heidegger's personal moral failings (or private sentiments) can be read into Heidegger's philosophy, and vice versa.

Three Positions on Heidegger

In the 83 years since Heidegger's public alignment with Nazism as it is evidenced in his *Rektoratsrede*, there have been several positions taken by philosophers, theologians, thinkers, scholars, and historians about how Heidegger's relationship with Nazism can be explained, interpreted, and criticized. My ***pragmatic-limited*** position attempts to contextualize and historicize Heidegger's Nazism with respect to Heidegger's philosophy—and, for that matter, consider what *Being and Time* has to offer philosophically and where the work fails, rather than imposing any hyper-ethical, hyper-historical reading based on Heidegger's Nazi involvement.

Two counterarguments to my ***pragmatic-limited*** position can be best described as "passive-dismissive" and "critical-condemning" positions.

The oldest and most populated with the longest lineage is what I have termed as the ***passive-dismissive*** position—it originates in 1933 in reaction to Heidegger's *Rektoratsrede* and his public alignment with National Socialism. This position, as it suggests, takes a passive or dismissive approach to confronting Heidegger's Nazism, which is based on both a lack of interest and an unwillingness to take it seriously. The major claims of those that advocate the *passive-dismissive* position are situated in the belief that Heidegger was never truly a Nazi and was, for that matter, only a superficial follower. In other words, this *passive-dismissive* position wishes to make a very clear separation between Heidegger's Nazism and Heidegger's philosophy, since, as Gadamer argues in *Heidegger's Ways* (1994), Heidegger's affiliation with Nazism was only a "political interlude." The main reason this position provides for their claims is that Heidegger was not the kind of man, both personally or intellectually, that would have believed in Nazi ideology, especially since Heidegger was more concerned with high philosophy instead of racist praxis. The evidence that this position uses to support their reasons is in Heidegger resigning his Freiburg Rectorate after only a year in the position and, essentially, discontinuing his attendance in Nazi meetings. The assumption underlying this argument, then, is that Heidegger resigned his Rectorate due to ideological differences with National Socialism and, more specifically, he discovered that his previous alignment with Nazism was a mistake.

The *passive-dismissive* position can be divided into four representative camps, each of which represent different types of stakeholders, since each "camp" has very different things at stake, depending upon what each has at jeopardy—each has something to lose as theologians, hermeneutists, philosophers, and scholars. The first camp includes the "existential" theologians, such as John Macquarrie as represented in his *Heidegger and Christianity* (1994). Similarly, the second camp includes hermeneutists such as Gadamer in his *Heidegger's Ways*. The third camp is comprised of post-World War II French philosophers, such as Jean-Paul Sartre, and later thinkers such as Foucault. Finally, the fourth camp includes older Heideggerian scholars, such as William J. Richardson and Theodore Kisiel, and younger scholars such as Richard Polt—only Polt has devoted a section of a chapter of his *Heidegger: An Introduction* (1999) to Heidegger's Nazism, with an additional discussion of the subject found in another small book by Jeff Collins, *Heidegger and the Nazis* (2000). Nevertheless, in *Heidegger and Christianity*, Macquarrie articulates the *passive-dismissive* position in a representative way, suggesting that Heidegger was a man "of superior intelligence [that] ought to have known better than to get involved with anything so disreputable and intellectually vacuous as National Socialism"—Macquarrie, then, concludes that Heidegger should be "judged primarily by his thinking and the results which are still flowing from it," rather than the faults and weaknesses resulting from his relationship with Nazism.

What I have described as a *critical-condemning* position, as the smallest population, include Victor Farías and Emmanuel Faye, which can be respectively identified in the arguments both make in *Heidegger and Nazism* and *Heidegger: The Introduction of Nazism into Philosophy*. The *critical-condemning* positions taken by Farías and Faye, in 1987 and 2006 respectively, not only sparked renewed interests in Heidegger's relationship with Nazism, but the two positions are particularly modern in condemnation, especially following Heidegger's death in 1976 and the continuing publication of Heidegger's *Gesamtausgabe* in special anticipation of the "Black Notebooks." The main claims of those that advocate the *critical-condemning* position are grounded on the inseparability of Heidegger's philosophy from Heidegger's Nazism. That is to say, even though *Being and Time* was published in 1927 and Heidegger aligned himself with Nazism publicly in 1933 with his *Rektoratsrede*, these are not mutually exclusive events in Heidegger's life but, instead, they are inextricably-linked, since Heidegger's speech serves as political affirmation for the philosophy of *Being and Time*. The reason this position provides for their claims is, in part, based on Heidegger's unwillingness to show contrition for his affiliation with Nazism and, to a greater extent, the findings of the Denazification Hearing of 1945 that ruled Heidegger a Nazi follower, or "*Mitlaüfer*." The evidence this position uses to support their reasons is with historical documents discovered after Heidegger's death, particularly Heidegger's abuse of his administrative powers as Rector of Freiburg against Jewish professors and students, and his anti-Semitic views that would not come to light until the publication of the "Black Notebooks." The assumptions that underlie this position's argument, then, is that there is a tangible connection between what Heidegger writes in the "Black Notebooks" and his lack of contrition about his alignment with Nazism in 1933—this assumption, more importantly, is quite clear, even in Heidegger's evasive explanation in the *Speigel* interview of 1966, which Heidegger insisted could not be published until after his death.

Aside from Victor Farías and Emmanuel Faye's respective works, the *critical-condemning* position is exemplified in Peter Trawny's most recently published *Freedom to Fail: Heidegger's Anarchy* (2015). As a representation of the *critical-condemning* position, in *Freedom to Fail*, Peter Trawny enters the issue of Heidegger's relationship with Nazism as editor of the Heidegger's newly-published, German edition of "Black Notebooks," which, as Trawny argues, shed new important light on Heidegger's personal thoughts about the prejudices and norms influenced by the National Socialist movement. Trawny's book assesses the "Black Notebooks" as expressions of Heidegger's "personal Nazism," which is part of Heidegger's "philosophical ethos"—for Trawny, though Heidegger's philosophy and his anti-Semitism are "mutually-exclusive" issues of concern, "overcoming anti-Semitism [in Heidegger's philosophy] can only succeed by drawing near to it."

While the *passive-dismissive* and *critical-condemning* positions intersect at the historical issue of Heidegger being a Nazi follower, the two positions greatly differ on how Heidegger's relationship with Nazism can be historically projected upon Heidegger's philosophy. That is to say, more importantly, both positions differ on how to answer the question: does Heidegger's relationship with Nazism matter? For the former, this question is dismissed altogether, whereby the *passive-dismissive* position itself is more concerned with ignoring historical facts and what those facts mean, in order to concentrate more narrowly on Heidegger's philosophical work, such as *Being and Time*. What makes this position especially extreme is that its "passive" approach to Heidegger, *Being and Time*, and Heidegger's Nazism does a disservice to this issue and, to a larger extent, minimizes the overall meaning of the controversy—this position has undoubtedly lost its authority with the 2014 publication of "The Black Notebooks" since that publication highlights its naivety. On the other end, however, the *critical-condemning* position maximizes the controversy and tends to bloviate it to an extended metaphor—for the *critical-condemning* position, *Being and Time* and Heidegger's Nazism are inseparable, and this inseparability means that *Being and Time* should be read as Nazi literature or National Socialist propaganda, functioning in a similar ideological register as Hitler's *Mein Kampf*. This seems especially cogent, if *Being and Time* and *Mein Kampf* are considered companion pieces published in 1927 and 1925 respectively. However, this sort of comparison is extreme, since the closeness in publication is merely coincidental and the authorial roots of both are quite different—for instance, while *Mein Kampf* is autobiographical, *Being and Time* is philosophical.

In light of *passive-dismissive* and *critical-condemning* positions, the *pragmatic-limited* position, though distinctly modern and developing mainly in reaction to Farías' *Heidegger and Nazism*, attempts to contextualize and historicize Heidegger's Nazism with respect to Heidegger's philosophy. The main claims of those that advocate this position

APPENDIX A: THE HEIDEGGER PROBLEM

is constituted by the need to strike a balance between Heidegger the man and Heidegger the philosopher—that is to say, the ***pragmatic-limited*** position tries to find a middle ground to adjudicate between Heidegger's philosophy and the ideology of National Socialism. The reason provided for this claim is that, if employing a pragmatic hermeneutical lens to read *Being and Time*, there should be a way to either redeem, reconcile, or rehabilitate Heidegger, the man. The evidence this position uses to support their reasons is the historical situatedness of the publication of *Being and Time* in 1927 and the *Rektoratsrede* of 1933—this is based on the assumption that these two historically occur in isolation and are mutually exclusive. This ***pragmatic-limited*** position is expressed most notably in Pierre Bourdieu's *The Political Ontology of Martin Heidegger* (1988), Karl Löwith's *Martin Heidegger and European Nihilism* (1995), Tom Rockmore's *On Heidegger's Nazism and Philosophy* (1992), Richard Wolin's *The Heidegger Controversy* (1993) and *The Politics of Being* (1990), and Slavoj Žižek's *In Defense of Lost Causes* (2008).

As a representation of the ***pragmatic-limited*** position, in *The Political Ontology of Martin Heidegger*, Bourdieu argues that Heidegger should not be considered as a Nazi ideologist and, as a result, there is no room in Heidegger's philosophy for a fascist/racist "conceptualization of the human being." More importantly, for Bourdieu, Nazism is only one manifestation of possible philosophies that can be derived from Heidegger's philosophy. As Bourdieu would likely agree, the ***pragmatic-limited*** position is mainly concerned with how to read Heidegger—it is not concerned with reading Heidegger from extreme positions, or superimposing history onto that reading, but simply doing the necessary hermeneutical dirty work by wrestling with the meaning in the text itself through a thorough investigative reading. Not only does this kind of reading of Heidegger's philosophy lend credence to the notion Slavoj Žižek makes in *In Defense of Lost Causes* that Heidegger takes "the right step in the wrong direction," but it does not mean that Nazism is in *Being and Time*—on the contrary, Nazism is only one way to read the philosophy in *Being and Time*, and only one way out of many possible readings. The ***pragmatic-limited*** position is not just historically concerned with how Heidegger being a Nazi follower can be projected upon his philosophy—that is to say, whether or not Heidegger's Nazi membership can be taken seriously and given a mouthpiece in *Being and Time*—but is more philosophically invested in how that association with Nazism can (or cannot) be interpreted ethically from his philosophy.

A ***pragmatic-limited*** position is the only logical approach to take when reading *Being and Time*, locating meaning in the text, and disseminating that meaning into the world of ideas, especially with the recent publication of "The Black Notebooks." This publication—almost 80 years in the making—should not mean we should take extreme positions of security, either by way of ***passive-dismissive*** or ***critical-condemning*** positions, but should mean, instead, that some of the answers we come up with are the ones we least expect, the ones we are most afraid of, and, of course, the ones that force us confront a deeply flawed text and its deeply flawed author.

APPENDIX B: KARL BARTH

INARGUABLY, KARL BARTH LOOMS largely on the landscape of twentieth-century theology as a significant maker of modern and, for that matter, postmodern theology. Barth's influence is similar to Heidegger's, particularly if we note their similar lifespans—Heidegger (1889-1976) and Barth (1886-1968)—as well as the close proximity of their major respective works—with Heidegger's *Being and Time* appearing in 1927 and the first volume of Barth's 12-volume *Church Dogmatics* appearing in 1932. These works, though Heidegger's is philosophical and Barth's is theological, both directly influenced what it meant to theologize in the 1930s, leading up to World War II. Both wrote on Pauline letters: Heidegger's interpretations can be notably found in *The Phenomenology of Religious Life* (GA 60), with the lecture on "The Introduction to the Phenomenology of Religion (Winter 1920/1921), while Barth's interpretations can be located in his *The Epistle to the Romans* (1918). Both have careers that intersect Bultmann—both Heidegger and Bultmann maintained a several decades of correspondence with Bultmann, ranging from the 1920s to the 1960s, which largely detail debates both had with Bultmann's theologizing. Indeed, while Heidegger's debates with Bultmann arise from the two being aligned, Barth's debates with Bultmann hinge on stark differences the two had. In this regard, perhaps through their respective relationships with Bultmann, Heidegger seems to have been as aware of Barth's theology as Barth was aware of Heidegger's philosophy.

Yet, when considering the various intersections between Heidegger and Barth, it seems that there would be a relationship between the two, if for no other reason than the two thinkers' desire to rethink what it means to theologize from the standpoint of the problems inherent in traditional thought. The most important point of comparison, predicated on how both attempt to rethink tradition, is with hermeneutics—allow me to contextualize Barth's specific approach to hermeneutics first, before looking more generally and more closely at the broader relationship between Heidegger and Barth.

APPENDIX B: KARL BARTH

Contextualizing Barth

Karl Barth rethinks the Reformed tradition on Scripture, inspiration, authority, and/or interpretation in direct opposition, first and foremost, to "Old Princeton Theology" of the late nineteenth century. As a hermeneutical movement, "Old Princeton Theology," with Charles Hodge (1791-1878) as an important representative figure, argued that the Bible was without error due to God's authorship of it. As a result, for Hodge and other figures of "Old Princeton Theology," the Bible contains truths. These "truths," as Hodge describes in his *Systematic Theology* published in 1872-1873, become the theologian's chief concern, where "the theologian has to collect, authenticate, arrange, and exhibit in their internal relation to each other."[1] In one sense, Hodge's view can be described as scientific and empirical—the role of the theologian, as Hodge describes in the above, is similar to that of a scientist, since the theologian must engage theology as a science. On the other hand, Hodge's view is particularly predicated on a, explicit positivist approach to hermeneutics, one that is grounded on the Bible being a totality of facts capable of building a hermeneutical case.[2]

Hodge's deeply positivist, scientific, and empirical approach to the Bible undergirded with Biblical infallibility or inerrancy is ultimately in the background to Barth's rethinking of the Reformed tradition on Scripture, inspiration, authority, and/or interpretation. Though Barth agrees, in theory, with Hodge and "Old Princeton Theology" about the authority of Scripture, Barth's point of departure and reconceptualization is with praxis. In effect, Barth is more concerned with what the Bible does. For Barth, what makes the Bible authoritative is not because of what it is (that is, in theory), but precisely because of what it does or how it functions (in praxis). To be clear, Barth does not dispute the authority of the Bible but, rather suggests that

---

1. Hodge, *Systematic Theology: Volume 1*, 1.

2. With "totality of facts" and "a hermeneutical case," I am specifically thinking about Ludwig Wittgenstein's articulation of this in *Tractatus Logico-Philosophicus*. I am condensing Wittgenstein I am condensing a series of claims made by Ludwig Wittgenstein. Though this work is much more positivist than Wittgenstein's later work and, by extension, re-thought through Wittgenstein's later work with language, this early work makes very interesting positivistic propositions. One by one, these propositions are as follows: 1.) the world is everything that is the case, 2.) the world is the totality of facts, not of things, 3.) the world is determined by the facts, and by these being all the facts, 4.) for the totality of facts determines both what is the case, and also all that is not the case, and 5.) the facts in logical space are the world. Wittgenstein, *Tractatus Logico-Philosophicus*, 31.

that authority is housed in what the Bible does as, in George Stroup's words, "the unique and indispensable witness to Jesus Christ."[3]

With this in mind, it is clear that Barth does finds value in conceptualizing the Bible as authoritative, but, for Barth, this conceptualization needs some constructive rethinking. What Barth is undeniably pushing back against is the sentiment that the authority of the Bible is both in reference to what it is and what it does. It is the notion that what the Bible is and what the Bible does are inextricably linked within the Bible's authoritativeness. Though this kind of constructive thinking is an important way to understand the Bible as the intersectionality of Scripture, inspiration, authority, and/or interpretation, Barth's need to rethink this constructive approach arises from what is missing in that original construction: genuine witness. As Stroup points out, Barth believes that "the Bible is not a book of oracles," and furthermore, in Barth's own words, " . . . it is not an instrument of direct impartation. It is genuine witness."[4]

At the heart of Barth's argument is the necessity to separate the Bible from the Word of God. Barth argues that these two elements (under the overarching intersectionality of Scripture, inspiration, authority, and/or interpretation) have been conflated in the earlier Reformed tradition, especially up to and including "Old Princeton Theology" of the late nineteenth century. Barth is very much invested in separating the Word of God from the human word. Or, in another sense, these can be explained in terms of the spoken Word of God and the written word of man. Barth believes that the latter does not replace or substitute for the former, since the latter. That is, the latter, or the Bible itself, cannot replace or substitute the former, the Word of God. Barth is clear about this, arguing the following: "the mere presence of the Bible and our own presence with our capacities for knowing an object does not mean and never will mean the reality or even the possibility of the proof that the Bible is the Word of God."[5] It is this situation—which I would call an *epistemological situation*—is one that we must recognize as being liminal, where our ability to prove that the Bible is the Word of God is impossible. Barth argues this, and more importantly, seems be aware that the Bible itself, as the written word made by man, is one level removed from the Word of God.

---

3. Stroup, ed., *Reformed Reader: A Sourcebook in Christian Theology: Volume 2 Contemporary Trajectories, 1799 to the Present*, 17.

4. Ibid., 21.

5. Ibid.

Such a sentiment, as found in Barth, is quite similar to Derrida's notion in *Of Grammatology* that writing is a language level removed from the spoken word. Of course, I do concede that it is necessary to say that Derrida is not making a theological argument, but he does, nevertheless, employ a very theocentric understanding of the spoken word as "Being" and the written word as a distillation, corruption, or pollution of "Being" into "being." Perhaps, Derrida would balk at my suggestion of his theocentric understanding. Yet, in the distinction Derrida draws between ontological language (the written word) and metaphysical language (the spoken word) is certainly framed from the top-down. This top-down approach is found in Barth. Granted, Barth does not assess the written word in the same manner as Derrida—one major point of difference is evident in the fact that the former has the aims of theologian while the latter's aims are at those of a philosopher. To be sure, both of them have different agendas and, though Derrida's agenda is highly influenced by Heidegger's hermeneutics, it is safe to say that Barth is not as influenced in the same way. That is, Barth would likewise balk at my finding any Heideggerian leanings in his hermeneutics. But, I do see in Barth a Derridian understanding about the differences between the written word and the spoken word. It is the former that Barth believes "is not an instrument of direct impartation [but rather] it is genuine witness."

For Barth, then, the Bible, as the written word, is an indirect impartation. In other words, it is not the direct Word of God, but is the Word of God witnessed to writers that have written the Word of God. Essentially, those that written the Word of God are intermediaries between the Bible as the manifestation of ontological language and the Word of God, as the ultimate metaphysical language. Again, there are traces of Derrida in such an understanding. Just as Derrida would argue that writing, in any form, is only an "indirect impartation" of the spoken word, Barth is operating in a corresponding manner about the Bible's "is-ness" and "what it ought to be." The Bible becomes, as Barth rightly argues, "by its very presence, by the fact that we can read it [something that] gives us a hearty faith in the Word of God spoken in it."[6] Accordingly, what undergirds Barth's understanding of the written word of the Bible is that it is "purely human word [since] it can be subjected to all kinds of immanent criticism, not only in respect to its philosophical, historical and ethical content, but

6. Ibid.

even of its religious and theological."⁷ In this way, what lies at the core of Barth's rethinking is the sense that the Word of God cannot be accurately captured by the human word. As a result, our ability to read what has been captured by the human word of those were genuine witnesses of the Word of God leaves us not just one level removed from the Word of God but, I would argue, two levels removed.

To begin, Barth's constructive understanding of Reformed theological hermeneutics of Scripture is in direct dialogue with Friedrich Schleiermacher's hermeneutics. This means, then, that Schleiermacher is undoubtedly in the background to Barth's hermeneutics, particularly with respect to the influence of Schleiermacher delineation of hermeneutics into grammatical interpretation (general hermeneutics) and psychological interpretation (specialized hermeneutics).

As Stroup describes, prior to the nineteenth century, hermeneutics was predominantly a franchise grounded in applying a series of grammatical rules to a text in order to interpret it—in the nineteenth century with Schleiermacher leading the way, hermeneutics "came to be understood in terms of the much broader process of *Verstehen*, or 'understanding.'"⁸ For Schleiermacher, the hermeneutist must employ both grammatical interpretations and psychological interpretations, where effective hermeneutics, as such, must embody a measured balance between both general and specialized hermeneutics respectively. So, for Schleiermacher, interpretation is an art, not just on the whole by way of striking a measured balance between the general and the specialized, but each side is itself an art."⁹ This sense of interpretation being an art is precisely what Barth rejects, which becomes an entry point in Barth's hermeneutics proper.

Not only does Barth reject, as Stroup writes, "the notion of a general or philosophical theory of hermeneutics [but] insist[s] that the interpretation of the Bible is governed by the name the Bible proclaims, that is, Jesus Christ."¹⁰ But, more specifically, Barth rejects any grammatical and psychological interpretations of the Bible, as found in Schleiermacher's hermeneutics, in favor of the content of Scripture itself. To this end, Barth's hermeneutics is simply predicated on the content of Scripture and the extent to which only from the content of Scripture "can it become really

---

7. Ibid., 22.
8. Ibid., 28-29.
9. Ibid., 30.
10. Ibid., 31.

intelligible."[11] What is inherent in this understanding, of course, is Barth's distinguishing between the human word and the Word of God. The former is not, as Barth argues, a "direct impartation" but is an expression of genuine witness. From this, it is possible to suggest that Barth would be reluctant to think of hermeneutics in a general way, or with respect to grammatical rules—this would make sense, since grammatical rules are human linguistic constructions and, therefore, can certainly not be constructions applied to the Word of God. In addition, Barth's rejection of a "philosophical" approach to hermeneutics, or Schleiermacher's "psychological side," is apparent in Barth's understanding of the written word being a level removed from the Word of God—it is the extent to which any "psychological understanding" on our part becomes problematic and impossible, since the written word is a secondhand account of the Word of God itself by those that are "genuine witnesses" to the Word of God itself.

Barth's hermeneutics is based on the Word of God itself. It is chiefly concerned with a primordial understanding of what the Bible is and what the Bible does. This is the main feature of Barth's constructive understanding of Reformed theological hermeneutics—his is a concern with, again, the primordial. This chief concern is, on one hand, about the overarching intersectionality of Scripture, inspiration, authority, and/or interpretation, but, on the other, is invested in the intersectionality of the Word of God, the object of witness, and the proclamation of the name Jesus Christ. Nevertheless, Barth's constructive understanding of Reformed theological hermeneutics is concerned with a primordial understanding about Scripture. In other words, what makes Barth especially "Reformed" is that his hermeneutics is not satisfied with the contemporary status quo—that is, the development hermeneutics up to the first half of the twentieth century—but, rather, he is interested in uncovering a more pure, more primordial notion of hermeneutics. This kind of hermeneutics, as such, can be described as "Reformed," since it is steeped in change, rethinking, and modification.

Accordingly, Barth's hermeneutics is "Reformed" because it seeks truth in hermeneutics, by using a "Reformed" approach to unconceal what traditional/historical hermeneutics has inadvertently concealed—for example, the concealment of the Bible as being the actual Word of God, when it is the human word relayed to humanity through genuine witness. In this way, I would argue that Barth's "Reformed" approach is Heideggerian. Obviously, such a comparison would obviously make Barth cringe.

11. Ibid.

However, I feel it is an important comparison to make, particularly with the purposes of expressing what makes Barth's constructive understanding of hermeneutics "Reformed." Any "Reformed" approach is concerned with truth, or, as Heidegger argues, αλεθεια. Allow me to take a moment to explain this. As Heidegger argues in his *Parmenides* lectures, αλεθεια is best translated as "unconcealness" or "unconcealment."[12] What this means, then, is when we say "truth," we are really stating that something has become "unconcealed" or that truth has shed a light of recognition on the darkness of miscomprehension. Of course, this is merely a distillation of Heidegger. Heidegger arrives at this analysis by dividing αλεθεια into α and λεθε: the former is like the prefix "un," while the latter is "concealment."[13] From here, Heidegger proceeds to explain that truth is not always truth, but a "concealment" for what must be "unconcealed." Granted, I must be brief with this, because, in order to give what Heidegger asserts a full-throated consideration about αλεθεια, it will require a much longer exposition on my part. I do not intend to do that here. I only wish to make a comparison between the "Reformed" approach in Barth and the Heideggerian necessity of αλεθεια. From there, the particular point I wish to again make clear is this: Barth's constructive understanding of hermeneutics is "Reformed" because it seeks to unconceal what traditional/historical hermeneutics has inadvertently concealed.

Barth and Heidegger

There is very little scholarship exploring the relationship between Heidegger and theology, with references to it appearing in John R. Williams' *Martin Heidegger's Philosophy of Religion* (1977) and Timothy Stanley's *Protestant Metaphysics after Karl Barth and Martin Heidegger* (2010). While Stanley's book is a comparative study on the individual influences and contributions Barth and Heidegger make to "protestant metaphysics," there is no cross-pollination between the two thinkers—that is to say, Stanley does not offer a direct discussion of Heidegger's influences on Barth and Barth's on Heidegger. It is not to say that this is even possible, since there is a consensus of circumstantial evidence that shows that Heidegger was not influenced directly by Barth any more than Barth was by Heidegger. In fact, the two

---

12. Heidegger, *Parmenides*, 11.
13. Ibid., 16.

APPENDIX B: KARL BARTH

thinkers are, essentially, in opposition to one another, such that Barth, as Williams notes, provided an "occasioned attack against [Heidegger]."[14]

It is certainly true that Barth attacked Heidegger, particularly in disagreement with Heidegger's thought. More importantly, this opposition to Heidegger arose out of Barth's own understanding of what it means to theologize and how Heidegger's infiltration into the field of theology—by the likes of Heidegger's philosophical influence upon the theologies of Rudolf Bultmann and Paul Tillich—tainted and contaminated modern theology. Indeed, given Barth's relationship with Bultmann, Barth expresses his opposition to Heidegger in a handful of letters exchanged between Barth and Bultmann, which are compiled in their collected correspondence from 1922 to 1966. Reference to Heidegger can be found in four letters of note, which include: 1.) from Barth to Bultmann, dated June 12, 1928, 2.) from Barth to Bultmann, dated May 27, 1931, 3.) from Bultmann to Barth, dated February 24, 1934, and 4.) from Barth to Bultmann, dated December 24, 1952—in each of them, particularly the three written by Barth, there is a subtle, but poignant rejection of Heidegger and Bultmann's use of Heidegger's thought theologically.[15]

Aside from these small references in letters written to Bultlmann, it seems, to the best of my knowledge, there are two noteworthy direct references that Barth makes about Heidegger—both references subjugate, compartmentalize, and harshly criticize Heidegger. The first is in Part Three of *Church Dogmatics: Volume III: The Doctrine of Creation* (first published in 1950, translated in 1960) and the other is in "Rudolf Bultmann—An Attempt to Understand Him," which appears in *Kerygma and Myth: Volume II* (1962). What is both significant and unfortunate about what Barth writes about Heidegger in these two direct references is that Barth ties Heidegger to existentialism and Sartre, to the extent that Barth refers to what he disagrees with as "Heidegger's existentialism"—this is especially unfortunate, because, in my view, Barth fundamentally misunderstands Heidegger.

In *Church Dogmatics*, within the volume devoted to "The Doctrine of Creation," in a section entitled "God and Nothingness," following the end of a subsection on "The Knowledge of Nothingness," Barth gives a lengthy discussion of Heidegger. In it, Barth begins by explaining that "we are in the fortunate position of being able to consult the short essay, which he

---

14. Williams, *Martin Heidegger's Philosophy of Religion*, 7.
15. See Barth and Bultmann, *Letters: 1922-1966*.

delivered as his inaugural lecture at Freiburg in Breisgau in 1929."[16] This "short essay" is *Was ist Metaphysik?* (or *What is Metaphysics?*), which Barth finds to be "a summary of what [Heidegger] says on the present theme in his greater work, [*Being and Time*]."[17] Setting aside what is undoubtedly Barth's rather limited view of Heidegger's work, which is verified, in part, by Barth admitting that "I shall not try to follow Heidegger's process of thought."[18] Indeed, for Barth, he seeks only "to describe the concept [of nothingness] which dominates [Heidegger's] exposition and then to show how it is developed in his teaching and how an answer is finally given to the question of discussion."[19] To say that the concept of nothingness "dominates [Heidegger's] exposition" in *What is Metaphysics?* is oddly (but unsurprisingly) narrow-sighted and seems to diminish not just what Heidegger specifically expresses in *Being and Time*, but also Heidegger's work more broadly. If Barth's intent is to, as he states, "show how [the concept of nothingness] is developed in [Heidegger's] teaching," limiting what he wishes to illustrate to only What is Metaphysics? poses significant problems for Barth's interpretation of Heidegger.

It must be noted, first, that the volume in question from *Church Dogmatics* appears in 1950, and Barth does not consult any other seminar, lecture, or talk Heidegger delivers leading up to 1950. To concentrate only on *What is Metaphysics?* places Barth (unknowingly) at a disadvantage in his use of Heidegger. Additionally, the fact that Barth is using a decidedly philosophical text to theologize about Heidegger's "concept of nothingness" can certainly be challenged, since Heidegger's more explicit theological texts dated to the same period as *What is Metaphysics?*—such as the talk on Augustine dated to October 26, 1930, the seminar on Augustine dated to Winter 1930/1931, and the talk, "Philosophizing and Believing: The Essence of Truth," dated to December 5, 1930—all seem to dispute Barth's assumptions about Heidegger. Furthermore, Barth's need to read a "concept of nothingness" into Heidegger seems to be more a reading of Sartre than Heidegger, particularly if we are reminded that Sartre's *Being and Nothingness* first appeared in 1943 and was subsequently translated into English in 1956—in this regard, it may be possible to suggest that Barth is conflating Heidegger with Sartre, given that Barth transitions

16. Barth, *Church Dogmatics: The Doctrine of Creation, Part 3*, 234.
17. Ibid.
18. Ibid.
19. Ibid.

from Sartre before discussing Heidegger, then returns to Sartre directly by referencing *Being and Nothingness* as well as Sartre's essay, "Existentialism is a Humanism" (1946). Barth's conflation of Heidegger and Sartre can be seen in the following:

> Our first main impression [being] that Sartre has behind him (as though obsessed by nothing and unable to see anything except in the light of it) what Heidegger has before him (as though obsessed by nothing and unable to look at any other goal. In other words, while noting is the basic concern of both, there is this difference in their respective attitudes towards it. In Heidegger we are concerned with the premise of Sartre, in Sartre with Heidegger's conclusion. Both deal with nothing as a principle, dimension and imperative.[20]

Here, we see Barth's conflation of Heidegger and Sartre, which suggests a much deeper relationship between than two than Heidegger himself would ever concede—this is so, if noting how Heidegger distances himself from Sartre and "Existentialism is a Humanism" in the "Letter on Humanism" (1946). Barth does eventually mention "Letter on Humanism," after extending "Existentialism is a Humanism" to include Heidegger. Even though Barth mentions Heidegger's "Letter on Humanism," he does so in passing, without recognizing that Heidegger meant for it to be a counterargument to everything Sartre espouses in "Existentialism is a Humanism." Barth completely misses (or avoids) the purpose of "Letter on Humanism," and how it likely refutes Barth's own reading of nothingness in Heidegger's thought.

Though Barth maintains that "the predominant concept is that of nothing"[21] and proceeds to directly cite Heidegger's words frequently from the *What is Metaphysics?* essay, there seems to be a concerted effort on Barth's part to support Barth's theological view of "the knowledge of nothingness," rather than more fully contextualizing Heidegger's philosophical understanding of nothingness as, in Barth's view, standing in close proximity to existentialism.

It is this assessment that finds its way into Barth's "Bultmann—An Attempt to Understand Him," which Barth's inability to understand what he refers to as "Heidegger's existentialism."[22] Though the purpose of the essay is to criticize Bultmann's use of Heidegger theologically, Barth provides an

20. Ibid., 338.
21. Ibid., 334.
22. Barth, "Bultmann—An Attempt to Understand Him," 114.

indictment of "Heidegger's existentialism" by way of Bultmann by writing "I do not see why I have to don this particular strait jacket in order to understand the New Testament."[23] In fact, Barth sees Bultmann's use of Heidegger as an "anthropological strait jacket."[24] We see that Barth furthers this criticism of Bultmann by marginalizing Heidegger in particular by finding that "neither Heidegger to-day nor Bultmann thinks that the Heidegger of 1927 has *the* philosophy, or that it dropped from heaven."[25]

While it appears that Barth fully understood Heidegger's philosophy, it is more apparent that he does not—Barth's understanding of Heidegger is, at best, limited. It is an understanding, on one hand, filtered through Bultmann's use of Heidegger, and, on the other hand, a filtered through Sartre's misuse of Heidegger. Because of this, Barth largely does not find much use for Heidegger in Barth's theologizing, insomuch as Barth seems to see Heidegger as obstructing modern theology more than positively influencing it. More importantly, because Barth opposes what Heidegger offers to modern theology, he abstains from theologizes through Heidegger (as Bultmann and Tillich do) and theologizes against Heidegger.

23. Ibid.
24. Ibid.
25. Ibid., 115.

BIBLIOGRAPHY

Adams, James L. *Paul Tillich's Philosophy of Culture, Science, and Religion*. New York, NY: Schocken, 1970.
Ashcraft, Morris. *Rudolf Bultmann*. Peabody, MA: Hendrickson, 1972.
Bainton, Roland H. *The Reformation of the Sixteenth Century*. Boston, MA: Beacon, 1952.
Barth, Karl. "Bultmann—An Attempt to Understand Him." In *Kerygma and Myth: A Theological Debate: Volume II*. Translated by Reginald H. Fuller. London: SPCK, 1962: 83-132.
———. *Church Dogmatics: Volume III [Part 3]: The Doctrine of Creation*. Translated by G. W. Bromiley and R. J. Ehrlich. Edinburgh: T & T Clark, 1960.
———. *Protestant Theology in the Nineteenth Century: Its Background and History*. Grand Rapids, MI: William B. Eerdmans, 2002.
Bonsor, Jack A. *Rahner, Heidegger, and Truth: Karl Rahner's Notion of Christian Truth: The Influence of Heidegger*. Lanham, MD: University Press of America, 1987.
Brentano, Franz. *The Origin of the Knowledge of Right and Wrong*. Translated by Cecil Hague. London, UK: Archibald Constable and Company, Limited, 1902.
———. *The Theory of Categories*. Translated by Roderick M. Chisholm and Norbert Guterman. The Hague: Martinus Nijhoff, 1981.
Bultmann, Rudolf. "The Historicity of Man and Faith." In *Existence and Faith: The Shorter Writings of Rudolf Bultmann*. Edited and Translated by Schubert M. Ogden. New York, NY: The World, 1966: 92-110.
———. *History and Eschatology: The Presence of Eternity: The Gifford Lectures 1955*. New York, NY: Harper and Row, 1957.
———. *The History of the Synoptic Tradition*. Translated by John Marsh. New York, NY: Harper and Row, 1968.
———. *Jesus and the Word*. Translated by Louise P. Smith and Erminie H. Lantero. London, UK: Charles Scribner's Son's, 1958.
———. *Jesus Christ and Mythology*. New York, NY: Charles Scribner's Sons, 1958.
———. "New Testament and Mythology," In *Kerygma and Myth: A Theological Debate*, Edited by Hans W. Bartsch. New York, NY: Harper and Row, 1961: 1-44.
———. *Primitive Christianity in its Contemporary Setting*. Translated by Reginald H. Fuller. Philadelphia, PA: Fortress, 1956.
———. "The Problem of a Theological Exegesis of the New Testament." In *Rudolf Bultmann: Interpreting Faith for the Modern Era*. Edited by Roger A. Johnson. San Francisco, CA: Collins San Francisco, 1987: 86-119.
———. *Theologie des Neuen Testaments*. Tübingen: J. C. B. Mohr, 1968.
———. *Theology of the New Testament Volume 1*. Translated by Kendrick Grobel. New York, NY: Charles Scribner's Sons, 1951.
———. *Theology of the New Testament Volume 2*. Translated by Kendrick Grobel. New York, NY: Charles Scribner's Sons, 1955.

Calvin, John. *Institutes of the Christian Religion*. Translated and Edited by John T. McNeill. Philadelphia, PA: Westminster, 1960.

Clayton, John P. "Questioning, Answering, and Tillich's Concept of Correlation." In *Kairos and Logos: Studies in the Roots and Implications of Tillich's Theology*. Edited by John J. Carey. Macon, GA: Mercer University Press, 1978: 121-140.

Congdon, David. "Is Bultmann a Heideggerian Theologian?" *Scottish Journal of Theology* 70, no. 1 (2017): 19-38.

―――. *The Mission of Demythologizing: Rudolf Bultmann's Dialectical Theology*. Minneapolis, MN: Fortress, 2015.

Cunningham, William. *The Reformers and the Theology of the Reformation*. Carlisle, PA: The Banner of Truth Trust, 1967.

Davidson, Donald. "Epistemology Externalized." In *Subjective, Intersubjective, Objective*. New York, NY: Oxford University Press, 2001: 193-204.

Deleuze, Gilles. *Immanence: Essays on a Life*. Translated by Anne Boyman. New York, NY: Zone, 2001.

Dennison, William. *The Young Bultmann: Context for His Understanding of God, 1884-1925*. New York, NY: Peter Lang, 2008.

Derrida, Jacques. *Of Grammatology*. Translated by Gayatri Chakravorty Spivak. Baltimore, MD: Johns Hopkins University Press, 1997.

―――. "Structure, Sign, and Play in the Discourse of the Human Sciences." In *Writing and Difference*. Translated by Alan Bass. Chicago, IL: The University of Chicago Press, 1978: 278-293.

Die Metaphysik Des Aristoteles. Tubingen: Druck und Verlag von L. Fr. Pues, 1847.

Edie, James M. "The Absence of God." In *Christianity and Existentialism*. Evanston, IL: Northwestern University Press, 1963: 113-148.

Foucault, Michel. *The Order of Things: An Archaeology of the Human Sciences*. New York, NY: Random House, 1970.

Frege, Gottlob. "On Sense and Reference." In *Translations from the Philosophical Writings of Gottlob Frege*. Edited by Peter Geach and Max Black. Oxford, UK: Basil Blackwell, 1960: 56-78.

Fritz, Peter J. *Karl Rahner's Theological Aesthetics*. Washington, D.C., The Catholic University of America Press, 2014.

Funk, Robert W. "Colloquium on Hermeneutics." *Theology Today* 21.3 (October 1964): 287-306.

Gadamer, Hans-Georg. *Truth and Method*. Translated by Garrett Barden and John Cumming. New York, NY: Crossroad, 1985.

Gilkey, Langdon. *Gilkey on Tillich*. New York, NY: Crossroad, 1990.

Gonzalez, Justo L. *The Story of Christianity: Volume II: The Reformation to the Present Day* New York, NY: Harper Collins, 2010.

Gordon, Haim, ed., *Dictionary of Existentialism*. Westport, CT: Greenwood, 1999.

Grigg, Richard. *Symbol and Empowerment: Paul Tillich's Post-Theistic System*. Macon, GA: Mercer University Press, 1985.

Hamilton, Edith and Huntington Cairns, eds., *The Collected Dialogues of Plato*. Princeton, NJ: Princeton University Press, 1982.

Hammann, Konrad. *Rudolf Bultmann: A Biography*. Translated by Philip E. Devenish. Salem, OR: Polebridge, 2013.

Heidegger, Martin. "Augustine and Neoplatonism." In *The Phenomenology of Religious Life*. Translated by Matthias Fritsch and Jennifer A. Gosetti-Ferencei. Bloomington, IN: Indiana University Press, 2010: 115-183.

———. "Augustine, Confessions 11: On Time" In *Seminare: Platon-Aristoteles-Augustinus*. Edited by Mark Michalski. Frankfurt: Klostermann, 2012: 41-70.

———. "Augustinus: Quid est tempus?: Confessiones lib. XI." In *Vorträge*. Edited by Günther Neumann. Frankfurt: Klostermann, 2016: 429-456.

———. *Being and Time*. Translated by John Macquarrie and Edward Robinson. San Francisco, CA: Harper San Francisco, 1962.

———. *Contributions to Philosophy*. Translated by Parvis Emad and Kenneth Maly. Bloomington, IN: Indiana University Press, 1999.

———. *Geschichte der Philosophie von Thomas von Aquin bis Kant*. Edited by Helmuth Vetter. Frankfurt: Klostermann, 2006.

———. *History of the Concept of Time: Prolegomena*. Translated by Theodore Kisiel. Bloomington, IN: Indiana University Press, 1985.

———. *Identity and Difference*, Translated by Joan Stambaugh. Chicago, IL: The University of Chicago Press, 1969.

———. "Introduction to the Phenomenology of Religion." In *The Phenomenology of Religious Life*. Translated by Matthias Fritsch and Jennifer A. Gosetti-Ferencei. Bloomington, IN: Indiana University Press, 2010: 3-89

———. *Kant and the Problem of Metaphysics*. Translated by Richard Taft. Bloomington, IN: Indiana University Press, 1997.

———. "Letter on Humanism." In *Basic Writings*. Edited by David F. Krell. San Francisco, CA: Harper San Francisco, 1992: 213-265.

———. *Logic: The Question of Truth*. Translated by Thomas Sheehan. Bloomington, IN: Indiana University Press, 2010.

———. *On the Way to Language*. Translated by Peter D. Hertz. New York, NY: Harper and Row, 1971.

———. *Parmenides*. Translated by André Schuwer and Richard Rojcewicz. Bloomington, IN: Indiana University Press, 1992.

———. "Phenomenology and Theology." In *Pathmarks*. Translated and Edited by William McNeill. New York, NY: Cambridge University Press, 1988: 39-54.

———. "Phenomenology and Theology." In *The Piety of Thinking*. Translated by James G. Hart and John C. Maraldo. Bloomington, IN: Indiana University Press, 1976: 5-21.

———. "Phänomenologie und Theologie." In *Vorträge*. Edited by Günther Neumann. Frankfurt: Klostermann, 2016: 179-212.

———. *Plato's Sophist*. Translated by Richard Rojcewicz and André Schuwer. Bloomington, IN: Indiana University Press, 1997.

———. *The Basic Problems of Phenomenology*. Translated by Albert Hofstadter. Bloomington, IN: Indiana University Press, 1982.

———. *The Concept of Time*. Oxford: Blackwell, 1992.

———. *The Concept of Time: The First Draft of Being and Time*. Translated by Ingo Farin and Alex Skinner. London: Contimuum, 2011.

———. "The Fundamental Question of Philosophy." In *Being and Truth*. Translated by Gregory Fried and Richard Polt. Bloomington, IN: Indiana University Press, 2010: 3-63.

———. "The Philosophical Foundations of Medieval Mysticism." In *The Phenomenology of Religious Life*. Translated by Matthias Fritsch and Jennifer A. Gosetti-Ferencei. Bloomington, IN: Indiana University Press, 2010: 131-154.

———. "The Problem of Sin in Luther." In *Supplements: From the Earliest Essays to Being and Time and Beyond*. Edited by John van Buren. Albany, NY: SUNY Press, 2002: 105-110.

———. "The Theological Discussion of 'The Problem of a Non-Objective Thinking and Speaking in Today's Theology'—Some Pointers to Its Major Aspects." In *Pathmarks*. Translated and Edited by William McNeill. New York, NY: Cambridge University Press, 1988: 54-62.

Heidegger, Martin, Elisabeth Blochmann, and Joachim W. Storck. *Martin Heidegger, Elisabeth Blochmann: Briefwechsel: 1918-1969*. Marbach am Neckar: Deutsche Schillergesellschaft, 1990.

Hegel, Georg W. F. *Phenomenology of Spirit*. Translated by A. V. Miller. New York, NY: Oxford University Press, 1979.

Hodge, Charles. *Systematic Theology: Volume 1*. Grand Rapids, MI: Wm. B. Eerdmans, 1872.

Honderich, Ted., ed. *The Oxford Guide to Philosophy*. New York, NY: Oxford University Press, 2005.

Hurst, John F. *Short History of the Christian Church*. New York, NY: Harper and Brothers, 1900.

Husserl, Edmund. *Ideas Pertaining to a Pure Phenomenology and to a Phenomenological Philosophy*, Translated by F. Kersten. Boston, MA: Martinus Nijhoff, 1983.

———. *The Crisis of European Sciences and Transcendental Phenomenology: An Introduction to Phenomenological Philosophy*. Translated by David Carr. Evanston, IL: Northwestern University Press, 1997.

Jasper, David. *A Short Introduction to Hermeneutics*. Louisville, KY: Westminster John Knox, 2004.

Jenkins, David. *The Scope and Limits of John Macquarrie's Existential Theology*. Stockholm: Uppsala, 1987.

Jonas, Hans. "Heidegger and Theology." In *The Phenomenon of Life: Toward a Philosophical Biology*. Evanston, IL: Northwestern University Press, 1966: 235-261.

Kant, Immanuel. *Critique of Pure Reason*. Translated by Norman Kemp Smith. New York, NY: St. Martin's, 1929.

Kegley, Charles W., ed. *The Theology of Paul Tillich*. New York, NY: The Pilgrim, 1982.

Kelly, Geffrey B. "Introduction." *Karl Rahner: Theologian of the Graced Search for Meaning*. Edited by Geffrey B. Kelly. Minneapolis, MN: Fortress, 1992.

Kierkegaard, Soren. *The Sickness Unto Death: A Christian Psychological Exposition for Upbulidng and Awakening*. Princeton, New Jersey: Princeton University Press, 1980.

Kisiel, Theodore. *The Genesis of Heidegger's Being and Time*. Berkeley, CA: University of California Press, 1993.

Kisiel, Theodore and Thomas Sheehan, eds. *Becoming Heidegger: On the Trail of his Early Occasional Writings, 1910-1927*. Seattle, WA: Noesis Press, 2007.

Kilby, Karen. *Karl Rahner: A Brief Introduction*. New York, NY: The Crossroad, 2007.

Künneth, Walter. "Bultmann's Philosophy and the Reality of Salvation." In *Kerygma and History: A Symposium on the Theology of Rudolf Bultmann*. Selected, Translated and Edited by Carl E. Braaten and Roy A, Harrisville. New York, NY: Abingdon, 1962: 86-119.

Leibniz, G. W. *Philosophical Essays*. Translated by Roger Ariew and Daniel Garber. Indianapolis, IN: Hackett, 1989.

Long, Eugene T. *Existence, Being, and God: An Introduction to the Philosophical Theology of John Macquarrie*. New York, NY: Paragon House, 1985.

Macgregor, Geddes. *Dictionary of Religion and Philosophy*. New York, NY: Paragon House, 1989.

Macquarrie, John. *Existentialism*. New York, NY: World, 1972.

———. *An Existentialist Theology: A Comparison of Heidegger and Bultmann*. New York, NY: The Macmillan Company, 1955.

———. *God-Talk: An Examination of the Language and Logic of Theology*. New York, NY: The Seabury, 1979.

———. *Heidegger and Christianity: The Hensley Henson Lectures 1993-94*. New York, NY: Continuum, 1994.

———. *In Search of Deity: An Essay in Dialectical Theism*. New York, NY: The Crossroad, 1984.

———. *In Search of Humanity: A Theological and Philosophical Approach*. New York, NY: The Crossroad, 1983.

———. *Martin Heidegger*. Richmond, VA: John Knox, 1969.

———. "New Frontiers in Theology: Vol I, The Later Heidegger and Theology, Edited by James M. Robinson and John B. Cobb Jr." Theology Today 20, no. 3 (October 1963): 420-422.

———. *On Being a Theologian*. Edited by John H. Morgan. London, UK: SCM, 1999.

———. "Pilgrimage in Theology." In *Being and Truth: Essays in Honor of John Macquarrie*. Edited by Alistair Kee and Eugene T. Long. London, UK: SCM, 1986.

———. *Principles of Christian Theology* (New York, NY: Charles Scribner's Sons, 1966).

———. *Studies in Christian Existentialism*. Montreal: McGill UP, 1965.

———. *Twentieth-Century Religious Thought: The Frontiers of Philosophy and Theology, 1900-1970*. London, UK: SCM, 1963.

———. *The Scope of Demythologizing: Bultmann and his Critics*. London, UK: SCM, 1960.

Martin, Bernard. *The Existentialist Theology of Paul Tillich*. New Haven, CT: College and University Press, 1963.

McKelway, Alexander J. *The Systematic Theology of Paul Tillich: A Review and Analysis*. Richmond, VA: John Knox, 1965.

Palmer, Richard. *Hermeneutics*. Evanston, IL: Northwestern University Press, 1969.

Peirce, Charles S. "Some Consequences of Four Incapacities." In *Philosophical Writings of Peirce*. Edited by Justus Buchler. Mineola, NY: Dover, 1955.

Plato. *The Republic*. Translated by Raymond Larson. Wheeling, IL: Harlan Davidson, Inc., 1979.

Reventlow, Henning G. *History of Biblical Interpretation: Volume 4: From the Enlightenment to the Twentieth Century*. Translated by Leo G. Perdue. Atlanta, GA: The Society of Biblical Literature, 2010

Richardson, William J. "Heidegger and God—and Professor Jonas." Thought 40 (1965): 13-40.

———. "Heidegger and Theology," Theological Studies 26(1), 86-100.

———. *Heidegger: Through Phenomenology to Thought*. The Hague: Martinus Nijhoff, 1963.

Rahner, Karl. "Concerning the Relationship between Nature and Grace." In *Theological Investigations Volume 1: God, Christ, Mary, and Grace*. Translated by Cornelius Ernst. Baltimore, MD: Helicon, 1961: 297-317.

———. "Experience of Self and Experience of God." In *Theological Investigation Volume XIII: Theology, Anthropology, Christology*. Translated by David Bourke. New York, NY: The Seabury, 1975: 122-132.

———. *Foundations of Christian Faith: An Introduction to the Idea of Christianity*. Translated by William V. Dych. New York, NY: The Seabury, 1978.

———. *Grundkurs des Glaubens: Einführung in den Begriff des Christentums*. Freiburg: Herder, 1977.

———. *Hearer of the Word: Laying the Foundation for a Philosophy of Religion*. Translated by Joseph Donceel. New York, NY: Continuum, 1994.

———. "Nature and Grace." In *Theological Investigations Volume IV: More Recent Writings*. Translated by Kevin Smith. Baltimore, MD: Helicon, 1966: 165-188.

———. *Nature and Grace: And Other Essays*. New York, NY: Sheed and Ward, 1963.

———. "Philosophy and Philosophising in Theology" In *Theological Investigations Volume IX: Writings of 1965-1967*. Translated by Graham Harrison. New York, NY: Herder and Herder, 1972: 46-63.

———. "Philosophy and Theology" In *Theological Investigations Volume VI: Concerning the Vatican Council*. Translated by Karl-H and Boniface Kruger. Baltimore, MD: Helicon, 1969: 71-81.

———. "Possible Courses for the Theology of the Future." In *Theological Investigation Volume XIII: Theology, Anthropology, Christology*. Translated by David Bourke. New York, NY: The Seabury, 1975: 32-60.

———. "Reflections on the Experience of Grace." In *Theological Investigations Volume III: The Theology of the Spiritual Life*. Translated by Karl-H and Boniface Kruger. Baltimore, MD: Helicon, 1967: 86-90.

———. *Spirit in the World*. Translated by William Dych. New York, NY: Continuum, 1994.

Ricoeur, Paul. *Hermeneutics and the Human Sciences*. Edited and Translated by John B. Thompson. New York, NY: Cambridge University Press, 1981.

———. "Preface to Bultmann." In *Essays on Biblical Interpretation*. Translated and Edited by Lewis S. Mudge. Philadelphia, PA: Fortress, 1980: 49-72.

Roberts, Robert C. *Rudolf Bultmann's Theology: A Critical Interpretation*. Grand Rapids, MI: William B. Eerdmans, 1976.

Robinson, James M. "The German Discussion." In *New Frontiers in Theology: Discussions among German and American Theologians: Volume 1: The Later Heidegger and Theology*. Edited by James M. Robinson and John B. Cobb Jr. New York, NY: Harper and Row, 1963: 3-76.

Saussure, Ferdinand de. *Course in General Linguistics*. Edited by Charles Bally and Albert Sechehaye. New York, NY: Philosophical Library, 1969.

Schilling, S. Paul. *Contemporary Continental Theologians*. Nashville, TN: Abingdon, 1966.

Schleiermacher, Friedrich. *The Christian Faith*. Edited by H. R. Mackintosh and J. S. Stewart Edinburgh, Scotland: T & T Clark, 1999.

Sheehan, Thomas. "Heidegger's Lehrjarhe." In *The Collegium Phaenomenologicum: The First Ten Years*. Edited by John C. Sallis, Guiseppina Moneta, and Jacques Taminiaux. Dordrecht: Kluwer, 1988: 77-137.

———. "Metaphysics and Bivalence: On Karl Rahner's *Geist in Welt*." *The Modern Schoolman*, no. 12 (1): 21-43 (1985).

———. *Karl Rahner: The Philosophical Foundations*. Athens, OH: Ohio University Press, 1987.

Stone, Jerome A. "Tillich and Schelling's Later Philosophy." In *Kairos and Logos: Studies in the Roots and Implications of Tillich's Theology*. Edited by John J. Carey. Macon, GA: Mercer University Press, 1978: 3-35.

Stroup, George, ed., *Reformed Reader: A Sourcebook in Christian Theology: Volume 2 Contemporary Trajectories, 1799 to the Present*. Louisville, KY: Westminster/John Knox, 1993.

Taylor, Mark K. "Introduction: The Theological Development and Contribution of Paul Tillich." In *Paul Tillich: Theologian of the Boundaries*. Edited by Mark K. Taylor. San Francisco, CA: Collins, 1987: 11-34.

Thiselton, Anthony. *Two Horizons: New Testament Hermeneutics and Philosophical Description with Special Reference to Heidegger, Bultmann, Gadamer, and Wittgenstein*. Grand Rapids, MI: William B. Eerdmans, 1980.

Thomas, George F. "The Method and Structure of Tillich's Theology." In *The Theology of Paul Tillich*. Edited by Charles W Kegley. New York, NY: The Pilgrim, 1982: 86-107.

Thomas, J. Heywood. *Paul Tillich*. Richmond, VA: John Knox, 1966.

Tillich, Paul. *A History of Christian Thought: From Judaic and Hellenistic Origins to Existentialism*. New York, NY: Simon and Schuster, 1968.

———. *Biblical Religion and the Search for Ultimate Reality*. Chicago, IL: The University of Chicago Press, 1955.

———. *The Courage to Be*. New Haven, CT: Yale University Press, 1952.

———. *The Eternal Now*. New York, NY: Charles Scribner's Sons, 1963.

———. *Mortality and Beyond*. New York, NY: Harper and Row, 1957.

———. *My Search for Absolutes*. New York, NY: Simon and Schuster, 1984.

———. "The Problem of Theological Method." In *Four Existentialist Theologians: A reader from the Works of Jacques Maritain, Nicolas Berdyaev, Martin Buber, and Paul Tillich*. Selected by Will Herberg. Garden City, NY: Doubleday and Company, 1958: 163-182.

———. *The Protestant Era*. Chicago, IL: The University of Chicago Press, 1957.

———. *Systematic Theology Volume 1: Reason and Revelation, Being and God*. Chicago, IL: The University of Chicago Press, 1951.

———. *Systematic Theology Vol. 2: Existence and the Christ*. Chicago, IL: University of Chicago Press, 1957.

———. *The System of the Sciences: According to Objects and Methods*. Translated by Paul Wiebe. East Brunswick, NJ: Associated University Presses Inc., 1981.

———. *Theology of Culture*. Edited by Robert C. Kimball. New York, NY: Oxford University Press, 1964.

———. *What is Religion?* Translated by James L. Adams. New York, NY: Harper and Row, 1973.

Urban, Linwood. *A Short History of Christian Thought*. New York, NY: Oxford University Press, 1995.

Van Buren, John. "Heidegger's Early Freiburg Courses, 1915-1923." *Research in Phenomenology* 23 (1993); 132-152.

———. *The Young Heidegger: Rumor of the Hidden King*. Bloomington, IN: Indiana University Press, 1994.

Van Buren, John, ed. *Supplements: From the Earliest Essays to* Being and Time *and Beyond*. Albany, NY: SUNY, 2002.
Wace, Henry and C. A. Buchheim, eds. *First Principles of the Reformation or the Ninety-Five Theses and the Three Primary Works of Dr. Martin Luther*. London, UK: John Murray, 1883.
Wheat, Leonard F. *Paul Tillich's Dialectical Humanism: Unmasking the God above God*. Baltimore, MD: Johns Hopkins, 1970.
Williams, John R. *Martin Heidegger's Philosophy of Religion*. Ontario: Wilifrid Laurier University Press, 1977.
Wittgenstein, Ludwig. *Tractatus Logico-Philosophicus*. Translated by C. K. Ogden. New York, NY: Harcourt, Brace, Company Inc., 1922.
Woessner, Martin. *Heidegger in America*. New York, NY: Cambridge University Press, 2011.
Woodson, Hue. *Heideggerian Theologies: The Pathmarks of John Macquarrie, Rudolf Bultmann, Paul Tillich, and Karl Rahner*. Eugene, OR: Wipf and Stock, 2018.
Young, Norman J. *History and Existential Theology: The Role of History in the Thought of Rudolf Bultmann*. Philadelphia, PA: The Westminster, 1969.

INDEX

a priori, 79, 80, 99, 113
A Thousand Plateaus, Deleuze/Guattari, 125, 127
Abraham, 88
Adaequatio, 63
aletheia, 101, 103, 128, 136, 143–45
Allegory/Simile of the Cave, 80
Anders, Gunther, 11
Angst, 146
anthropological, 191
Aquinas, Thomas, 1–3, 5–6, 27–28, 54–55, 59–63, 78, 80, 134, 149, 157
Arendt, Hannah, 11
Aristotle, 5–6, 28, 40–41, 45, 54, 55, 58, 62–63, 70, 78, 80, 89, 113, 120, 136, 149, 155–56
Aristotlianism, 25
attunement, 147, 150–53
Augustine, 5–6, 39–46, 48, 68–70, 78, 80–81, 83–84, 134, 189, 195
Augustinianism, 41
authenticity, 136, 144, 146, 153, 161

Bahktin, Mikhail, 93
Barad, Karen, 156, 159
Barth, Karl, 5–7, 16, 18, 27–28, 97–98, 181–82, 185–91, 193
Becker, Oskar, 38, 40, 43–44
Begriff, 10, 55, 71, 198
Being and Nothingness, Sartre's, 143, 155, 189, 190
Being and Time, 6–8, 12–13, 28, 34, 38, 45, 51, 55–56, 68, 71, 76, 100–101, 105, 123, 126–27, 129, 131, 134–40, 144, 146, 148, 154–59, 162–63, 170–75, 177–81, 189, 195–96, 200
being-in-the-world, 88, 126, 142–43

Bible, 5, 6, 85–88, 91–93, 96–97, 182, 185–86
biblical hermeneutics, 83
biblical interpretation, 80–83, 96–97
Black Notebooks, 11, 29, 169–74, 177–78, 180
boredom, 151–54
Bourdieu, Pierre, 179
Braig, Carl, 31–32
Brentano, Franz, 21, 131, 193
Bultmann, Rudolf, 2–13, 15–18, 23, 28, 48–50, 68, 78, 95, 99, 104–5, 109, 112, 134, 145, 161–64, 167, 181, 188, 190–91, 193–94, 196–200

Cajetan, Thomas, 5, 54–55
Calvin, John, 6, 84–85, 87–91, 95, 146, 194
Calvinist, 87
Campbell, Charles, 2–3, 13, 18
Cartesian, 14, 132, 140–41, 156
Cartesian Meditations, Husserl's, 140
Catholicism, 22, 32, 53, 61
Chalcedon, Council, 83
Christ, 5, 7, 85, 104–5, 107, 185, 186, 193, 198–99
Christian, 5, 8–10, 13–16, 25, 27, 29, 31–32, 35–37, 41–42, 45, 48, 54, 57, 62–63, 67, 73–74, 78, 80–81, 83, 85–92, 94, 97, 102, 105, 126, 146, 193–94, 196–99
Christian faith, 57, 81, 91
Christian God, 74
Christian life, 37, 45, 48
Christian theology, 14–16, 25
Christian thought, 9, 54, 78
Christian tradition, 80, 83, 86

INDEX

Christianity, 10, 20, 28, 43, 66, 73, 80, 83, 85–87, 91, 95, 176, 193- 194, 197–98
Christianization, 72–73
Christianness, 67
christliche, 42
Church, 13, 22, 31, 41, 83, 84, 91, 94, 181, 188–89, 193, 196
Classicism, 116
Cobb, John, 16, 19, 21, 23, 197–98
cogito, 146, 156–57
cogito ergo sum, 146, 156–57
concealed, 23, 78, 101, 147, 151, 161, 168, 186–87
concealment, 99, 101, 103, 136, 161, 186–87
Concept of Anxiety, Kierkegaard's, 143
Congdon, David, 5–6, 194
conscience, 48, 144, 146
conservatism, 93, 95
Constantinople, Council, 83
Contributions to Philosophy, 101, 114, 195
corruptio, 52
Course on General Linguistics, Saussure's, 119
Critique of Pure Reason, Kant's, 79, 99, 100, 113, 131, 196
curses interruptus, 38

Dasein, 58, 113, 114, 121, 126–28, 130, 136–37, 139–54, 156, 163, 165
Davidson, Donald, 7, 130–33, 194, 197
De trinitate, Augustine's, 43
deconstruction, 120–21, 167
Deleuze, Gilles, 7, 93, 105, 114–15, 125–27, 194
demythologizing, 2, 5, 12, 164
denazification, 12, 76, 169
denkenden, 61
Dennison, William, 4, 10, 194
Derrida, Jacques, 6, 7, 118–24, 146, 167, 194
Descartes, Rene, 41, 61, 63, 140, 146, 154–57
Deutsche Literaturarchiv in Marbach, 33, 36, 47, 49, 55–56, 59, 64, 68, 71

dialectic, 107–110, 115, 120, 126, 128, 159
Didache, 102
Die Gottesbeweise, 63
différance, 119
Dilthey, Wilhelm, 28, 40–44
disclosedness, 144, 146
discourse, 9, 15, 27, 78, 116, 121, 142, 146
Dogmatic, 32
dogmatics, 31, 181, 188–89, 193

Ebbinghaus, Julius, 46, 48
Ebeling, Gerhard, 18–19
Eckhart, Meister, 35
Eichhorn, Johann, 6, 92–93
empiricism, 132
Enlightenment, 31, 92, 197
entities, 15, 109, 135, 139–45, 155, 159
entity, 15, 87–88, 120, 126–27, 139, 140–41, 145, 165
episteme, 136
epistemological, 42, 88–91, 99–100, 106, 110–11, 116–17, 120, 125, 131, 162, 165
eschatology, 38
estrangement, 105
Evangelical-Theological Association, 70
everyday existence, 13
everydayness, 139, 142–44, 146, 148
exegesis, 30–31, 50, 193
existence, 13, 15, 19, 43, 53, 57, 64, 70, 88, 90–91, 104–9, 111–12, 116–17, 120, 125, 139, 149, 155–59, 161–62, 165
existence precedes essence, 155, 157–59
existential, 8, 11, 13, 44, 88–90, 99, 101, 104–8, 112, 125–27, 129- 130, 141, 142, 144–46, 156, 163- 168, 176
existentialism, 1, 8–9, 12, 16, 17, 77, 95, 155, 157, 188, 190–91
existentialist, 2, 3, 9–10, 12, 130
existentialist theology, 3
experiential-existential, 165
externalism, 130

factical, 37, 45, 129, 145

INDEX

facticity, 45, 48, 88, 106, 108, 129, 146
fallen-ness, 142
Farias, Victor, 20
Faye, Emmanuel, 169–70, 177
finitude, 108, 111, 148–49, 153–54
formal indication, 38–39, 45
Foucault, Michel, 7, 116–17, 120–23, 176, 194
Frei, Hans, 96
Freiburg, 5–6, 9–12, 30–34, 37, 45–48, 67, 71–72, 76, 136, 147, 154, 169, 173–76, 177, 189, 198–99
Fuchs, Ernst, 18
fundamental attunement, 147–54
Funk, Robert, 25–26, 194

Gabler, Johann, 93
Gadamer, Hans-Georg, 7, 56, 99, 104, 112–15, 146, 170, 176, 194, 199
Galatians, 37, 48
Geist, 1–3, 8–9, 61, 199
Geisteswissenschaften, 43
genitivus objectivus, 75
genitivus subjectivus, 75
German Library Archive, 60
German people, 75
German state, 75
Gesamtausgabe (Heidegger), 33, 49, 55, 59–60, 64, 68, 174, 177
God, 2, 4–7, 9, 15, 22, 25, 26–29, 31, 38, 43–44, 48–49, 50–53, 56–57, 63- 64, 73–75, 82, 85–92, 96, 105, 107- 112, 114, 146, 162, 185–86, 188, 194, 197–200
godlessness, 64
Göller, Emil, 31
Gospel of John, 5, 32, 86
Gott-losigkeit, 64
grace, 41–42, 165
Greek, 24, 30, 54, 72, 82, 101, 103, 113
Grundlagen, 33
Guattari, Felix, 7, 125–27
guilt, 48, 92, 144

Hammann, Konrad, 6, 10, 194
Harnack, Adolf, 40–42, 95
Hebrew, 30, 82

Hebrew Bible, 82
Hegel, Georg, 10–11, 28, 35, 61, 69, 70, 72–75, 96, 109, 115, 155, 163, 196
Hegelian, 73, 96, 109
Heideggerian Theologies, 1–5, 10, 162- 163, 167, 200
Heidelberg Disputation, 53
Henderson, Ian, 2–3, 13, 18
Heraclitus, 101–2, 135
Hermenetiucs and the Human Sciences, Ricoeur's, 124
hermeneutical lenses, 81, 96
hermeneutics, 5–6, 10, 22, 78–87, 89–91, 93–101, 103–5, 107, 109, 111–13, 115, 117–19, 121, 123–25, 127, 129, 131, 133, 181, 182, 185–87
hermeneutics of faith, 97, 124
hermeneutics of suspicion, 97, 124, 125
Heyne, Christian, 6, 92–93
high scholastic, 54
high scholasticism, 54
historical-existential, 164
Historicism, 116
Hitler, Adolf, 11, 72
Hoberg, Gottfried, 30–31
Hochscholastik, 54
Hodge, Charles, 95–96, 182, 196
Hölderlin, Friedrich, 11, 28
Holy Spirit, 87, 91
Honecker, Martin, 1–2
human being, 49–53, 90–91, 104, 106–7, 109, 139–40, 155, 173, 179
human existence, 3, 12–13, 57, 88, 91, 104–7, 109–110, 126, 140, 162
human experience, 15
human reason, 87
humanism, 155–61
Humanism, 7–8, 16–17, 127, 134, 154–59, 190, 195, 200
humanitas, 158–60
humanity, 43, 50–53, 88–92, 105–112, 165, 186
Husserl, Edmund, 11, 32–33, 36, 47–48, 67, 100, 110, 136, 140, 143, 155, 196
Husserl Archive, 36

INDEX

ideology, 169–74, 176, 179
Institutes of the Christian Religion,
    Calvin's, 88–90, 146, 194
intentionality, 140, 143
is-ness, 128–29, 139,
iustitia originalis, 51–53

Jaspers, Karl, 8, 37
Jaspert, Bernd, 50
Jesuit, 1, 20, 21, 54
Jonas, Hans, 11, 23–27, 196–97
justification of faith, 48

Kairos, 145, 194, 199
Kant, Immanuel, 5, 10, 35–36, 44–45,
    46–48, 60, 61, 63, 67, 73, 79–80,
    85, 94–95, 99–100, 108, 113, 130–
    131, 154–56, 195–96
Kant Society, 47
Kantian, 33, 79, 99, 108–9, 113, 115, 123
Kierkegaard, Soren, 37, 53, 106, 126, 130,
    143, 146, 163, 196
Kisiel, Theodore, 6, 13, 34, 38–39, 45–46,
    50–52, 54, 59, 64, 67–68, 71, 176,
    195–96
Klages, Ludwig, 151

Lacoue-Labarthe, Philippe, 20
language, 7, 9, 13, 15, 82, 84, 100, 101,
    114, 116–19, 124, 132–33, 163–
    64, 182,
Leibniz, Gottfried, 63, 98–99, 197
Letter on Humanism, 190
Levinas, Emmanuel, 11, 28
Levi-Strauss, Claude, 121
Liberal Christianity, 95
liberalism, 95
Life of Jesus, Strauss's, 96–98
linguistical-existential, 164
linguistics, 119
Logical Atomism, Russell's, 7, 128–29
Logical Investigations, Husserl's, 47
logos, 24, 74, 113, 136–37, 163
lower-level, 60, 69
Löwith, Karl, 11, 40, 179
Loyola, Ignatius, 54

Luther, Martin, 5–7, 28, 46–54, 78, 84–
    88, 91, 134, 196, 200
Lutheran, 29, 36, 47, 84–86, 93

Macquarrie, John, 2–5, 6–9, 10–21, 27–
    28, 104–5, 109, 112, 134, 161–64,
    167, 176, 195–97, 200
Malebranche, Nicolas, 41
Marburg, 4–7, 10–11, 18, 47, 55, 59, 64,
    67–68, 136
Marburg Theological Society, 55
Maréchal, Joseph, 1–4
Mayer, Julius, 30–31
McNeill, William, 64, 194–96
medieval, 25, 35, 40, 61, 156–57
Melanchthon, Philip, 46
metaphysical, 29, 35, 73, 79–80, 90,
    106–7, 121–22, 126–29, 149, 153,
    155, 157–58, 160
metaphysician, 122–23
metaphysics, 15, 31, 72–75, 113, 123,
    126–27, 129, 132, 138, 147–49,
    154, 157–61, 187
Middle Ages, 5, 35, 59–63
Mitläufer, 12, 169, 175
moral theology, 31
Mysticism, 5, 7, 31, 33–35, 37, 196

National Socialism, 11–12, 20, 72, 75, 77,
    169, 172–75, 176, 179
Nationalsozialismus, 175
Natorp, Paul, 34
natura hominis, 53
natural theology, 74
Nazi, 11, 12, 20, 72, 76, 169–79
Nazi Party, 11, 72, 76, 169–72, 175
Nazism, 7, 11–12, 20, 27, 169–79
Neoplatonism, 5, 39–40, 45–46, 48, 195
New Testament, 2–3, 5–6, 9–10, 12, 31,
    50, 82, 99, 104–5, 191, 193, 199
Nicaea, Council, 83
Nicomachean Ethics, Aristotle's, 45, 136
Nietzsche, Friedrich, 11, 122–23
nihilism, 14
non-being, 135–37

INDEX

Of Grammatology, Derrida's, 118–20, 122–24, 146, 194
Old Princeton Theology, 95–96, 182
On Being and Essence, Aquinas's, 5, 54–55, 59
On the Analogy of Names, Cajetan's, 5, 54–55
On the Way to Language, 100–101, 195
ontics, 126–27, 164–65
ontological, 67, 79–80, 90, 99–100, 106–8, 122, 126–28, 129, 137, 139, 143–46, 155–56, 159, 173, 174
ontological priority, 139
ontology, 33–34, 37–38, 59–60, 63, 65, 112–13, 137–38, 140, 148, 156-157
orthodox, 9, 95
Ott, Hugo, 16–18, 19, 20, 28
Otto, Rudolf, 36–38

Parmenides, 69–71, 101–3, 135- 136, 138, 143, 187, 195
Parmenides lecture, 135, 138
Paul, Saint, 28, 30, 37–38, 45, 48–50, 78, 181
Peirce, Charles, 124, 197
Pfeilschifter, Georg, 31
phänomenbegriff, 63
Phänomenologie, 33, 36, 64, 195
phenomenological research, 35, 47
Phenomenology, 5–6, 21, 23–24, 28, 33–34, 36–40, 45, 48, 55, 64–65, 68, 71, 76, 100, 110, 115, 154, 157, 181, 195–97, 199
phenomenology of religion, 34, 37
Phenomenology of Spirit, Hegel's, 115, 196
phenomenon, 13–14, 37–38, 63, 137, 139–40, 144–46, 150
philosophizing, 11, 25, 57–58, 78, 81, 134, 148–49, 161–63
phronesis, 136
Physics, Aristotle's, 47
physis, 149
Plato, 6, 7, 55, 59–60, 69–70, 78, 80, 81, 85, 101, 112–15, 121–23, 125, 129, 132, 134, 135–38, 156, 160, 194–97

Plato's Sophist, 7, 55, 134, 136, 195
Platonism, 41, 78
Pöggeler, Otto, 38
positive sciences, 62, 65
positum, 65, 67
postlapsarianism, 52, 89
prelapsarianism, 52
primordial, 35, 51, 102, 121, 135, 142–45, 161–67, 186
primordial being, 145, 163–67
primordial thinkers, 102, 135
primordiality, 11, 145–46, 162–65, 167–68
Privatdozent, 2, 33
Protestant, 5, 28, 37, 47, 84, 87, 97–98, 187, 193, 199
Protestantism, 53, 61–62, 95
psychological, 35, 185–86

question of the meaning of Being, 138, 154, 156
Quid est tempus, 68–69, 195
Quine, Willard, 131–32

Rahner, Karl, 1–4, 6, 8–11, 27–28, 104, 107–110, 112, 134, 161–63, 165, 167, 193–94, 196, 198–200
rational-existential, 164–65
Rauschenbusch, Walter, 95
reduction, 110, 119
Reformation, 84–87, 90–91, 94–95, 193–94, 200
Reitzenstein, Richard, 32
Rektoratsrede, 174–75, 177, 179
religion, 20, 30–32, 34–37, 39, 45–46, 62, 147
Religion within the Limits of Reason Alone, Kant's, 5, 45–46
religiösen, 33
Renaissance, 31, 116
res extensa, 141, 157
revealed theology, 74
rhizome, 125–28
Richardson, William, 13, 20–23, 25–27, 71, 176, 197
Ricoeur, Paul, 7, 97, 124–25, 198

INDEX

Robinson, James, 8, 13, 16–22, 195, 197–98
Russell, Bertrand, 7, 28, 128–30

salvation, 85, 92
Sartre, Jean-Paul, 8, 12, 16, 77, 143, 155–60, 176, 188–91
Sauer, Joseph, 31
Saussure, Ferdinand de, 80, 119, 123–24, 198
scepticism, 43
Schadewaldt, Wolfgang, 69
Schalk, Fritz, 40
Scheler, Max, 41, 67, 151
Schelling, Friedrich, 7, 11, 199
Schleiermacher, Friedrich, 6, 35–36, 44, 85, 93–95, 185–86, 198
scholasticism, 52, 54, 61
Schwartz, Edward, 32
Schwarze Hefte, 169
science of faith, 66–67
scientific theology, 62
Scotist, 54
Scotus, John Duns, 33, 54, 157
scripture, 5, 11, 29–31, 42, 84, 86–87, 88, 92–95, 97, 105, 163–68, 182, 185–86
Sein und Zeit, 8, 10–13, 16–18, 29, 67
self-communicate, 108
self-consciousness, 74–75, 94
selfhood, 13–15, 105, 107, 144
semantic, 82–83
Sheehan, Thomas, 6, 13, 30–33, 38, 46, 50, 52, 54, 59, 64, 67, 195–96, 198
signified, 84, 119, 121–22
signifier, 84, 119, 121–22, 124
sin, 42, 49–53, 78, 107, 143
sinfulness, 107
solicitude, 141
Sophist, 112, 134–37
sovereignty, 90–91
Spengler, Oswald, 151
Spinoza, Baruch, 63
Spivak, Gayatri, 118, 122–24, 194
St. Peter, 86
Straubinger, Heinrich, 31
Strauss, David, 6, 96–98, 121

Stroup, George, 5, 185, 199
structuralism, 121
subjectivization, 83, 85, 94
Summa contra gentiles, Aquinas's, 5, 59
Summa Theologica, Aquinas's, 55
summum bonum, 52
systematic theology, 6–8, 87

techne, 117, 126, 136
temporal, 11, 14, 20, 57, 99–100, 104, 107, 143, 146, 148, 156, 166-168
temporal-existential, 167
temporality, 11, 13–15, 58, 64, 100, 106, 140, 143–44, 146, 152, 154, 156, 166–68
The Christian Faith, Schleiermacher's, 36, 94, 198
The Forms, 101, 114–15
The Fundamental Concepts of Metaphysics, 7, 134, 147
The Heidegger Circle, 76
The Order of Things, Foucault's, 116–17, 121, 194
The Republic, Plato's, 80–81, 101, 197
The Sickness Unto Death, Kierkegaard's, 126, 196
Theaetetus, Plato's, 134–35
theo-logic, 73–75
theologize, 9–10, 27, 75, 78, 134, 161–63, 181, 188–89
theologizing, 3, 9–13, 15, 20, 22, 25, 57–58, 71, 75, 78, 134–35, 137, 139, 141, 143, 145, 147, 149, 151, 153, 155, 157, 159, 162, 163, 165, 167, 181, 191
Thessalonians, 37, 48
thing-in-itself, 94, 99
Thiselton, Anthony, 13, 96, 99, 104, 119, 199
Thomist, 54
thrownness, 89, 142–44, 159
Tillich, Paul, 4, 6–11, 27–28, 85, 87, 91, 95, 104–9, 112, 134, 143–45, 161–65, 167, 188, 191, 193–94, 196–200
Tractatus Logico Philosophicus, Wittgenstein's, 129

transcendental, 1, 72, 79–80, 100, 108, 110, 140
transcendental dialectic, 108
transcendental idea, 79, 100
transzendentalphilosophie, 63
Trawny, Peter, 177–78
Trinity, 9, 86
Troeltsch, Ernst, 37, 40–42, 47
Truth, 3, 6, 55, 70–72, 113, 145–46, 154, 189, 193–97
two-horizons, 99

ultimate concern, 107, 143–45, 161
unconcealment, 6, 7, 101, 130, 131, 133, 143, 145, 164–65, 168, 187
unconcealness, 103, 187
unconceals, 162
upper-level, 45, 54, 59–60, 67, 69
Urstand, 51

Van Buren, John, 13, 30–34, 37–38, 46, 48–50, 54, 59, 199–200
Vernunft, 61
Vertitas, 63
Volksstrum, 12, 76

Warfield, Benjamin, 95
Was ist Metaphysik?, 189
Weber, Simon, 30–31

Wegmarken, 64
Weltanschauungsproblem, 38
Wesen, 33, 71
Wesleyan Quadrilateral, 162
What is Called Thinking?, 149
Wissenschaft, 71
Wittgenstein, Ludwig, 99, 104, 129, 182, 199–200
Woessner, Martin, 26, 200
Wolff, Christian, 63
Word of God, 27, 85–88, 185–86
worldhood, 51, 139–41
worldlessness, 51
worldview, 38, 65, 147

Young, Julian, 169

Ziegler, Leopold, 151
Žižek, Slavoj, 179
Zwingli, Ulrich, 6, 85, 91, 92

ἀλήθεια, 131, 133, 163–68
θεός, 74
καιρος, 164–68
κηρυγμα, 164, 167–68
ληθε, 168
λόγος, 163–64, 167–68
χάρις, 165, 167–68

www.ingramcontent.com/pod-product-compliance
Lightning Source LLC
Chambersburg PA
CBHW070320230426

43663CB00011B/2182